Liberia and the Dialectic of Law

It is the condition of modernity that an institution cannot depend on a god, tradition, or any other transcendental source to secure its foundations, which thereby come to rest upon – or rather in, and through – its subjects. Never wholly separated from its subjects, and yet never identical with them: this contradictory condition provides a way of seeing how modern law gives form to life, and how law takes form, enlivened by its subjects. By driving Theodor Adorno's dialectical philosophy into the concept of law, the book shows how this contradictory condition enables law to become instituted in ways that are hostile to its subjects, but also how law remains open to its subjects, and thus disposed towards transformation. To flesh out an understanding of this contradiction, the book examines the making and remaking of "Liberia", from its conception as an idea of liberty at the beginning of the nineteenth century to its reconstruction at the beginning of the twenty-first with the assistance of an international intervention to "establish a state based on the rule of law". In so doing, the book shows how law is at the epicentre of a colonising power in Liberia that renders subjects as mere objects; but at the same time, the book exposes the instability of this power, by showing how law is also enlivened by its subjects as it takes form in and through their lives and interactions. It is this fundamentally contradictory condition of law that ultimately denies power any absolute hold, leaving law open to the self-expression of its subjects.

Shane Chalmers is a McKenzie Postdoctoral Fellow at Melbourne Law School, The University of Melbourne.

Liberia and the Dialectic of Law

Critical Theory, Pluralism, and the Rule of Law

Shane Chalmers

Routledge
Taylor & Francis Group
LONDON AND NEW YORK

First published 2018 by Birkbeck Law Press

2 Park Square, Milton Park, Abingdon, Oxfordshire OX14 4RN
52 Vanderbilt Avenue, New York, NY 10017

Routledge is an imprint of the Taylor & Francis Group, an informa business

First issued in paperback 2019

British Library Cataloguing-in-Publication Data
A catalogue record for this book is available from the British Library

Library of Congress Cataloging-in-Publication Data
Names: Chalmers, Shane, author.
Title: Liberia and the dialectic of law : critical theory, pluralism, and the rule of law / Shane Chalmers.
Description: Abingdon, Oxon ; New York, NY : Birkbeck Law Press, 2018. | Based on author's thesis (doctoral – Australian National University, 2016) issued under title: Law's rule : Liberia and the rule of law. | Includes bibliographical references and index.
Identifiers: LCCN 2018006324 | ISBN 9781138545731 (hardback)
Subjects: LCSH: Law–Liberia. | Rule of law–Liberia. | Legal polycentricity–Liberia. | Effectiveness and validity of law–Liberia.
Classification: LCC KSK440 .C48 2018 | DDC 340/.11–dc23
LC record available at https://lccn.loc.gov/2018006324

ISBN: 978-1-138-54573-1 (hbk)
ISBN: 978-0-367-89312-5 (pbk)

Typeset in Galliard
by Taylor & Francis Books

For Lindy and Jim

Painting of Liberian women by F B Yekehson (2010)

Contents

Illustrations

Figures

Acknowledgements

Jeremy Farrall's supervision of my doctoral project created the conditions for this book. Jeremy's trust in the project, open mind, close engagement, and when necessary, pointed advice, provided the wonderful combination of openness and closure that enabled me to go in creative directions without losing total sight of the assignment. Thank you.

Inspiration for the book has come from many people, places, and parts. I'm sure I'm barely aware of the source of much of this inspiration. What I am aware of is the inspiring influence of Desmond Manderson. His approach to scholarship, his work and advice are embedded in these pages. Veronica Taylor is another source of inspiration, as a leader and a scholar, as well as a generous advisor in my doctoral journey. Some of the most critical interventions have come from Kate Henne, whose admirable capacity to use critique to open up new possibilities has shaped this work from its earliest days. I thank all three for their contributions.

It was a great privilege to have had the convivial and intellectually stimulating tent of RegNet (now the School of Regulation and Global Governance) at The Australian National University as a base for this project during my doctorate. Hilary Charlesworth's Centre for International Governance and Justice in particular created the kind of academic cacophony that is so essential to a vibrant place of learning. I thank those who made my time at RegNet such a special one. I also acknowledge with gratitude the support provided during this time by the people of Australia through the grant of an Australian Postgraduate Award, as well as the opportunities and support provided by The Australian National University.

Travelling afield, I thank the generosity and hospitality of the many people who welcomed me to their parts of the world. Above all I acknowledge with great respect and admiration the peoples of Liberia, and thank the women and men there who opened their country up to me and helped to make this research project possible. The Oñati International Institute for the Sociology of Law in Euskadi has offered recurrent hospitality throughout the project and an incredibly inspiring place to work; it is there that I completed the manuscript in early 2017 with the support of an Australian Endeavour Research Fellowship. I also thank Peter Fitzpatrick for his generous advice and warm welcome offered during a summer's visit at Birkbeck Law School in 2014; and I thank Birkbeck for hosting me and the Australian Bicentennial Scholarship for helping to make that visit possible. The

Max Planck Institute for Social Anthropology in Halle and the Osnabrück Summer Institute on the Cultural Study of Law also generously opened their doors to me at different points in the journey. I thank these institutions for welcoming a wondering scholar. I thank too the Liberian Collections at the University of Indiana, Bloomington, for providing access to their archives.

Going further back in time, I have to acknowledge the seminal influence of McGill Faculty of Law. It was there, in the course of an LLM, that I was exposed to the work of Theodor Adorno, critical theory, and legal pluralism and the anthropology of law. For this I am indebted in particular to the teachings of Richard Janda and Ronald Niezen.

In the final stretch it was the support of Routledge's Birkbeck Law Press that enabled this book to take its ultimate form, with much thanks to the BLP editorial board and to Colin Perrin and the team at Routledge. I am also very grateful to Shaun McVeigh, Peter Rush, Alain Pottage, as well as two anonymous reviewers, who took the time to read drafts of the manuscript at different stages and provide deeply thoughtful feedback.

But it is friendship that makes the journey a human one. One special friendship in particular made the final stages a new process of discovery and learning; to Valeria, thank you for making this project one of law and love. And to Lindy and Jim, for opening up the world and making it for me a place of wonder and possibility; to Petr and Ben for sharing the exploration of that world as brothers and friends; and to all the friends who made this process so lively, fun, and thought provoking – thank you.

The book reproduces published material. Chapter 3 reproduces material published in Shane Chalmers, 'Civil Death in the Dominion of Freedom: Liberia and the Logic of Capital', *Law and Critique*, vol 28, no 2 (2017). Chapter 4 reproduces material published in Shane Chalmers and Jeremy Farrall, 'Securing the Rule of Law through UN Peace Operations', *Max Planck Yearbook of UN Law*, vol 18 (2014) and Shane Chalmers, 'The Visual Force of Justice in the Making of Liberia', in Desmond Manderson (ed), *Law and the Visual: Representations, Technologies, and Critique* (University of Toronto Press, 2017). Chapter 5 reproduces material published in Shane Chalmers, 'Law's Imaginary Life on the Ground: Scenes of the Rule of Law in Liberia', *Law and Literature*, vol 27, no 2 (2015). The Conclusion reproduces material published in Shane Chalmers, 'Law's Pluralism: Getting to the Heart of the Rule of Law', *Law, Culture, and the Humanities* (2017): online dx.doi.org/doi:10.1177/1743872117707276 [print forthcoming].

Introduction

Being detained

Monrovia Central Prison, Liberia, August 2013

The Training and Development Officer from the Corrections Advisory Unit of the United Nations Mission in Liberia is standing outside the prison gate, her white skin marking her out as much as her blue insignia. I have crossed this street numerous times before, but I have never noticed the corrections facility. Its towering perimeter wall blends into the Ministry of Defence and military barracks that run alongside, but even these do not stand out in Monrovia; this could have been any other international NGO compound. Standing in contrast to the squatter settlements that serve the rest of the city's nearly two million inhabitants – who reside in the hollowed out remains of war-torn buildings or in recycled shacks crowded into vacated plots of land and swamp – these walled compounds are one of most visible markers of urban life in post-war Liberia.

A man stands guard at the prison gate. He does not speak as the UN officer signs us in and escorts me through the outside perimeter. Inside we come to the gate of a second walled perimeter. In the narrow yard between the two walls stands a UN Formed Police Unit. Passing through this second gate we come to a third perimeter, a high metal fence with a gate that opens into the main prison yard. In the centre of this sandy yard I am introduced to two male UN corrections officers who act as mentors to the Liberian staff. As they offer statistics about the individuals who are contained in the prison, to illustrate the object of their rule-of-law reform mission, I become distracted by the sight of the shipping containers that serve as their office. There is something about these structures, in their constancy, in their iterability – capable of being hauled away at any moment, loaded on the back of a ship, to be set down in another country, in another hemisphere, to be of service again at any time – that jars with what I am being told about the need to address the plight of the individuals contained in the prison … but before I can develop that thought the Superintendent arrives and I am called to attention.

After the introductions, the UN officer and a Liberian guard escort me into the main prison building, the few clothes hanging from the rusty bars of its second-story windows the only hint of life inside. The large concrete building has several cell-blocks, including two for armed robbery and a juvenile block. All of the men in here are "pre-trial detainees"; although of the more than 960 children, women, and men in the Central Prison, some 800 are being detained pre-trial. Many have been in here for months and years, most without access to legal representation or contact with the outside. As we pass through one of the corridors a man calls out to me from behind the bars of his cell. He demands to know who I am and what I am doing here. I explain that I am a researcher from a university studying the legal system reform process. His answer holds me in contempt: "*What more has to be studied? You don't need to do more research to see that the justice system is broken here*". He underlines this sentence with his own experience as a pre-trial detainee: being detained for months (or was it years?), with neither trial nor access to a lawyer nor contact with anyone beyond these walls – "*and you speak of 'the justice system'? There is no justice system here!*"

With his voice still reverberating through the corridor I am escorted into a second, smaller building. It is even more chilling than the first. As I enter I am struck by an odour of stagnation, the smell of living bodies slowly rotting, of men struggling to stay alive. When my eyes adjust to the dim light I see the condition of the cells, perhaps one and a half meters wide and two and a half meters long. Without space on the floor for each of the cell's five or six inhabitants to sit and sleep together, the men have set up a system of layered hammocks, three hammocks high, one above the other, the top hammock strung up three or more meters off the ground. The hammocks appear to have been made by hand out of sacking, felt, and other recycled materials. I am told they break every now and again.

Unlike the other building, the walls in this one are covered in drawings. One piece in particular catches my eye as we are leaving. Drawn on the wall of an alcove off the main corridor it is an exact representation of the Liberian coat of arms, with its image of a ship sailing towards the west African shore carrying the free people of colour who would establish what would become the Republic of Liberia. Hanging over this coat of arms is a slightly larger than usual banner – and here the prisoner's hand must have lingered a moment, a flicker of a smile must have crossed his face, for a moment, if not a great burst of laughter, shaking the foundations of the Prison as he reprinted the line: *The love of liberty brought us here.*

International Institute for the Sociology of Law, Euskadi, February 2017

This book is concerned with a contradiction in law, although the contradiction is not particular to law. It is the very condition of modernity, when an institution cannot depend on a god, tradition, or any other transcendental source to secure its foundations, which ultimately come to rest upon – or rather in, and through – its subjects.[1] As a result, the institution can never be wholly separated from its subjects, who constitute its grounds, and yet it also can never be made identical

1 See, e.g., Jacques Derrida, 'Declarations of Independence', in Elizabeth Rottenberg (ed), *Negotiations: Interventions and Interviews, 1971–2001* (Stanford: Stanford University Press, 2002) 46–54.

Figure I.1 Liberian coat of arms[2]

with them, whose differences defy such unity and closure. This contradictory condition might not be particular to law, but it does provide a way of understanding and examining it as a modern proposition – to see how law gives form to life, and how law takes form enlivened by its subjects.

The purpose of the first two chapters of this book is to stake out this contradiction by driving Theodor Adorno's dialectical philosophy into the concept of law. The result is a view that resembles Peter Fitzpatrick's theorisation of modern law and confirms the urgency of his work on law's responsiveness and "responsability". It shows how the contradiction in law, whereby law remains both separate and inseparable from its subjects, is law's *enlivening* condition, for worse, but always also for better. For worse, because it means law can become instituted in

2 Attribution: FXXX (own work) [public domain], via Wikimedia Commons.

ways that are hostile to its subjects, despite the best intentions; but always also for better, because the contradiction makes such ordering unstable and therefore disposed to transformation, and moreover, it ensures law remains open to its subjects. Adorno's contribution is a philosophy, concerned with the "primacy of the object", that works to ensure this responsiveness – law's very *pluralism* – remains critical to "the law", by working to hold the law open to subjects who give it its name while remaining abject before it.

I will return shortly to the scene of Liberia's Central Prison to give a more concrete view of this, but the necessity of turning to such a scene to grasp the problem also points to the book's broader concern. While bringing Adorno's critical social philosophy together with Fitzpatrick's legal theory provides a general understanding of law's contradictory form, enabling a view of its violence as well as its nonviolence, its capacity for domination as well as its emancipatory potential, it reveals nothing of the singular ways in which law actually takes form, which of course remain circumstantial, contingent on place and time, not to mention the humans who give it life. That is the purpose of the remaining four chapters: to flesh out an understanding of this contradictory law through a study of the making and remaking of "Liberia", beginning with its conception as an idea of liberty.

The idea's first settlements were established in the early 1820s by the American Colonization Society, a philanthropic organisation constituted for the purpose of "colonizing the free people of color" of the United States "in Africa, or elsewhere".[3] When the settlers declared their erstwhile colony a Free, Sovereign and Independent State in 1847,[4] they did so as an African-American republic. The Constitution the Americo-Liberian rulers adopted at independence therefore unsurprisingly recalled the US Constitution, including its national legal system and Common Law tradition.[5] This Constitution provided the foundation for the national law for the next 137 years. At the same time, the vast majority of Liberians – west Africans whose ancestors knew the lands of Liberia long before the republic was an idea, and who were largely excluded from its realisation as a nation-state – were not included as signatories of either the Declaration of Independence or the Constitution. Rather they were systematically excluded by design and/or effect from being rightful subjects of Liberia, while for most of the nineteenth and twentieth centuries the national law was used to secure order and stability, ensuring the Republic's ruling minority could extend and maintain their control over the country's lands and peoples.

Thus grounded as a normative matter in less than 5 percent of the subjects over whom it claimed and exercised jurisdiction, the Americo-Liberian state failed to

3 See Article 2 of the Constitution of The American Society for Colonizing the Free People of Color of the United States, published in *A View of Exertions Lately Made for the Purpose of Colonizing the Free People of Color, in the United States, in Africa, or Elsewhere* (Washington, DC: printed by Jonathan Elliot, 1817), 11–12.

4 Declaration of Independence of Liberia (1847).

5 See Constitution of the Republic of Liberia (1847); see also Charles Henry Huberich, *The Political and Legislative History of Liberia: Volumes 1 and 2* (New York: Central Book Company, 1947).

maintain within itself the basis of its ongoing existence as a modern institution, leaving its foundations effectively groundless. The result was revolution and the eventual overthrow of the republic in 1980 with a *coup d'état* led by a young "indigenous" man, Master-Sergeant Samuel Doe. The *coup* precipitated the devastating civil wars of the 1990s and early 2000s that killed a quarter of a million people, displaced millions more, and destroyed the institutions and infrastructure of the state.[6] The year 2013 – the year I conducted fieldwork in the country – marked a decade of post-war government committed to instituting "the rule of law" as a core pillar of its state-building and development agenda. It also marked a decade of a UN peace operation in the country with a mandate to support "the establishment of a State based on the rule of law".[7] If this marks a break in the history of Liberia, then the extent to which the old contradiction remains makes the question of what is taking place in this attempt to remake the nation-state of critical importance.[8]

In answering that question, the book's concern is how the contradiction in law opens it to mediation by different logics: how these logics can be seen to inform the ways in which law takes place, while law can be seen to provide a medium for these logics to operate. The book is especially concerned with how law is at the epicentre of a colonising power that makes subjects into living dead through acts of sovereign expression. This "colonising power" is not a state, or an organisation, or an institution. It is a logic – the logic of capital. Operating through law as its forceful medium, this logic renders subjects as mere objects, creating the kind of death world encountered in Liberia's Central Prison. At the same time, the book is concerned with how two other logics are informing law in Liberia. One is the logic of security, which makes law into an instrument for securing order and stability – indeed, for securing the logic of capital. The other is the logic of a liberal-internationalist regime that tends to treat every recognised subject as equivalent, thereby reducing them to an empirical individuality that denies their subjective differences. As an "empirical individual", the subject becomes the object of a universal subjectivity that makes it not only legitimate but a categorical humanitarian imperative to assist in developing it to its full potential as such.

Taken together these three logics can be seen to inform law in Liberia, and yet there is another side to the story. This follows the book's more general argument: as much as law is a means of governing over subjects, holding the potential to become an instrument of domination, law is also enlivened by those very subjects,

6 According to one report: "virtually all of the country's approximately 3 million people had to flee their homes at one time or another, sometimes for a few weeks and in many cases for several years. However, official figures estimate that 1.2 million were internally displaced and 700,000 were refugees at the war's end". Shelly Dick, *FMO Country Guide: Liberia* (Refugee Studies Centre, 2003), 11: http://repository.forcedmigration.org/show_metadata.jsp?pid=fmo:5126

7 UN Doc S/Res/1509 (19 September 2003), preambular para 7.

8 As this book goes to press, the UN Mission in Liberia is scheduled to withdraw completely by the end of April 2018: UN Doc S/Res/2333 (23 December 2016), para 10.

taking form in and through their lives and interactions. It is this fundamentally "illogical" or contradictory condition of law that ultimately denies these logics any absolute hold, leaving law open to be a medium for the self-expression of its subjects – an opening that is at its most frustrating in the case of Liberia.[9]

But let us return to a scene that offers a glimpse of all this: Liberia's Central Prison. What this scene shows above all is an institution of law, populated by bodies that give it life as an institution, that simultaneously denies their subjectivity. Thus, as a matter of *fact*, the children, women, and men who populate the prison have been brought within in the most physical way, as beings detained. The living bodies rotting in the damp pit of its deepest recess testify to that fact. And yet as a matter of *right*, these children, women, and men remain outside, being detained "pre-trial" not only in the sense that they have yet to see a lawyer, that they are yet to see a judge, that they are yet to see a law, but being detained pre-trial also in the sense that they are yet to be included as a normative matter within the institution that would judge them. Franz Kafka's parable of the countryman who is left waiting outside the gate of the law might come to mind. Where Kafka's countryman remains suspended in his own pre-trial limbo, the children, women, and men in Liberia's Central Prison have passed through three of its gates only to find themselves in the same position. But it is not quite the same position. It is much worse: a depersonalised position, in which their bodies have been brought forcefully inside the law, made identical with its institution in the most visceral way, while their subjectivity remains outside, non-identical in the most violent way. Thus, as subjects they remain pre-trial while as empirical individuals their bodies undergo the most intense trial every moment of day and night.

It is obvious that Liberia's Central Prison manifests a serious problem in law. As the prisoner said to me with contempt from behind the bars of his cell: "*you don't need to do more research to see that the justice system is broken here!*". The question is not whether there is a problem here but how to understand the problem, and how to respond. At least that is the question for the Liberians and their international partners who are working to establish a state based on the rule of law, for whom the problem is precisely that there is no "rule of law" in Liberia. Here we hear the voice of the lawyer: in a state based on the rule of law, these prisoners would have natural justice, they would be accorded due process by law. Fixing the dysfunction in the legal system would therefore resolve the problem by bringing the prisoners within the law as a matter of right as well as a matter of fact. But hearing this, the sociologist and anthropologist interject at once: such a response would not resolve the problem; quite the opposite, it would exacerbate a problem that is not technical but social/cultural. That these prisoners remain outside the institution as a matter of right reflects the fact that the national law of Liberia is

9 For an analysis of international law that pursues a similar logic of openness and closure, whereby international law has both "imperial" and "counter-imperial" dimensions, see Sundhya Pahuja, *Decolonising International Law: Development, Economic Growth and the Politics of Universality* (New York: Cambridge University Press, 2011).

not *their* law, not in any deep, normative sense. What is more, the historian points out, since the Declaration that founded the republic, the overwhelming majority of Liberians have been "pre-trial detainees", included as a factual matter within the bounds of the nation-state while being excluded as a normative matter from its institutions. Indeed, the philosopher adds: as sociology/anthropology and history show, the problem is not just how to strengthen the objective conditions of the national legal system, so the bodies of its subjects might access it more easily; the problem is how to respond to an essential dissonance in law, whereby the law remains separate from the very humans who enliven it. The answer, then, the lawyer concludes, is not only to fix the dysfunctional legal system but at the same to educate Liberians about it, to bring their bodies *and* their minds within the law!

Like these imaginary but also very real characters, this book is concerned with how to make sense of the problem seen in the prison, and how to respond. But to answer that question, the book asks another one: how might these responses *be shaping the problem?* Confronted with a contradiction in law, whereby subjects of law never fully enter into the law, how are actors such as government and UN officials responding, and how are their responses informing the ways in which law manifests? In short, how might the responses *be the problem*, and how to respond to the responses?

Of course, the prison itself is already a response to the contradiction that makes law always also "not law". For those who are concerned with securing the absolute position of the national law as the law, the prison provides a resolution to manifestations of deviancy. It provides the *corrections facility* – bringing those who contradict "the law" within it, physically if not normatively. That is the dominant response in Liberia to the fact that the national law is also obviously not law, forming a core part of the rule-of-law reform agenda of the government and its international supporters. The response is to (re)enforce the identity between the national law and its subjects, to resolve the contradiction by finally overcoming their separation. To assist in achieving this the prison system is being strengthened to ensure detainees are duly processed while being held in model human-rights facilities. And yet this does not address the underlying contradiction. Hauling bodies from padded cells to stand before a judge might bring offensive bodies within the law but it does not resolve the normative problem of being detained "pre-trial", that is, the fact that the national law of Liberia is not their law as a matter of right. Rather than resolving the problem, the result is a form of civil death, with the bodies kept alive while being denied their rightfulness as subjects who know the law in other ways. What is more, in this form law might serve a regime that requires living bodies that obey the law but not necessarily subjects who identify with it.

This points to how law might become a medium for a colonising power that makes subjects into living dead through acts of sovereign expression – and how this might be the result of a particular response to the contradiction in law. When I entered the cell-blocks of Monrovia Central Prison, it certainly *smelt* like I had entered an epicentre of what Achille Mbembe has called a "death-world": a form of "social existence" created through an expression of sovereignty "in which vast populations are subjected to conditions of life conferring upon them the status of *living dead*".[10] When my eyes grew accustomed to the dim light the sight only reinforced the smell. Describing how "necropower" operates Mbembe recalls Frantz Fanon's description of "the town belonging to the colonized people".[11] What I saw fit his description: "a place of ill fame, peopled by men of evil repute", "a world without spaciousness; men live there on top of each other", "starved of bread, of meat, of shoes, of coal, of light".[12] What I saw was a prison whose inmate population, by legal definition people of ill fame, is kept alive on one meal a day,[13] deprived of exercise in the yard,[14] stacked one on top of the other in their cells. And what I heard was a sound that still reverberates through the prison's corridors, questioning the justice of the institution that detains them. The shipping containers that serve as the offices of the UN rule-of-law reformers manifest no less this logic that treats humans in a universally exchangeable manner, in which subjects become numerous bodies strewn across the globe. No matter how well-intentioned this response is, the result is a twisted answer to Mbembe's critique of the West's seeming inability to appreciate that all humans – including Africans – "have, concretely and typically, the same flesh".[15] Systematically this critique is turned around by a logic that operates on every body in the same way. What Mbembe's "flesh and body" was supposed to signify – "the *idea of a common human nature, a humanity shared with others*" – is stripped of its humanity, leaving a response that concretely, and typically, deals in bodies but not subjects.[16]

The scene of Liberia's Central Prison thus offers a glimpse of how law can become animated in a way that makes it hostile to its subjects. Above all it points to how a certain logic – what I argue is the logic of capital – might inform law. It also indicates how the government and its international supporters are focusing on reforming Liberia's prison system in order to strengthen "the rule of law", which points to a certain security focus. And it suggests that, to the extent the prison is anything more than an instrument of order and stability, the aim is to transform the minds of Liberians, to bring them within the national law as a normative matter. In these ways the prison scene points to the co-implication of law and the

10 Achille Mbembe, 'Necropolitics', *Public Culture*, vol 15, no 1 (2003): 40 (italics in original).
11 Cited in ibid, 26–27.
12 Ibid.
13 As I was told during the visit to the Central Prison.
14 As I was also told during the visit to the Prison, the threat of riots and prison breaks, combined with the lack of corrections officers, meant that prisoners were being denied regular exercise in the yard.
15 Achille Mbembe, *On the Postcolony* (Berkeley: University of California Press, 2001), 2.
16 Ibid, 2 (italics in original). This result resembles Mbembe's later work on necropolitics, where he develops his concern with "figures of sovereignty whose central project is […] *the generalized instrumentalisation of human existence and the material destruction of human bodies and populations*", and how these figures of sovereignty "are what constitute the *nomos* of the political space in which we still live": Mbembe, 'Necropolitics', 14 (italics in original).

logics of "capital", "security", and "liberal internationalism". But there is more to this scene than that. Inside, at the very core of Liberia's Central Prison, sits a man drawing a picture on its wall – a picture that shows what no response can stop from manifesting, the very contradiction that makes law potentially hostile to its subjects. The drawing exposes the unstable grounds of the national law: a law that was brought to west Africa with the promise of liberty, that has become the opposite. In this man's response, however – in his act of talking back – the contradiction provides a window to see another possibility. The prisoner's drawing confronts the institution with its history. It requires this history to be seen from the perspective of the prisoner within this institution; and it requires this institution to be seen from the perspective of this history. The effect is to place the institution *in history* – to make it a matter not only of the here and now but also a matter of what has been; and the effect is to draw out the history from the institution – to make the history of Liberia a matter of what is taking place *here and now*. And the effect shakes the foundations. The man's image can be whitewashed; the institution's cracks can be plastered over; but as long as law remains an essentially contradictory proposition, its subjects can talk back. *This* is the emancipatory possibility, the response to the responses, denying the logics that inform law their hold, leaving law open to be a medium for the self-expression of the subjects who enliven it.

Chapter 1 opens with a reading of "negative dialectics" that draws out five aspects of Adorno's philosophy, which I then drive into the concept of law in Chapter 2. This provides the theoretical approach and conceptual framework for the study of law in Liberia, set out in the four chapters that follow. The first of these, Chapter 3, focuses on the logic of capital and the making of "Liberia". This shows how the logic of capital informed the colonial origins and consolidation of the nation-state in the nineteenth and twentieth centuries, and how it is informing the remaking of Liberia in the twenty-first century. Chapter 4 continues the analysis of post-war Liberia, focusing on the logic of security and how it is informing the government's work to establish a state based on the rule of law with the assistance of a UN peace operation. Chapter 5 then considers how the contradiction in law nonetheless remains integral to its life in Liberia, enlivened by subjects in ways that defy any logical hold on law. Finally, Chapter 6 brings the study to a close by reconsidering how actors in Liberia are responding differently to this persistent contradiction. This shows how the logic of liberal internationalism is informing the attempt to institute "the rule of law" in response to the contradiction in law; but it also shows other responses that point to a radically different rule of law. It is upon this that I reflect in the Conclusion – on what the contradiction in law might mean for law's rule.

A final note on research methods. I collected the material for this book through a combination of fieldwork, archival research, as well as deskwork. The fieldwork included four months living in Monrovia in 2013 where I examined the work being done to establish "the rule of law" by the government, the UN Mission in Liberia (UNMIL), bilateral development agencies, and international and national NGOs. During this time I collected research material from interviews,[17] official

17 See the Appendix for a list of interviews.

documents, newspaper articles, and radio programs. The fieldwork also included two months in eight sites outside Monrovia (see Figure I.2),[18] collecting material using a combination of observation and interviews with actors engaged in the implementation of rule-of-law reform programs, including government and UN officials, international and national NGOs, civil society actors, journalists, as well as through conversations with people in the communities. Outside of Liberia I conducted interviews with officials in the UN Headquarters in New York City working on global issues of rule-of-law assistance, and gathered documents from the Liberian archives at the University of Indiana in Bloomington.

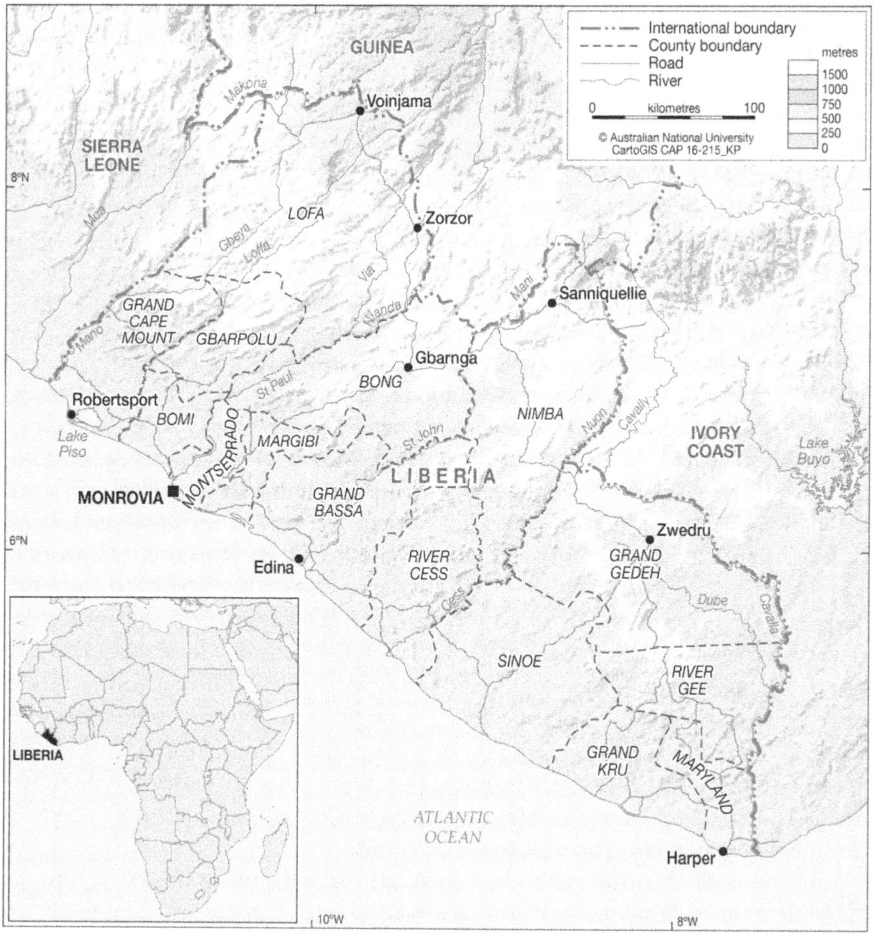

Figure I.2 Fieldwork sites in Liberia[19]

18 Edina, Gbarnga, Harper, Robertsport, Sanniquellie, Voinjama, Zorzor, Zwedru.

19 Attribution: Karina Pelling, CartoGIS, College of Asia and the Pacific, The Australian National University.

Figure I.3 Benson Street, central Monrovia[20]

Figure I.4 Voinjama, capital of Lofa County and one of the biggest towns in Liberia[21]

20 Attribution: Erik (HASH) Hershman [CC BY 2.0 (http://creativecommons.org/licenses/by/2.0)], via Wikimedia Commons.

21 Attribution: Shane Chalmers (2013). The population of Voinjama is approximately 30,000.

1 Negative dialectics

Introduction

A basic philosophical problem underlies this study: how to respond to the dialectic of subject and object. This recalls the problem of institutionalisation highlighted in the Introduction, whereby an institution cannot be identical with its subjects – indeed its integrity as an institution depends on this separation; and yet it cannot be wholly separate from these subjects either, who, as subjects and not as a mere sum of bodies, constitute its grounds as an entity. Thus, as an objective social form, an institution might remain constant while the subjects that enliven it come and go; while at the same time, the integrity of the institution depends on it maintaining within it these subjects who are of its essence.[1]

This dialectic, whereby subject and object remain simultaneously separate and inseparable, is not problematic in itself. The problem arises when there is an insistence on *identity*. This can happen in two ways: by separating subject and object and making them identical with themselves, and by collapsing the two and making them identical with each other. The problem of analytical separation can be seen in the study of law in particular, in the tendency to approach law either as an "object of study" or as a "subject of study".[2] In the first case, approaching law

1 To reiterate another image to signify this point, an image evoked by "Proust's narrator" and reiterated by Spivak in her 'Translator's Preface' to Derrida's *Of Grammatology*:

> I was not one man only [...] but the steady advance hour after hour of an army in close formation, in which there appeared, according to the moment, impassioned men, indifferent men, jealous men... In a composite mass, these elements may, one by one, *without our noticing it*, be replaced by others, which others again eliminate or reinforce, until in the end a change has been brought about which it would be impossible to conceive if we were a single person.

"What, then", Spivak asks, "is the [...] identity?". Gayatri Chakravorty Spivak, 'Translator's Preface', in Jacques Derrida, *Of Grammatology* (Baltimore: Johns Hopkins University Press, 1997), xi.

2 For a discussion of these different approaches to law in the fields of socio-legal studies and law and the humanities, with a tendency in the former to approach law as an object of study and in the latter as a subject of study, see Desmond Manderson,

as an object of study risks losing sight of its subjective qualities: it risks treating law in a way that reifies its institutional separation from the subjects who enliven it. In the second case, approaching law subjectively risks losing sight of its objective qualities: it risks treating law in a naïvely relativistic way that fails to maintain how it has a social structure that makes it more than its subjects. The problem is that in each case the response fails to maintain within it the truth of the other. Because law has both subjective and objective dimensions, the question is how to bring the two together in the study of law. The answer is not to attempt to overcome the differences between these dimensions, however, by merging subject and object into some third basis for studying law (producing a kind of Gonzo methodology).[3] The question is how to avoid separating the two and privileging one over the other, without collapsing the two in disregard of their differences – how to maintain their differences while bringing them together in their critical relation to each other.

The philosophy set out by Theodor Adorno in his work *Negative Dialectics* is directed at this problem. At its crux, "negative dialectics" is simply "the consistent consciousness of nonidentity".[4] This is "dialectical" in the sense that it places every thesis, or identity, in relation with its antithesis, or nonidentity. However, this is a *negative* dialectic, rather than a "positive" one, in that the equation of thesis and antithesis, identity and nonidentity, is not seen to end in synthesis. The equation, which would make the two identical, is always seen to be inadequate. Every synthetic end is seen as another identification, the truth of which remains in relation to the ways in which it is more and other than identified. This results in a restless negativity, a constant overturning of one-sided positions.[5]

The purpose of this chapter is to elaborate this approach by drawing out five aspects of negative dialectics from Adorno's philosophy: (1) the subject of experience, through a discussion of the subject-object dialectic; (2) how understanding this is a matter of justice; (3) the problem of conceptualisation; (4) the logical law of contradiction; and (5) the dialectical dimensions of determination and infinitude. In the next chapter I then drive these aspects of negative dialectics into the concept of law, and through that, into the realities of law in Liberia.

Negative dialectics

As a philosopher, as a sociologist, and as a scholar of the humanities, Adorno's critical concern was the violence that is done to life the moment undialectical

'AD 2014: A Review essay of Eve Darian-Smith, *Laws and Societies in Global Contexts – Contemporary Approaches* ', *Law and Humanities*, vol 8, no 1 (2014).

3 The reference is to Hunter S Thompson's style of journalism which was famous for bringing together the most precise factual investigation with his freakish experience of the facts.

4 Theodor W Adorno, *Negative Dialectics* (Dennis Redmond, members.efn.org, 2001), 16–18.

5 In this Adorno's *Negative Dialectics* sits alongside Jean-Luc Nancy's *Hegel: The Restlessness of the Negative* (Minneapolis: University of Minnesota Press, 2002).

"identity thinking" is reified in society. Adorno saw this in Nazi Germany, where it facilitated the Holocaust through the ideological equation of the proper subject of human life with the *Volksgemeinschaft*, rendering non-identical forms of subjectivity eliminable. He saw it in the capitalist-economic rendition of everything as universally exchangeable units. He saw it in the scientific mode that treats the isolated object as matter of fact. Above all he saw it in the modern bureaucratic state, in its drawing together of these conceits in the administration of life: identifying subjectivity according to circumscribed categories, rationalising everything instrumentally according to a logic of exchangeability, based on a model of truth that resembles an "ideology of the positive" that equates what is real with what is analytically identified.[6]

The subject of experience

Underlying each of these concerns is an awareness of the violence that is done to an object the moment the subject attempts to make sense of the experience of it; the attempt to grasp it reducing it to a concept that is held out as its equivalent.[7] I turn to the centrality of the "concept" in a moment. Before that, however, it is necessary to understand what is meant here by "experience".

This is the experience of contradiction that arises out of the confusion of being (subjectively) and existing (objectively), in which the two are never completely separate (a subject being always informed by an objective existence, which is likewise informed by the subject who acts) but also never in perfect harmony or unity (objective existence always being made sense of subjectively).[8] This is the experience of the subject-object dialectic, whereby subject and object inform each other without becoming identical. As such, the concept of experience in Adorno's negative-dialectical philosophy does not seek to capture a pure or original knowledge, nor a perfect state of being, but rather a condition of not knowing and not being in any absolute way.[9] As Adorno writes, "what experience is concerned with at any particular moment is the animating contradiction of such absolute truth".[10] Thus, not only is this *not* an experience of oneness, but it is an experience of knowing existence and being at one with it in neither knowing nor being at one with it – a contradiction that resurrects the spirit of what has been gripped in truth by rigor mortis.

But just as subject and object are never at one with each other, the subject is also never at one with itself. This is not the kind of monadic experience of the autonomous and self-determining liberal subject. For Adorno, as for Hegel, the subjectivity of the individual is always also contingent and objectively determined, "the subject" being an objective form, constituted historically and in relation to

6 Adorno, *Negative Dialectics*, 61–63.
7 Ibid, 19–21.
8 See, e.g., ibid, 104–136; Theodor W Adorno, 'The Actuality of Philosophy', *Telos*, vol 31 (1977).
9 See also Theodor W Adorno, *Hegel: Three Studies* (Cambridge: MIT Press, 1963), 53.
10 Ibid. See also Adorno, *Negative Dialectics*, 21–22.

nature, and therefore never absolutely individual.[11] And yet the subject also comprises self-conscious individuals who recognise themselves and demand to be recognised as singular beings. Thus, subject (like object) is both objective and subjective, both generic and singular, determined and self-determining, and none of these in itself. An objective part of a whole – and therefore knowable only through empirical study of the whole – and yet irreconcilably apart from this totality – and therefore knowable only in its singular situation,[12] the subject remains suspended in an experience that is of the animating contradiction of absolute truth.

A matter of justice

In this, negative dialectics shares common ground with poststructuralism. In contrast to the postmodernists who became enchanted by the thought of indeterminacy, and the trenchant modern positivists who cannot let go of the desire for certainty and stability, the critical concern of negative dialectics, as that of poststructuralism, is not to resolve the subject's contradictory experience but to make it critical to every resolution. Adorno's negative-dialectical philosophy, like Derrida's philosophy of deconstruction, thus works against the domination that results from any attempt at resolving the contradictory experience that leaves subject and object as separate as they are inseparable. And for both, this is a matter of justice.[13]

For Adorno, any attempt to resolve or dismiss the subject-object dialectic would either separate the two entirely, in an analytical fashion that conceives of the subject as wholly subject and the object as wholly object; or else it would elide the one in pronouncing a unity of the two, in a totalitarian fashion that conceives of an equivalence of subject and object.[14] An example of the analytical separation is the subject of Enlightenment who sees the world as his object and whose rights as an individual are inviolable – in both cases failing to recognise the extent to which his subjective existence is constituted in the very objective spheres, natural and historical, from which he thinks himself free as a rightful individual. An example of the totalitarian elision would be the state in which the individual subject is no

11 See Adorno, *Hegel*, 63. Nancy's articulation of the Hegelian concept of the "subject" is also instructive here: see Nancy, *Restlessness of the Negative*, 4–5. The concepts of "nature" and "history" are central to much of Adorno's work; for an overview see Susan Buck-Morss, *The Origin of Negative Dialectics: Theodor W Adorno, Walter Benjamin, and the Frankfurt Institute* (New York: The Free Press, 1977), Chapter 3.

12 See also Adorno, *Negative Dialectics*, 21–22.

13 On the relation between Adorno's negative dialectics and Derrida's deconstruction, see Jacques Derrida, *Fichus* (Paris: Galilee, 2002); Jean-Philippe Deranty, 'Adorno's Other Son: Derrida and the Future of Critical Theory', *Social Semiotics*, vol 16, no 3 (2006). On the relation between negative dialectics and poststructuralism more generally, see Peter Dews, 'Adorno, Post-Structuralism and the Critique of Identity', *New Left Review*, vol 157 (May–June 1986). For a critical reading of this relation that instead situates Adorno's work in a Marxian vein, see Fredric Jameson, *Late Marxism: Adorno, or the Persistence of the Dialectic* (London: Verso, 1990).

14 See Adorno, *Negative Dialectics*, 176–177.

longer recognised apart from the whole, which is held up as the objective form of the absolute subject – failing to recognise the extent to which "the whole realizes itself only in and through the parts, only through discontinuity, alienation, and reflection".[15] This is a matter of *justice* in that to speak of "the subject" in absolute or universal terms is to ignore the ways in which individual manifestations of subjectivity diverge from it, becoming objects of indifference, and as such, being, exposed to violence. Likewise, to speak of "objectivity" in absolute terms is to overlook the ways in which objects are constituted subjectively, thus concealing their historical concretion, and as such, exposing the subject to violence through its historical exclusion from what is objective while allowing for the perpetuation of domination within the production of the object/ivity.

Derrida's philosophy of deconstruction works in a similar way to expose the untruth of binary oppositions and the exploitation that congeals in the space between them. However, in revealing the untruth of binary thinking Derrida neither collapses the two into one nor dismisses their relation outright. Deconstruction does not aim to do away with difference any more than negative dialectics; the opposite, it is motivated by a concern for the singularity of the other in its utter difference – hence the two are never reduced to the one. And yet the justice of deconstruction is not to be found in suspending the subject in an infinite plurality of difference – hence the two are never cleaved from one another either. Rather the justice of deconstruction, like that of negative dialectics, is in the experience of contradiction: in *recognising* difference, always *different* from its recognition.[16]

There are two sides to this, neither tenable on its own. On one side: in *recognising* difference, difference is affirmed (cognised) – thus what is different is cut short by the identification of what is different. This is difference as "distinction, inequality, or discernibility".[17] On the other side: recognising what is different as *unrecognisably* different, difference is not affirmed (not cognised) – thus what is different is left open to what is different. This is difference as "deference", deferring what is different to what is different to its cognition here and now, expressing "the interposition of delay, the interval of a *spacing* and *temporalizing* that puts off until 'later' what is presently denied, the possible that is presently impossible".[18] Critically neither position holds on its own. What is different must be articulated for it to be meaningfully spoken of – but this reduces difference to a self-referential identity, to absolute sameness, "the order of the *same*"[19]; and so the meaning must be deferred – but this suspends what is different indeterminately, as absolute difference, "nonidentity"[20]; and so what is different must be articulated.... To cut things short, there can be no justice in either affirming difference or in

15 Adorno, *Hegel*, 4. See also Adorno, *Negative Dialectics*, 18–19, 21–22.

16 See Jacques Derrida, 'Force of Law: The "Mystical Foundation of Authority"', *Cardozo Law Review*, vol 11 (1989–1990).

17 Jacques Derrida, 'Differance', in Julie Rivkin and Michael Ryan (eds), *Literary Theory: An Anthology* (Malden: Blackwell, 2004), 279.

18 Ibid.

19 Ibid.

20 Ibid.

deferring difference. Justice requires bringing the polarised positions together (in *différance*).[21]

Justice, whether approached by way of negative dialectics or deconstruction, thus requires respecting this contradictory experience, which requires a restless process of recognising how the subject is other than its identified forms. This does not mean refraining from the act of articulation, which for Adorno would mean to stop thinking altogether, which would mean "not even the simplest operation could be thought through, there would be no truth, everything would be emphatically nothing"[22]; and for Derrida would mean suspending the possibility of justice indefinitely, which would be unjust, "for only a decision is just".[23] This is the paradox for both Adorno and Derrida: the decisive cognition is as *necessary* as it is *violent*, moving towards truth as much as it is untrue in itself, as *just* as it is never "*presently* just, fully just".[24] As Derrida writes: "the ordeal of the undecidable [...] must be gone through by any decision worthy of the name" – an ordeal that "is never past or passed", never "surmounted or sublated" in the decision, but "remains caught, lodged, at least as a ghost – but an essential ghost – in every decision, in every event of decision".[25] Truth and justice are *in* this experience of contradiction, an experience that animates every act, every judgment.

Concepts and the nonconceptual

I began by saying that underlying Adorno's concerns is an awareness of the violence that is done to an object the moment a subject attempts to make sense of the experience of it; the attempt to grasp it reducing it to a concept that is held out as its equivalent. Having set out what is at stake, both in terms of the subject's contradictory experience and how dealing with the contradiction is a matter of justice, I now turn to the root problem: conceptualisation. This is also where negative dialectics diverges from deconstruction. In sum, where Derrida's philosophy ultimately remains focused on the subject and its acts of articulation, Adorno's negative dialectics seeks to maintain focus on the object of articulation. In this Adorno's philosophy is "materialist", without slipping into a naïve realism.

The German word *begreifen* is a keyword for Adorno, as it was in Hegel's philosophy, and plays on the dual meaning of "grasp" as both a physical and mental enclosure.[26] This is "understanding" as an act of turning objective sense over to conscious thought, in order to make sense of the subject's experience. This is never an entirely abstract act, thinking always involving taking hold of objects, sensationally, in the attempt to comprehend the experience of them, consciously. For Adorno there is no concept without an objective basis, just as "thinking

21 Ibid.
22 Adorno, *Negative Dialectics*, 18–19; see also 114–116.
23 See Derrida, 'Force of Law', 963.
24 Ibid, 963 (italics in original).
25 Ibid, 965.
26 See also Nancy, *Restlessness of the Negative*, 5.

without the concept is nothing of the sort".[27] That is, concepts are never purely subjective but always in relation to an object, as little as it might be recognised, while the relation between thought and object is also never immediate but mediated conceptually. As such, concepts, as technological innovation as much as a way to appreciate existence, provide the cognitive tools that facilitate the subject's conceited mastery of the world, that is, domination. And yet Adorno's critique of conceptual violence does not aim to do away with concepts, seeing such an end as no less conceited, and no less violent, leaving the subject blind as to how things continue to be mediated subjectively and therefore prone to domination without second thought. The driving concern of negative dialectics is to work against the *privileged thought* of the subject, which always comes at the expense of the object. The aim, in other words, is to maintain an uncompromising respect for the primacy of the object, not by withdrawing from the expressive act that would violate it, but by making the negative-dialectical relation of subject and object critical to every conceptual schema. This is what it means for negative dialectics to be directed at "the consistent consciousness of nonidentity".[28]

Key to making sense of this is the concept of the nonconceptual. This is the "more" in the formulation, "what is, is more, than it is".[29] What *is*, conceptual, "is", and what is *more*, remains nonconceptual. For Adorno this is where philosophy has persistently failed, either dismissing from the outset the nonconceptual as "transient and inconsequential" and of no interest or else, when it has taken an interest it has done so "in vain", merely ending up with new conceptualisations of the nonconceptual.[30] Adorno criticises Hegel's dialectic, like every version of dialectics before and since, for this reason. Adorno's critique is that the Hegelian system lost sight of its object the moment it was held out as wholly identifiable with the subject. This fails to maintain the dialectic's negative thrust and ultimately affirms the possibility of a synthesis of subject and object, an identity of identity and nonidentity.[31] The result is domination of the object by the "primacy of the subject",[32] the experience of contradiction ultimately resolved by sublating the object as an aspect of the subject.[33]

Having said that, Hegel's dialectic remains critical. Adorno's aim in critiquing it is not to trash it but to *release* it, in both meanings of the word: to free it from its

27 Adorno, *Negative Dialectics*, 104–107; see also 114–121.
28 Ibid, 16–18.
29 Ibid, 163–164.
30 Ibid, 19–21. By "philosophy" Adorno has in mind a European tradition of philosophy "since Plato", and German idealism in particular.
31 Ibid, 18–19. But compare Nancy, *Restlessness of the Negative*, and Slavoj Žižek, *The Sublime Object of Ideology* (London: Verso, 2008), xxix. In their own ways both Nancy and Žižek see contradiction and negativity as not only the process but also the "end" of Hegelian dialectics; indeed for Žižek it was Marx and not Hegel who "sutured" the dialectical antagonism, making Hegel in a sense "the first post-Marxist": see Žižek, *The Sublime Object of Ideology*, xxix.
32 Adorno, *Negative Dialectics*, 18–19; see also 48–50.
33 In this, Adorno writes, "Hegel is, like Kant and the entire tradition, including Plato, a partisan of the One": ibid, 158–161.

confinement and to work upon it as one's own. Adorno's critique aims to retrieve the negativity in Hegel's philosophy that was so essential in his *Phenomenology*, [34] and push it to its logical end-point, which is without end, a restless overturning of every point. Just as Adorno's negative dialectic aims to open thought to the non-conceptual through concepts, to release what is dynamic in them, the same is true of Adorno's *Negative Dialectics* with respect to Hegel's philosophy. It is in releasing Hegel's dialectical system through its critical treatment in *Negative Dialectics* that Adorno aims to open up the conceptual to the nonconceptual without making them the same.

The law of contradiction

The contradiction is central to this mode of thinking, as the "index of non-identity",[35] and it is therefore important to introduce it here in greater depth. For this it is useful to consider Adorno's formulation: "Since however this totality [of the concept] is formed according to logic, whose core is constructed from the proposition of the excluded third, everything which does not conform to such, everything qualitatively divergent assumes the signature of the contradiction".[36]

In the study of logic, at least in the European tradition since Aristotle, the "law of the excluded third" purports to establish a clear line of separation between two contradictory propositions: "X" is either true (it is "X") or it is not true (it is "not X"). Whatever fails to live up to the categorical demands of this distinction is relegated to the condition of the contradiction, which is the excluded third proposition: "X" is true *and* it is not true (it is "X" and it is "not X"); and conversely, what is expressed as "X" is *neither* true *nor* not true (it is neither "X" nor "not X"). Thus, from the first of these two perspective – that of the expressive subject – "X" *is* "X", precisely as it says it is. To dispute the logic of that, from a conceptual point of view, would be self-contradictory, which is absurdity.[37] And yet, even though the concept "must always hold forth as if it had such completely in hand", nonetheless "the non-naïve thought knows how little it encompasses what is thought".[38] While "X" *is* "X", as it says it is, it remains patently obvious to the expressive subject that "X" is also not exactly what it seeks to express, despite what it says. That is why understanding *conceptually* what it means for "X" to be "X" requires understanding the absurdity in which the concept is at the same time not what it expresses itself to be – how "X" is "X" and "not X" simultaneously.

That is the contradiction from the conceptual perspective of the expressive subject. However, as noted, there is a second perspective on the contradiction, from the standpoint of what is expressed as "X". From this view – the nonconceptual perspective – the object that is represented by the concept "X" is neither wholly

34 Ibid.
35 Ibid, 16–18.
36 Ibid.
37 On absurdity as self-contradiction, see Thomas Hobbes, *Leviathan* (Oxford: Oxford University Press, 2008), 88.
38 Adorno, *Negative Dialectics*, 24–27.

"X" nor wholly "not X". On one hand, an object is never *identical* with its concept, which is merely a representation of it; on the other hand, an object is also never entirely *nonidentical* with its concept, insofar as it represents it. Thus the object remains: suspended in a state of abjection, neither wholly "X" nor wholly "not X". Both of these perspectives on the contradiction are instructive and need to be kept in mind,[39] for reasons that will become clear when I turn to the concept of law in the next chapter.

Negative dialectics does not aim to break the law of the excluded third or have it struck off the books; it is much more radical than that. Against the ideology of the positive it makes the contradiction central to thought, as the index of non-identity.[40] In this the contradiction is not seen as something to be ashamed of and hidden from sight or to be cleaned up with obsessive scrubbing; either way it remains, perhaps better hidden or else as the stubborn stain one tries to ignore. Negative dialectics has no interest in cleaning the surface of thought through analysis; the opposite, it works against the subject's desire to control existence through its conceptual mastery by foregrounding the absurdity, and the violence, of such conceit. Of course, dialectics cannot do without positive distinctions: the concept is no less the material of dialectical analysis than is the object that contradicts it. But rather than fetishise the concept, negative dialectics focuses on the confusion that results when concepts clearly face their contradiction.

Determination and infinitude

At its most basic "negative dialectics" is therefore just another name for "critical thinking" – indeed for Critical Theory – striking at the limits of thought, demanding attention to what is excluded from and oppressed by every attempt at identification.[41] As a critical mode of thinking it is a constant reminder that concepts are wholly inadequate to their task of determining the truth of things, that the truth of a concept lies and lies in its relation with its contradiction. This is what Adorno means when he writes: "its name says to begin with nothing more than that objects do not vanish into their concept, that these end up in contradiction with the received norm of the *adaequatio*".[42] What *is*, grasped by thought, always ends up in contradiction with what thinking mistakes for its truth according to the maxim *veritas est adaequatio rei et intellectus* ("truth is the equation of thing and intellect"). This is where negative dialectics "transgresses" against the dominant European tradition of dialectical philosophy.[43] Unlike the positivist versions of dialectics that Adorno critiques, exemplified by the formulation of the "negation of the negation" as a method of determining the truth of the matter,

39 See also Adorno, *Hegel*, 78.
40 Adorno, *Negative Dialectics*, 16–18.
41 On Critical Theory, see Max Horkheimer, 'Traditional and Critical Theory', in *Critical Theory: Selected Essays* (New York: Continuum, 1972).
42 Adorno, *Negative Dialectics*, 16–18.
43 Ibid, 'Prologue'.

negative dialectics focuses on how little of the object is present in the material.[44] "Dialectics not a standpoint", Adorno emphasises.[45] Dialectics does not culminate in a truthful exposition any more than it might be used to defend a proposition. There is no such position, no point at which one might stand and look back having finally reached "the truth"; there is only the constant overturning of the ground on which one stands, as the overturning of the truth in light of its untruth. To take dialectics as a standpoint for determining what is true would be to grind to a halt in a cloud of dust while the world carries on.

The constant movement of negative dialectics and its attention to untruth is not a hopeless descent into relativism, however. While negative dialectics does not come to rest on a determinate truth it also rejects relativism's false individualism in which the autonomous and self-determining subject is the locus of truth.[46] For Adorno there is an actuality beyond the self-conscious subject that informs the subject while being transformed by it. The point is not that there is no objective truth; the point is that what is objectively true cannot be *grasped* – existence reducible to a concept of being no more than knowledge is reducible to a determinate system of thought. This also does not end in a nihilistic position of indeterminacy, however. As Adorno writes, this approach seeks to emancipate dialectics from any form of affirmation "without relinquishing anything in terms of determinacy".[47]

What Adorno means by "determinacy", and how negative dialectics moves thought towards the determinate without simply affirming it, is what makes this mode of thinking so critical and so necessary to intellectual work. One way to think about this is the relation just touched upon, between what is "real", as a claim to *the* truth, and what is "actual", *in* truth. Thus on one side: what is actual, rendered as what is real, reality represents existence in stucco finish, plastered over with a calcareous substance that imitates stone. On the other side: truth in actuality, always more than realised, always penetrates through; the cement wears away with time, dissolves under changing conditions, an interior becomes exposed to an exterior, revealing the gaps, requiring a fresh rendering. Again there are two dimensions: what is actual, which is infinitely realisable, always *more* in truth than what "is" said to be the truth; and what is real, which is by definition how things are, precisely what "is" without *more*. In poststructuralist terms these two dimensions correspond to the poles of determinacy and indeterminacy, as the relation between what is fixed in itself and what is beyond itself, outside of itself, exterior to itself.[48] For negative dialectics, as for poststructuralism, both dimensions are always in play. *Reality*: never an ambivalent statement, always an expression of what "is" actual; while what *is* actual: never restricted by its definition as "is", always overflows the order of things, always takes form in other ways.

44 Ibid.
45 Ibid, 16–18.
46 For Adorno's critique of relativism, ibid, 45–48.
47 Ibid, 'Prologue'.
48 See Peter Fitzpatrick, *Modernism and the Grounds of Law* (Cambridge: Cambridge University Press, 2001), 52, 62.

This is not a binary code, switching from one to the other. The *point* is dialectical, posing truth in-between the proposition and the exposition, in-between real definition and actual infinitude, in-between finite reality and infinite actuality. The point is the *movement* towards truth: exposing the truth to its untruth, as what is beyond its determinate position, the truth, made to tremble, must move out of itself, beyond itself, towards another position, if it is to not turn to dust. And yet there is no movement without position; infinitude without definition, even less substantive than dust.[49] The truth must stake its claim in real ground, take up position, against the thought of infinity, so that it might tremble in-between, resting on neither one nor the other, becoming, in truth, neither wholly determinate nor wholly indeterminate.[50]

49 Adorno, *Negative Dialectics*, 174–175.

50 See Nancy, *Restlessness of the Negative*, in particular on "restlessness" (3–7), "becoming" (8–13), and "trembling" (40–45). On "truth", see also Adorno, *Negative Dialectics*, 21-22, 43–45, 50–53, 57–58, 61–63, 107–111, 114–116 and 132–134, and on "infinity", ibid, 124–127.

2 The concept of law

Law as is

In the third part of *Negative Dialectics* Adorno sought to model his philosophy by driving it, "according to its own concept, into the realm of reality".[1] This included several passages on the "juridical sphere" and "law and equity".[2] My aim in this chapter is to develop that analysis by driving the account of negative dialectics developed in the previous chapter further into the realities of law.[3]

To do that I begin here with a simple structure, the predicate sentence, of the form subject–copula–predicate: "it is this". I then argue that this is the structure of law – indeed that *law is the copula writ large*, a dialectical medium connecting subject and object, making an existential judgment as to how things "are" into a corporeal sentence on and of what *is*, at the same time making a grammatical sentence on and of how things "are" into an actual judgment as to what *is*. I then develop the argument by examining law as "the articulation of normativity", from three perspectives: from the standpoint of law as the expressive subject that articulates the sentence "the law is this"; from the standpoint of the subject whose experience is the object of law; and from the perspective of the process that plays

1 Theodor W Adorno, *Negative Dialectics* (Dennis Redmond, members.efn.org, 2001), 'Prologue'.
2 Ibid, 303–305 ("Die juridische Sphäre") and 305–306 ("Recht und Billigkeit").
3 Adorno's work has received almost no attention from English-language scholars of law, with some recent exceptions: see Craig Reeves, 'Adorno, Freedom and Criminal Law: The "Determinist Challenge" Revitalised', *Law and Critique*, vol 27, no 3 (2016); Craig Reeves, 'Criminal Law and the Autonomy Assumption: Adorno, Bhaskar, and Critical Legal Theory', *Journal of Critical Realism*, vol 13, no 4 (2014); Craig Reeves, '"Exploding the Limits of Law": Judgment and Freedom in Arendt and Adorno', *Res Publica*, vol 15, no 2 (2009); Andreas Fischer-Lescano, 'A "Just and Non-violent Force"? Critique of Law in World Society', *Law and Critique*, vol 26, no 3 (2015); Robert Fine, 'Natural Law and Critical Theory: Bringing Rights Back In', *Journal of Classical Sociology*, vol 13, no 2 (2013); Robert Fine, 'Debating Human Rights, Law, and Subjectivity: Arendt, Adorno, and Critical Theory', in Lars Rensmann and Samir Gandesha (eds), *Arendt and Adorno: Political and Philosophical Investigations* (Stanford: Stanford University Press, 2012); Alan Norrie, *Law and the Beautiful Soul* (London: The Glasshouse Press, 2005).

out between the "subjective" expression of law as the law, and the "objective" experience of law as always also otherwise.

The result is a view of law as both the positive expression and what remains more and other than expressed. Just as negative dialectics is directed at the consistent consciousness of nonidentity, a negative-dialectical approach to law is directed at making the non-identical aspect of law critical to its concept. In more concrete terms, this is directed at making the prisoner's experience central to the concept of law rather than treating him as excess that must be remanded in a corrections facility in order to uphold the rule of law – a point I return to in the chapter's concluding section in outlining the relevance of this discussion to the study of law in Liberia.

The predicate sentence

But first the predicate sentence, and never far from the scene, Adorno:

> The cult of being lives by the ancient ideology of the *idola fori*[4]: that which thrives in the darkness of the word being and the forms derived from it. "Is" establishes the context of the existential judgment between the grammatical subject and the predicate and thereby suggests something ontic. At the same time, taken purely by itself, as the copula, it means the general categorical matter-at-hand of a synthesis, without representing something ontic. Heidegger draws the ontological purity from the logicity of the copula, thus suiting his allergy against the factical; from the existential judgment however the memory of the ontic, which then permits it to hypostasize the categorical achievement of the synthesis as a given fact. To the "is" there does indeed correspond a "matter-at-hand": in every predicative judgment the "is" has its meaning just as much as the subject and the predicate. The "matter-at-hand" is however intentional, not ontic. The copula fulfils itself according to its own meaning solely in the relation between the subject and the predicate. It is not independent.[5]

In this passage Adorno identifies two aspects of the copula. *In-between* the grammatical subject and predicate it establishes "the context of the existential judgment". It holds up the sentence as a sentence on and of life, convicting "it", what *is* in actuality always more than predicated, of being, identifiable, accountable, expressible: "it is this". At least that is what it holds up – life behind bars. *By itself*, however, as a grammatical operative, the copula merely performs a synthetic

4 Francis Bacon considered "four classes of idols which beset men's minds", one of which is the *idola fori*, or "idols of the market place", "formed by the intercourse and association of men with each other": see Francis Bacon, *The New Organon, or True Directions Concerning the Interpretation of Nature* (Adelaide: ebooks@Adelaide, 2014), Aphorisms, XXXVIII-XLIV.

5 Adorno, *Negative Dialectics*, 107–111.

function, combining "it" and "this", subject and predicate, in a single sentence on and of words, convicting it of this, sententiously.

Thus by itself the copula represents nothing actual, or nothing more than what "is", in its purest form, discourse – the stuff of ideology as much as idols. And yet this word-play is almost never *for itself.* Used seriously its intention is to make sense of existence; like the idol it is intended to signify nothing in itself and always something more. Thus the two aspects of the copula are not simply separate but also inseparable. Crossing one way: the intention of the linguistic synthesis is to perform a real function, to determine the matter-at-hand: "it is *this*?" – a serious question. Crossing the other way: from the existential judgment a memory of the ontic pervades what remains purely synthetic, the grammatical construct becoming real: "it *is* this" – a serious answer. Now both are real: the actual problem that needs to be judged, a sentence handed down, as much as the sentence that allows for the matter to be spoken of, and therefore taken in hand and dealt with.

Thus the copula, most meaningful by itself, "is not independent", its meaning always in-between what *is*, in actuality, and how it "is", expressed, enlivening both through the contradiction. What *is*, in actuality, contradicting how it "is", expressed; what "is", expressed, contradicting how it *is*, in actuality. The "matter-at-hand": always this contradictory configuration of what is objective and what is subjective. Holding this material, as an idol, the subject does not have in hand what it intends to grasp, as *is*. To think the matter-at-hand as *is* the subject makes the fatal mistake, making the sentence on and of words into a sentence on and of life. That is why it must not be forgotten that the matter-at-hand is intentional and not ontic, intending to hold up what "is" as how things *are*, without actually upholding how things *are* as what "is". To forget this is to forget that "the *Idols of the Market Place* are the most troublesome of all – idols which have crept into the understanding through the alliances of words and names", words and names that beget other words and names, defining each other and not the objects with which they deal.[6] And yet the configuration is no idle form. What *is*: brought into being through an act of copulation. Mediating between what *is* and how it "is" expressed, copulation gives existence a name, "being", even more apparent, more alive even, at the same time condemning it to idol form, at risk of existence, being, no more than a fetish.

And so the copula, is, a dialectical medium, making an existential judgment as to how things "are" into a corporeal sentence on and of what *is* – out of the subjective verdict, an objective sentence; at the same time making a grammatical sentence on and of how things "are" into an actual judgment as to what *is* – out of the subjective sentence, an objective verdict. "Is": connecting subject and object through the lines of the conscious mind.

There is perhaps no better example than the Aboriginal songlines that connect people and country in the most radical way, songlines that are of the land as much

6 Bacon, *The New Organon*, Aphorisms, XLIII.

as its people, the two as inseparable as they are separate – lines sung out over the world, singing its existence into being. Songlines that are, as such, also of law.[7]

The predicate sentence of law

If that is the copula, a dialectical medium, synthesising sentences on and of words that are sentences on and of the world, reflecting the subject's experience of separation and yet inseparability, then what does it mean to say that law is the copula writ large? It means the same, with one forceful difference: *the law is this* – a sentence over life, like every other, and yet like no other. "The law is this": a sentence like every other, it remains *intentional* and not ontic, *normative* and not definitive; like no other, its hypostasization is rock-solid. And yet, rendered in stucco finish, the sentence plastered over with a calcareous substance that imitates stone, the basis always penetrates through; the cement wears away with time, dissolves under changing conditions, an interior becomes exposed to an exterior, exposing the gaps, requiring a fresh rendering.

To examine the theoretical implications of this – of seeing law as the copula writ large – the rest of the chapter considers law as "the articulation of normativity" from three perspectives. The first is from the standpoint of law as the expressive subject that articulates the sentence, "the law is this". This means looking at things through law – seeing law not as an object of study ("the law") but as an expressive subject ("law") that gives form to existence as its object. This is the "conceptual perspective" introduced in the previous chapter,[8] the view from the exterior: law, as subject, looking upon its legal creation non-naïvely. And the view from here is unsettled. The subject can see how every act of articulation, of expressing what "is" (the law), is an idolistic leap of faith over what remains in between what *is* and what is predicated as "is" – how "this" is and is not what it is expressed to be by law.

The second perspective then takes the standpoint of the subject whose experience of law is neither wholly circumscribed by the law as expressed nor wholly outside the law. Rather than seeing "law" as subject, this second perspective views "the law", as object, from the standpoint of the subject whose existence is the object of law. This is the inside perspective of the grammatical subject of the predicate sentence that experiences the reality of the sentence, "the law is this". This is the nonconceptual perspective introduced in the previous chapter,[9] the abject perspective of the subject whose experience of law is neither as predicated nor simply free from predication.

These first two viewpoints are concerned with law as a "subjective" and as an "objective" phenomenon: from the first perspective, how law gives form, as a

7 See, e.g., Irene Watson, *Aboriginal Peoples, Colonialism and International Law: Raw Law* (Abingdon: Routledge, 2015), 22–24 and Chapter 3. See also Christine Black, *The Land is the Source of the Law: A Dialogic Encounter with Indigenous Jurisprudence* (Abingdon: Routledge, 2010).

8 See 19–20.

9 Ibid.

subjective matter; and from the second perspective, how the law takes form, as an objective matter. And yet, "dialectics not a standpoint".[10] Having considered law from these two separate standpoints, in positive-analytical fashion, a third perspective is needed to see how they come together, in negative-dialectical fashion. The aim here is to view the *process*: how law becomes "the law" and how "the law" becomes law, and how this becoming takes place in the interplay between the two standpoints, which is no place at all but a constant movement.

The articulation of normativity

The conceptual perspective

Law is articulate. As an expressive subject law articulates how things are to be, giving form to reality through its expression as "the law". By law: *this is the law*. This is law as "articulation" in the most basic sense of the term: "to give expression". This is law, without definite article, without determinate form in itself – an act of making express, of giving form.

Law is also imaginative, its expressive scope as limited as the human imagination. Thus law might articulate linguistically through acts of speaking, writing, singing, as well as through other expressive modes such as painting, weaving, sculpture, dance – indeed through any cultural artefact, through any spatial arrangement, through any act by which the subject gives form to reality.[11]

Infinitely imaginative, law nonetheless has an object in mind: to articulate normativity. By "normativity" I mean the quality of being normative: as *prescription* it is the subjective sentence on life, which subscribers render real by acting upon with conviction, making what is intentional into what appears ontic. To the serious question, "it is *this*?", the serious answer, "it *is* this". What "is": always a normative statement rendered real by its affirmation, as *is*. Thus the child asks: "the tree is the soil?" The parent answers negatively, cutting the tree from the ground it inhabits, from the air it breathes, from the birds it nests, and affirms, "the tree is *this*". Expressing what "is": always an act of articulating normativity. Likewise law: giving form to how things *are to be* by expressing how things ought to be; giving form to how things *ought to be* by expressing how things are to be. Thus the expression of law "gives legal form to life and life to law", as matter of jurisdiction.[12] Juris-diction – the expressive act of law – "gives us the structure of our existence".[13]

If "law" (without definite article) is a subjective-expressive act of giving form to what is real and what is ideal, jurisdictionally, in a way that the two – reality and how it is imagined ideally according to law – cannot be separated or finally

10 Adorno, *Negative Dialectics*, 16–18.

11 See Roderick A Macdonald, 'Custom Made – For a Non-chirographic Critical Legal Pluralism', *Canadian Journal of Law and Society*, vol 26, no 2 (2011).

12 Shaunnagh Dorsett and Shaun McVeigh, *Jurisdiction* (Abingdon: Routledge, 2012), 1.

13 Ibid. See also Peter D Rush, 'An Altered Jurisdiction: Corporeal Traces of Law', *Griffith Law Review*, vol 6 (1997).

resolved, then "the law" (with definite article) is the expression that takes form in this act of articulation. As an expression of law, the law takes form as a dialectical image of how things *are to be* and how things *ought to be*, brought together in a flash, creating a distinct sense of how things are to be *because that is how they ought to be* and of how things ought to be *because that is how they are to be.*[14] Expressed together authoritatively in an imaginative act of law, what remains normative becomes a matter of common sense: "this *is* the law"; while, as an image, the matter of the law is also actually real, giving form to existence regularly.

This is the fantastic reality of law as an imaginative act of articulating normativity. But like the most powerful fairy tales there is a violent side to this. To the extent that law is imaginatively articulate, law *articulates*, which is not only "to give expression" but at the same time and in the process, "to bend at the joint".[15] Thus what is expressed by law as the law is bent in the act of articulation. The expression that takes form as the law is an image of things articulated: giving form, law, the expressive subject, does not simply express how things are because that is how things *are*, objectively speaking, but represents how things are to be because that is how they *ought to be.* This is the origin of the "originary violence" of law discussed by Walter Benjamin, Jacques Derrida, and Peter Fitzpatrick. Before getting to them, however, first Adorno, who also points to this, the originary violence of law, when he addresses "the juridical sphere" in reflection on Hegel's *Philosophy of Right.*

> Law [Recht] is the Ur-phenomenon of irrational rationality. In it the formal principle of equivalence becomes the norm, everyone is measured by [the] same standard. Such equality, in which differences perish, gives a secret impetus to inequality; persisting mythos in the midst of an only apparently demythologized humanity. The norms of law [Rechtsnormen] cut short what is not covered, every experience of the specific which is not preformed, for the sake of the seamless systematic, and then raises instrumental rationality to a second reality *sui generis.* [...] The entire juridical realm is one of definitions. Its systematic commands, that nothing shall pass into it, which could escape from its closed circle, *quod non est in actis* [which is not in the act/deed]. This enclosure, ideological in itself, exerts real violence through the sanctions of law [Sanktion des Rechts] as the socially controlling authority, particularly in the administered world.[16]

In its "*very form*", Adorno goes on to write, law "*expresses domination*, the yawning difference of individual interests from the whole".[17] Thus as an expressive form – as an instrument of rationality – "the norms of law cut short what is not

14 On "dialectical images", see Walter Benjamin, *The Arcades Project* (Cambridge: Belknap Press, 1999), 463.

15 See also Lawrence Grossberg, 'On Postmodernism and Articulation: An Interview with Stuart Hall', *Journal of Communication Inquiry*, vol 10, no 2 (1986): 53–55.

16 Adorno, *Negative Dialectics*, 303–305.

17 Ibid, 305–306 (italics added).

covered, every experience of the specific which is not preformed" – precisely what is non-identical to the law – and raises this rationalised reality, this legal identity, to the level of second nature. Whatever fails to live up to this reality, this second nature, given form through its expression as the law, experiences law antagonistically. Thus law "expresses domination": the law, always an inadequate expression of what *is*, nonetheless imposed on things, demands categorical conformity under real threat of penalty.

In outlining this view of law Adorno cites Hegel, specifically Hegel's observation that "law [Recht]" and "the real world of law [Rechts]" are "grasped through thought",

> that through thought the form of rationality, namely universality and determinacy, is given, this, the law [Gesetz], is what that feeling which reserves itself at will, that conscience which places law [Recht] in the subjective conviction, looks at with grounds as what is most hostile to itself. It perceives the form of legality [Form des Rechten], as one of duty and one of the law [Gesetzes], as a dead, cold letter and as a fetter; for it does not cognize itself in it, hence is not free in it, because the law [Gezetz] is the rationality of the thing, and this latter does not permit the feelings to warm to its own particularity.[18]

The distinction here between Recht and Gesetz is critical, as the distinction between law and the law. Recht, as law – *expressing* right – gives form as a conceptual matter to things, as "this, the law [Gesetz]"; thus the law, as Gesetz – an *expression of* right – takes form as "the rationality of the thing", as a matter of law. And as the rationality of the thing – as a conceptualisation of how things are to be by right – the law is experienced hostilely by a life that overflows rationality, that refutes its sentence and continues to play out beyond the grasp of every rational order. Everything remains nonidentical to law's imagination of things, and so nothing is recognisable in the law apart from its image, which is never adequate. Law, addressed to its images of *things*, dominates *everything*. And so the subject who experiences law in the form of what "is", expressed as the law, experiences it "as a dead, cold letter and as a fetter".

Adorno points to both meanings of articulation in these passages, as an act of giving expression and bending at the joint. Adorno's apparently pessimistic verdict is concerned with the real consequences of articulation, in this case the consequences of law as the articulation of normativity. *Everything*, cut short by the norms of law: every *thing*, raised to a second reality sui generis, as the material of law. In giving expression to existence in terms of the law, acts of law, as acts of articulation, are seen to bend it, giving form to it as what, from the conceptual perspective, *is*, imagined to be its proper, natural form. In the act of articulation, what "is" is raised to a second nature, that of *the law*; and in the process what *is*, now identified with the rational reality of a law that is expressed sui generis, is cut

18 Ibid, 303–305.

short, becoming nonidentical with what is the law. What is *more*: becoming the stubborn stain of an irrational rationality that will not entirely vanish.

The conceptually inflicted violence of law thus has its origin in the contradictory experience of being, inseparably apart. Copulation, which holds out the hope of an existential synthesis, producing the one out of the two, produces difference as much as sameness, a third that is neither the one nor the other nor simply whole in itself, but what *is*, inseparably apart. The law that takes form through the Act is this: no synthesis in fact, but a configuration that nonetheless establishes the context of the existential judgment. "The law is the law", as the sentence holds out, but what "is" the law *is* also always otherwise, as experienced by its subjects. The violence of law originates *in* this contradiction, in-between the synthesising act and the demand that what has been disseminated must conform to the synthetic prescription in the way it lives. Thus the violence is in the statement, "the law is *this*", intensified and made terrifyingly real in the re-statement, "*the law* is *the law*", silencing the voices that say "*this* is not law".

And so the conceptual violence of law has its origin in the contradiction, but the contradiction also originates the law. Put simply: there would be no law to speak of without it being spoken of. Inarticulate, law remains implicit at best, sensed but its sense never made explicit. The act of articulation is therefore *required* for law to be the law. As such, the violence that flows from law's contradictory nature is not simply a matter of law-as-subject dominating its object. It is also *hopeful*, also potentially emancipatory. Adorno does not examine this directly, in terms of law, but this is the implication of his treatment of conceptualisation as a means of both domination and emancipation. Thus, as an act of domination a concept cuts short what it intends to express, as its object; and yet, without giving form to the object conceptually, the object would remain unrecognised, sensed but not made sense of. Rather than existence cleaved into what is conceptual and what remains nonconceptual, existence would remain meaningless, never being, made sense of (being as nothing). Or rather, because humans as conscious subjects are thinking subjects, always making sense of existence, the result of not actively thinking would be to abandon the object to how it is nonetheless recognised by other subjects (being as given). Conceptualisation, as *re*conceptualisation, is therefore emancipatory to the extent that it works to overturn the untruth of what has been given, moving the concept towards its nonconceptual aspect.

Bringing this to bear on the concept of law: merely sensing what is law as a normative matter might be sufficient most of the time, but when my sense of what is law and your sense of what is law come into conflict, a decision has to be made as to what *is* "the law". While this decision necessarily cuts short both senses of law, yours and mine, to a greater or lesser extent, in articulating a common sense of law ("the law is this"), the decision is nonetheless necessary if the conflict is to be resolved by law. The legal decision might substitute a harshly singular untruth – "the law is *this*" – for the amorphous truth that is most just in respect of an infinite plurality of difference, but, as Derrida has shown, the definite injustice of a decisive law is nonetheless more just than the indefinite justice of an indecisive law.[19] The decisive cognition is as *necessary* as it is violent, as *just* as it is never fully just. As Fitzpatrick writes, "the 'original' violence pertaining to law" is the "incessant violence which inevitably follows from there not being an origin and from law having to originate in each act of legal decision".[20] Thus every act of legal decision-making – stating "the law is *this*" – gives form to law as a "fresh judgement".[21] And yet, what is "the law" remains intentional and not ontic. The result is that what "is" the law remains in need of a fresh judgment, either to affirm that "the law" *is*, in fact, "the law", or else to amend the initial act, to answer the question, "the law is this?", with a new statement, "the law is *this*".

Articulating what is the law becomes even more imperative when the situation is not one where you and I, amongst others, have a sense of law as a normative matter and every now and again need to articulate what is the law to avoid or resolve conflict, but when what is the law has *already* been articulated. In this situation the question of justice is not to decide what is the law for the first time – to make common sense of what is law in relation to your sense and my sense – but to do this in relation to a previous expression of law. The legal decision is emancipatory in this situation in that it is an act of "beginning again",[22] holding out the potential of deciding again what is the law in response to its subjects. This is what it means to overturn the untruth of the law, as the injustice of the law, by moving it towards what is more, true and just.

The nonconceptual perspective

That is from the standpoint of the expressive subject: a view of law as the articulation of normativity. From this perspective "the law" *is* law but it is also not identical with what law seeks to express. This makes law's acts of articulation both potentially dominating, with the law cutting short its object, and emancipating, as an act that might reform the law to move it closer to its object, by remaining consistently conscious of nonidentity. So much can be seen by taking the standpoint of law as the expressive subject looking upon its legal creation non-naïvely. However, there is another side to this, which is the experience of the subject within jurisdiction. The question here is: what does the contradiction that animates law, making it both potentially dominating and emancipating, look like from an "objective" standpoint? This question switches perspectives to make law in its given form the object to be comprehended from the standpoint of the subject that finds itself before the law. This perspective focuses on how "the law", never simply as *is*, is never simply experienced as given.

19 Jacques Derrida, 'Force of Law: The "Mystical Foundation of Authority"', *Cardozo Law Review*, vol 11 (1989–1990).

20 Peter Fitzpatrick, *Modernism and the Grounds of Law* (Cambridge: Cambridge University Press, 2001), 80–81.

21 Ibid.

22 See Ben Golder and Peter Fitzpatrick, *Foucault's Law* (Abingdon: Routledge, 2009), 123.

For the subject who experiences law in this way, as otherwise than given, and yet must answer to the law, as given, this is an abject experience of being, "cast off or away, esp. as being vile or unworthy; refuse, scum, dregs. Chiefly *fig.* of persons".[23] This experience of abjection is the *objective* experience. In the inspired act of giving form to the law, the object of law – the very existence of its subjects – is both law's vital material and its toxic waste ("refuse, scum, dregs"). Thus the subject, who experiences law objectively, experiences it abjectly. Adorno, commenting on Hegel's *Philosophy of Right*, sums up the absurdity, and the violence, of this experience:

> That the individual feels so easily wronged, when the antagonism of interest drives it into the juridical sphere, is not, as Hegel would like to argue, its own fault, such that it would be too deluded to recognise its own interest in the objective legal norm and its guarantee; rather it is that of the constituents of the legal sphere itself.[24]

The abjection felt by the subject that fails to recognise its existence in the objective legal norm is not delusional but entirely *rational*; it is not a symptom of the irrationality of the subject but of the law itself. Thus it is in the experience of the subject that the rationality of the objective norms of law is shown to be irrational – that what is rational to the law is irrational to what is before it. And this – being, nonidentical before the law, as a normative matter – is the original and unshakeable legal experience: "Law is the Ur-phenomenon of irrational rationality".[25]

And so the subject finds itself abject before the law, *physically* – as the subject who is being detained in Liberia's Central Prison; but also *temporally* – as the subject whose sense of normativity precedes what is now articulated as the law[26]; as well as *sequentially* – as the subject whose sense of normativity is given form by law and superseded in the process.[27] Coming before the law in every sense, as "worthy" of a law that takes its name, and yet – being "vile or unworthy; refuse, scum, dregs" – never able to finally enter into it, physically, temporally, sequentially, the subject of law remains suspended on the threshold. And perhaps this is the experience of Kafka's countryman who never passes into the law nor walks away from its gate. If Adorno could have spoken with Kafka's countryman he might have said up front: "Its systematic commands, that nothing shall pass into it, which could escape from its closed circle"[28]; which would be to say: under the order of law, only *nothing* shall pass into the law *ultimately*, while being, suspended on the threshold. The gate, as the concept, opens to its object at the same time as it

23 'Abjection, *n.*', Oxford English Dictionary Online, December 2015.
24 Adorno, *Negative Dialectics*, 303–305.
25 See note 16 above.
26 See Macdonald, 'Custom Made', 311.
27 However, it is important to note the meaning of "supersede" as a sequential movement that does not simply mark the end of what is being superseded but rather its *deferral*: see 'supersede, *v.*', Oxford English Dictionary Online, December 2015.
28 See note 16 above.

refuses entry to that which remains abject before it; and so this law, which takes your name, is neither for you nor not for you.[29]

A perspective on the process

"Dialectics not a standpoint", and yet so far this discussion of law as the articulation of normativity has approached law from two standpoints. This is necessary to see law as the copula writ large, but wholly inadequate. The problem with points of view, even when precariously grounded in contradiction, is their fixation: they still seek to put things in their place. "Law" and "not law", "identity" and "non-identity", "subject" and "object", and every perplexing combination of these: the result remains a punctuated arrangement. What is missing is the very *process* – the passage in-between law's states of fixation. In part this is about the emancipatory force of law, which makes every act of law an act of beginning again, holding out the possibility of deciding again what is "the law" in response to the abject experience of the subjects of law. As discussed, this is about overturning the untruth of the law, as the injustice of the law, by moving it towards what is more, true and just. However, it is also about the *nonviolence* of law.

If the violence of law is its rational aspect as the articulation of normativity – law's every act cutting short its object – then the nonviolence of law is its nonrational aspect: its openness to what remains its object.[30] As discussed above, while law, as the copula, is most meaningful by itself, its expressions are nonetheless mere word-play if it does not also establish "the context of the existential judgment".[31] For law, as the copula, to be *really* meaningful, its sentences on and of words must be sentences on and of life. But this means law must be *open* to life, as its object, as much as its acts cut life short by rendering its own sentences as what is real. In other words, for law to become the law in fact and not just in word, law must remain open to becoming the law always in respect of the fact of its being otherwise.[32] Following Adorno, this means ensuring law remains open, as a conceptual matter, to what is not the law, as a nonconceptual matter – ensuring law remains "consistently conscious of nonidentity" in the act of articulating identity lawfully. This is also to follow Fitzpatrick in thinking about the responsiveness of law. However, before I get to Fitzpatrick, I need to continue with Kafka, because perhaps what is most interesting about his parable here is what it suggests about law's nonviolent aspect, and therefore its emancipatory possibility.

In *Before the Law* Kafka's gatekeeper tells the countryman at the outset that he cannot be admitted to the law "at the moment", although "it is possible" he will

29 See also Peter Fitzpatrick, 'Necessary Deceptions: Kafka and the Mystery of Law', in Maria Aristodemou, Fiona Macmillan, and Patricia Tuitt (eds), *Crime Fiction and the Law* (Abingdon: Routledge-Birkbeck Law Press, 2017).

30 See Peter Fitzpatrick, 'Why the Law is also Non-Violent', in Austin Sarat (ed), *Law, Violence and the Possibility of Justice* (Princeton: Princeton University Press, 2001); Fitzpatrick, *Modernism and the Grounds of Law*, 78.

31 See note 5 above.

32 See also Macdonald, 'Custom Made'.

be allowed entry later. From the abject perspective this possibility seems like an insidious conceit. For the countryman before the law it is this possibility that makes law seem *omnipotent*, giving its gatekeeper – which is only its first gatekeeper – an overbearing power to refuse entry. This appears to be an insidious conceit because, if the possibility of entering was not held out, it would not be possible for the gatekeeper to withhold entry. It is the very possibility of admission that gives law its power to exclude; and so the countryman sits and waits in abjection, refused entry for the moment but in anticipation of the possibility of being admitted later, through a gate that was, after all, made for him. From this perspective it is the possibility of law giving form to how things ought to be, determinately, as an objective matter, that enables "the law" to take form, to transform everything into "the norms of the law" while leaving its object at the gate, as "unworthy" of finally entering into the law. And perhaps that is the contradictory possibility of law, seen nonconceptually: a violently insidious conceit, a trick that allows law to constitute itself as *the law* out of its object at the expense of its object.[33] And yet, shifting standpoints to take the conceptual perspective, the opposite is also apparent. From this point of view, the possibility of law being open to its object is not its power to exclude its subjects from the law but rather a reflection of its need to be attuned to what it is *powerless* to include: the existence of its subjects. From this perspective a subject cannot finally pass into law not because law is omnipotent but because law is *impotent.* From this perspective, even if Kafka's gatekeeper wanted to admit the countryman, he would have been powerless to do so – law, the expressive subject, always ultimately failing in its effort to articulate things objectively.

Thus, what appears to be an insidious conceit, is, from one perspective, and from another, is a reflection of law's insatiable need to reach out to what it is powerless to grasp. "You are insatiable", Kafka's doorkeeper says to the countryman at the end of the parable. The sentence hangs between the doorkeeper and the countryman, implicating them both. The subject before the law is insatiable, spending his life seeking entry into a law that neither admits him entry nor refuses him absolutely (the possibility is there; the gate is made for him). But so too is law as the expressive subject insatiable, unable to grant admission to what, by its own designs, it is intended to admit. Without the possibility of satiation hanging between them, bringing them together in this maddening way, the countryman would go elsewhere, seeking law in other ways, and the law would become uninspired, taking one last breath before becoming entirely instrumental rationality without any redeeming quality.

It is in light of this absurd portrayal of law that Fitzpatrick's work on responsiveness becomes urgent. Fitzpatrick's theorisation of modern law is very similar to the one that I have outlined here, in terms of a polarity between an indeterminate law, an illimitable law, that is not circumscribed by grounds of its own, on one

33 See also the discussion of "the paradox of sovereignty" and the "form of law" in Giorgio Agamben, *Homo Sacer: Sovereign Power and Bare Life* (Stanford: Stanford University Press, 1998).

side, and on the other side, the determinate laws that lay down the law in the most definite terms.[34] In Fitzpatrick's work these two polarised dimensions are as integral to each other as they are disparate. Law would remain impotent if it was entirely beyond delimitation, just as the laws would begin to crumble if they were absolutely fixed. Law must be grounded just as the grounded laws must remain responsive to what remains indeterminate. In the terms I have been using here: law (without definite article) must take form as the law (with definite article), and yet to be *law*, it must always also be more than the law as expressed. This is about law becoming the law in ways that respect its being otherwise. As Fitzpatrick puts it:

> "The law" thence would be an unconditional law of utter responsiveness to the other, a responsability, to revive an old usage. This could only be a law incapable of containment. Yet, without more, such a law would be a mere dissipation. So, that law would depend for its realization on the conditional and conditioned "laws" to give it determinate effect. The determinate laws, in turn, depend on the unconditional law, the responsive law, for their own continuing existence.[35]

This law, "incapable of containment", is law in its nonconceptual aspect. And yet, "*without more*, such a law would be a mere dissipation": what is more, must be breathed in and given expression to as "the law", if it is to be more than indeterminate vapour. But – and this is the critical move – "the determinate laws, in turn, depend on the unconditional law, the responsive law, for their continuing existence": expressed as "the law", law is stripped of its vital substance, and again "such a law would be a mere dissipation". That is why law in its conceptual aspect, as the articulation of normativity, must remain responsive, to ensure its expressions do not cease to be law. Just as the nonconceptual *more* requires concepts of what "is", concepts of what "is" must remain open to what *is* beyond their order. In this sense "responsive law" is inspired law: a law that remains open to its nonconceptual aspect at the same time as it gives expression to the law determinately.

Thus the problem of law, which is also its possibility, is in the *process* that plays out in-between infinitude and determinacy, in-between law and the law. This process makes law an abject experience for subjects before the law, but it also holds open the law to being otherwise. The process makes the law a terribly fallible conceit, and a potentially violent instrument of domination. As Fitzpatrick writes of Kafka's *The Trial*: "There is no trial. Or the title could be translated as 'the process'. There is no process".[36] *The Trial*, or *Der Prozess*, has this closed dimension to it, describing a legal process that refuses entry to a subject who remains abject before it. The process, by which law becomes not law the moment it opens its mouth to articulate the law, is, from this perspective, not a genuine process at

34 See, e.g., Fitzpatrick, *Modernism and the Grounds of Law*.

35 Peter Fitzpatrick, 'The Revolutionary Past: Decolonizing Law and Human Rights', *Metodo: International Studies in Phenomenology and Philosophy*, vol 2, no 1 (2014): 128.

36 Fitzpatrick, 'Necessary Deceptions'.

all. Never admitting its object, it remains a closed circle. But there is of course more to the process – just as there is more to *The Trial*. Fitzpatrick draws this out by showing how in Kafka's writing, "with law, there is always an 'opening' as well as a 'closing', a possibility somehow embedded there".[37] This is the possibility of law being in a position of "beginning again", opening it to being more and other than the law as expressed. Importantly this is not a proposition (a beginning-position) for finally reaching the truth of the matter of law. Being, always in the position of beginning again, is no such position at all: it is not a standpoint but an insistence on the constant overturning of the grounds of the law in respect of the ever-new ways of "relating to others and being-together".[38]

This is the *critical* aspect of the process: remaining consistently conscious of how law, as the articulation of normativity, is an opening and a closure, and making one critical to the other. Law, as the articulation of normativity, can never be wholly open, because then the process would be as good as closed, "interminable" in the sense of always being without closure, difference deferred indefinitely, being as nothingness. But law, as the articulation of normativity, can also never be wholly closed, because then the process would become wholly irrelevant; never open to its object, law would become objectless absurdity, and total violence. Never one nor the other by itself, but also never absolutely fused together, the two becoming one only to blind the subject as to how the unity is like the promise of false idols. Or as Fitzpatrick writes, reflecting on *The Trial*: "The opening and the closing fuse in our being drawn into the emanant radiance of the law – 'a radiance that streams forth inextinguishably from the door of the Law'".[39] The radiance of the law that appears to transcend its contradictory condition is blinding, leaving the subject no less abject, but much less capable of mediating the contradiction.[40]

Framework

Through this chapter I have sought to show from three perspectives a contradiction in law, and to argue that it is irresolvable – indeed that it is law's *enlivening* condition. This argument, and these three perspectives, frame the study of law in Liberia in the four chapters that follow. Chapters 3 and 4 take the first ("articulate" or "conceptual") perspective in examining how the idea of Liberia was given form by law in the nineteenth and twentieth centuries, and how it is being given form again in the twenty-first century; while Chapter 5 switches to the second ("abject" or "nonconceptual") perspective in examining how law is taking form in Liberia post-war. To put this another way: if Chapter 3 is concerned with an affirmation, "Liberia is *this*" (by law); and if Chapter 4 is concerned with a *re*affirmation,

37 Ibid.
38 Golder and Fitzpatrick, *Foucault's Law*, 123.
39 Fitzpatrick, 'Necessary Deceptions'.
40 See also Panu Minkkinen, 'The Radiance of Justice: On the Minor Jurisprudence of Franz Kafka', *Social and Legal Studies*, vol 3, no 3 (1994).

"*Liberia* is *Liberia*" (by law); then Chapter 5 is concerned with the voices that are talking back, requiring a response that is more than yet another affirmation of what is by law. Chapter 6 then takes the third perspective, on the "process of law", to examine these responses to the contradiction.

This perspectival framework is only the start, however – a theoretical device for examining law's contradictory life in Liberia. As stated in the Introduction, in itself, law's contradictory form is not the problem. The problem is the violence it enables as well as the emancipatory possibilities it holds out. *This* is the book's critical concern: not the contradiction in law, but its implication. By "implication" I mean specifically how the contradiction opens law to mediation by different logics, which inform how law takes place while taking place through law. Thus Chapter 3 focuses on the "logic of capital" in examining the making of Liberia; Chapter 4 focuses on the "logic of security" in examining the remaking of Liberia; Chapter 5 focuses on the "illogic of law" in examining how law is taking form in nonrational ways postwar; and Chapter 6 focuses on the "logic of liberal internationalism" in examining the work that is being done to institute the rule of law in response to the contradiction in law. In each instance the positive logics can be seen to operate in the chasm that separates and joins subject and object, either exploiting their separation ("capital"), their nonseparation ("security"), or both at the same time ("liberal internationalism"); although in each instance the contradiction remains unresolved, with subject and object remaining as separate as they are inseparable, as the negative logic (or "illogic") serves to remind.

3 Civil death in the dominion of freedom

Overlooking the capital

Three castles stand on the rise of Cape Montserrado. Looking up from amongst the market women on Benson Street they can be seen looming over Liberia's capital city.[1] There is not a road or laneway in central Monrovia without a view of at least one of these towering structures, and if there is, I am sure it does not escape their shadow.

When I say three castles I mean an embassy, a temple, and a hotel. Looking up Benson Street one's gaze is arrested first by the embassy. Operated by the United States of America, this newly completed complex shines white on the hill. On the other side of the street and slightly higher up the rise stands the Grand Lodge of Masons of the Republic of Liberia. The Masonic Temple's run-down exterior, still visibly scarred by munitions from the civil wars of the 1990s and early 2000s, reflects the overthrow of the "Americo-Liberian" regime that once governed the Republic from within its walls. However, it is on the rise. Like the embassy it is once again functioning as a stronghold, its membership representing power in Liberia.[2] Above both, standing on the very top of the hill, is Ducor Hotel, or what remains of the five-star resort. Once owned by Intercontinental it is now a hulking eight-story concrete shell.

For several years after the cessation of armed conflict in 2003 the hotel was occupied by homeless Liberians, only for them to be evicted by the Government in anticipation of its renewal as a glamorous resort, a symbol of "Liberia Rising".[3]

1 The market on Benson Street can be seen in Figure I.3 (Introduction).

2 The Roster of Grand Masters of Liberia provides an inventory of some of the most powerful figures in Americo-Liberian history, from the inaugural president of the "First Republic", Joseph J Roberts, to the last, William R Tolbert Jr. See Grand Lodge of Masons, AF & AM, Republic of Liberia: www.grandlodgeofliberia.org/. While the Masons lost power with the *coup* that overthrew the Americo-Liberian oligarchy, its power as an institution in Liberia is increasing again. As a Lebanese-Liberian businessman put it to me, if one wanted to succeed in Liberia one had to be a member of the Masons.

3 See Republic of Liberia, *Agenda for Transformation: Steps Toward Liberia Rising 2030. Liberia's Medium Term Economic and Development Strategy (2012–2017)* (Monrovia: Republic of Liberia, 2012), 9.

In the years before the overthrow and killing of Muammar Gadhafi in 2011, Libya and Liberia had re-established relations, and Libya was in the process of investing in Liberia. One investment was to be the restoration of the Ducor Hotel. This would have been Colonel Gadhafi's castle on the hill but for the US-led intervention in Libya. The significance of this would not have been lost on Liberians whose country was, throughout the second half of the twentieth century, both a base for the US to advance its cold-war interests in the region,[4] and on the front lines of Libyan-trained revolutionary movements in west Africa.[5] For Liberians looking up from the market on Benson Street, these three castles – representing the USA, Colonel Gadhafi, and Liberia's ruling class – would have reflected this familiar history of the three powers that had shaped the Republic in the twentieth century. Instead, three months after the killing of Gadhafi, the US opened its new embassy complex on the hill overlooking Monrovia, leaving two castles and the crumbling shell of a hotel.

But this crumbling shell of a hotel must not be overlooked as a mere structure. It is precisely as a hollowed-out site, a remnant of something more, that the hotel is the castle of the three to which the most critical attention should be paid. That is because of its radical difference from both the embassy and the temple. Unlike them it is a *res fungibilis* – a thing entirely fungible – a castle that defies its very castle-ness. As "castles" the embassy and the temple are immovable by institution; they could of course change locations, but they must remain the Embassy of the United States in Monrovia and the Grand Lodge of Masons of the Republic of Liberia. They have an essential institutional nature that binds them in certain ways to the places they occupy and the subjects who inhabit them. This is also their weakness, to the extent that, should their institutions be destroyed, so too would be the power they represent. The hotel by contrast is a movable species of thing without any essential nature in itself. It is a capital investment that takes the form of a castle on the hill, its "essential nature" remaining separate from the object it encases in marble and glass, and when it moves on it leaves behind a hollowed-out site, a form of death. Parasitic, it lives off other objects, destroying them in the process. And because, as a species, the thing that once animated the site of the hotel is without its own actual or institutional nature, the power it represents cannot be destroyed by destroying either object or institution. As a power over life, it is essentially a logic; and it is a logic that can be found to operate through law.

What exactly is this logic, and how does it operate through law? I address these questions in this chapter in two ways. One is through a study of the making of Liberia, an historical examination that focuses on the practical operation and effect of the "logic of capital". The other way is through a more general study of jurisprudence that provides an examination of this logic's theoretical basis in law through a reading of John Austin's lecture on "things", published in his influential

4 See D Elwood Dunn, *Liberia and the United States during the Cold War: Limits of Reciprocity* (New York: Palgrave Macmillan, 2009).

5 See, e.g., Colin M Waugh, *Charles Taylor and Liberia: Ambition and Atrocity in Africa's Lone Star State* (London: Zed Books, 2011), Chapters 5 and 9.

nineteenth century treatise on English law, *Lectures on Jurisprudence*. In bringing these two analyses together, the purpose is not to establish an historical or genealogical connection between mid-nineteenth century English law and the making of Liberia, but to consider the two homologously. That is, the analysis of Austin's lecture on "things" provides a view of a logic operating through law that I argue can also be seen at work in the making of Liberia. The result, in other words, is a view of the logic at work *in* law (Austin) and *through* law (Liberia).

The logic of capital

In his *Lectures on Jurisprudence, or the Philosophy of Positive Law*, Austin defines a "fungible thing" as "a thing whose place, lieu, or room, may be supplied by a thing of the same kind, or even by a thing not of the same kind, as money in the form of damages".[6] How he reaches this definition is instructive, because what it reveals is a logic that, at its extreme, can render an object a thing that is indeterminate, movable, general.

A thing of law: indeterminate, movable, general

Austin begins his lecture "on certain distinctions among things" by showing how in Roman law, a thing, or *res*, in "the most extensive sense", "embraces every object [...] which may be the subject or object of a right or duty", including persons; thus "a slave is styled a thing".[7] He contrasts this extensive meaning of "thing" with how the word is used in "ordinary discourse or parlance": "When we speak of a thing, we usually mean an object which is sensible and permanent, and which is not a person".[8] He then contrasts the Roman law meaning and the ordinary meaning with the meaning in English law, which, he concludes, oscillates between the two. The result, he writes, is that, "[i]n the language of English law, it would not appear that the term '*thing*' has any determinate import". "In short, the extension of the term *thing* is so extremely uncertain, that if it were expelled from the language of law, much confusion would be avoided".[9]

Rather than expel the term "thing" from the language of law, however, Austin limits his analysis of things to "permanent sensible objects which are not persons".[10] He then goes on to describe the division of such things into "things immovable" and "things movable". On one side: "Physically, Immovable things are such as cannot be moved from their present places; or cannot be moved from their present places without an essential change in their actual natures". On the other side: "Physically, Movable things are such as can be moved from the places which they presently occupy, without an essential change in their actual natures". This

6 John Austin, *Lectures on Jurisprudence, or the Philosophy of Positive Law: Volume 2* (London: John Murray, 1873), 807.
7 Ibid, 802.
8 Ibid.
9 Ibid, 803.
10 Ibid, 804–805.

division is qualified by a third category that cuts across both, containing "things which are physically movable" but which are "immovable by institution". That is, "the thing, though physically movable, is arbitrarily annexed to an immovable thing, so as to be considered as a part of it, and to be comprised in its name" (such as an heirloom).[11] So here we learn that a thing might have an "actual nature" and an "institutional nature" – which is not so remarkable, merely pointing to a thing that acquires its "essential nature" through an actual or social fixation. But we also learn of a category of thing that is thought to be movable without an essential change to either its "actual" or "institutional" nature. *This* is a remarkable thought: a thing that remains essentially the same in any context; a thing with a constancy in itself that makes it infinitely iterable.[12]

Austin then considers a further division of things into "specifically determined" things (*the* house) and "generally determined" things (*a* house).[13] What is remarkable here is what is meant by "specific". Austin begins by telling us that, "in the language of logicians", "specific performance would mean something totally different from what it actually denotes" in the language of jurisprudence.

> It would not mean a performance of an obligation in the very terms of it; for instance, by conveying *that* specifically determined house; but would be equally applicable if I merely conveyed *a* house, or something in lieu of one.[14]

This leads Austin to conclude that "specific", although general as a matter of logic, is particular as a matter of law.[15] And yet things are not quite so clear. As Austin goes on to explain, "almost the only ground for enforcing specific performance is, that nothing else can completely supply the place of that very thing for which the party contracted", which, he emphasises, is almost never the case, for the reason that "money in the form of damages" would almost always suffice. In other words, while a "specific thing" means *this* thing, and not another like it, this thing is almost never so singular that it cannot be replaced by money, that is, given a general (exchangeable) value. But yet again, there remains the division

11 Ibid, 805.

12 If this does not strike you as remarkable – if, that is, you hold the common-sense view that an object does not necessarily change its essential nature when moved in time and space (the chair in one corner of the room remaining the same when placed in any other corner of the room), I recommend reading Jorge Luis Borges, *Funes the Memorious* (1942), about a man:

> almost incapable of ideas of a general, Platonic sort. Not only was it difficult for him to comprehend that the generic symbol dog embraces so many unlike individuals of diverse size and form; it bothered him that the dog at three fourteen (seen from the side) should have the same name as the dog at three fifteen (seen from the front).

13 Austin, *Lectures in Jurisprudence*, 805–806.

14 Ibid, 806.

15 Ibid, 806–807.

with which Austin begins, between "specifically determined" things (*the* house) and "generally determined" things (*a* house). If this division is to be meaningful then the two (specific and general) cannot simply be the same. And so, it would seem, there is a third possibility: a "thing" that is *both* particular and general – its singularity always determinable to an extent by a general value.[16]

Rendering things: the representational framework of law

This lecture by Austin thus reveals a logic operating through the "philosophy of positive law" that, at its extreme, can render an object entirely fungible while maintaining the appearance of object-ness. Understood as a "movable species", a thing is simultaneously the opposite of a thing, understood as a "sensible permanent object". Austin summarises this when he notes with approbation how, "[i]n the language of the German jurists, fungible things are styled '*vertretbar*' – representable".[17] What is able to be represented, *ad infinitum*, without any essential change to its nature, is the thing styled *vertretbar*. What is representable is not an object in its singularity but a thing that combines a particular object with a general value, making the object generalisable through the representational framework. The object represented is not actually present as "the thing", and is only presented as such, rendered synonymous in the language of the law.[18] Indeed this is,

16 This finding would not have been surprising to Austin's contemporary, Karl Marx. In his analysis of commodities in *Capital*, Marx shows how commodities are:

> two-fold, both objects of utility, and, at the same time, depositories of value. They manifest themselves therefore as commodities, or have the form of commodities, only in so far as they have two forms, a physical or natural form, and a value form.
>
> Karl Marx, *Capital: A Critique of Political Economy: Volume 1* (London: The Electric Book Company, 1998), 33

Thus, as in Austin's analysis of a thing, Marx shows how a commodity is both "singular" in its physical form, which gives it its particular utility, and "general" in its value form, as an exchangeable object. Importantly, this value is not *intrinsic* to the object but reflected onto it, as a "mode of expression", specifically a mode of expressing equivalence: ibid, 27. Indeed, according to Marx,

> the value of commodities is the very opposite of the coarse materiality of their substance, not an atom of matter enters into its composition. Turn and examine a single commodity, by itself, as we will, yet in so far as it remains an object of value, it seems impossible to grasp it. If, however, we bear in mind that the value of commodities has a purely social reality, and that they acquire this reality only in so far as they are expressions or embodiments of one identical social substance, viz., human labour, it follows as a matter of course, that value can only manifest itself in the social relation of commodity to commodity.
>
> Ibid, 33

17 Austin, *Lectures in Jurisprudence*, 807.

18 Again, in Marxian terms, what is being dealt with is no longer the bodily form of the object but an abstracted exchange value that is "totally independent" of the object's particular qualities and yet exists as the object's mode of expression: see Marx, *Capital*, 28.

according to Louis Marin, "the first effect of representation in general [...] not presence but effect of presence. It is surely not the same, but it is as if it were, and often better than, the same".[19] But it is not just a matter of substitution: to represent is also "to show, to intensify, to duplicate a presence".[20] The thing, presented as the same as the object, authorises the actual presence of the object. In other words, the object acquires its *legitimate* presence, *as a thing*, through the representational framework.[21] "Such would be the second effect of representation in general, to constitute a subject through reflection of the representational framework".[22] Thus the thing appears to be *more* real than the object it represents, through the reflection of the framework onto the object, which renders the two synonymous (in the language of the law).

This suggests an elaboration to Austin's division of things into "things movable" and "things immovable". On this analysis a fungible thing is the opposite of a thing "immovable by institution": it is a thing movable by institution. Recall: a thing *immovable* by institution is a physically movable object that is "arbitrarily annexed to an immovable thing, so as to be considered as a part of it, and to be comprised in its name" (such as an heirloom). In reversal of this, a thing *movable* by institution is an object that cannot be moved from its present place, here and now, without an essential change in its actual nature, that is arbitrarily annexed to a movable thing, so as to be considered as a part of it, and to be comprised in its name. Thus an object is made fungible by making it synonymous with (comprised in the name of) a movable thing with a general value – the two remaining separate and yet annexed through the representational framework of law. As a movable species, the actual object takes on the appearance or outward form of a fungible thing, much like the sacrament of the Eucharist, which makes the very body and blood of Christ representable "under the *Species* of bread and wine".[23]

In sum, the representational framework examined by Austin in his lecture "on certain distinctions among things" – specifically, the representational framework of English law in the nineteenth century – reveals a logic that can transform singular objects into their opposite, movable species. Functioning at levels of generality,

19 Louis Marin, *Portrait of the King* (Minneapolis: University of Minnesota Press, 1988), 5.

20 Ibid.

21 Or, in Marxian terms, an object acquires its value, as a commodity, through the framework of exchange: see Marx, *Capital*, Chapter 1. Thus the round piece of metal in my pocket acquires its legitimate presence, as money, by being stamped with the markings proper to this framework (which is itself constituted through the network of social relations).

22 Marin, *Portrait of the King*, 5–6.

23 'Species, *n.*', Oxford English Dictionary Online (September 2015). The result is a kind of Marxian "*inversion* through which what is sensible and concrete counts only as a phenomenal form of what is abstract and universal": Marx cited in Žižek, *The Sublime Object of Ideology*, 29. Rather than the "thing" deriving its properties from the particular object that it circumscribes, the object now derives *its* properties from the thing. Thus, to paraphrase Marx, at this point, could things themselves speak, they would say, "in the eyes of each other we are nothing but exchange values": Marx, *Capital*, 52–53.

this logic substitutes for the object a thing that remains essentially the same in any context, with a constancy that makes it infinitely iterable, and presents that thing as if it were the object. By reflecting this logic onto the object, as one might paint a structure with blindingly bright light, the object acquires its *real* objectivity as a thing of the law.[24] In Slavoj Žižek's terminology, it becomes a *sublime* object: an object that is no longer bound by its materiality, having been freed into the "form of thought", and yet retains a material body.[25]

Logical consequences: capital punishment

But what of the actual object? What happens when the light goes out? What is left of the object when the thing moves on? Marin tells us: "[t]he first effect of the

24 Incidentally, this is also what it means "to invest". Although no longer usually understood in this way, an "investment" is literally an outer covering; in the words of the Oxford English Dictionary, it is "refractory material which can be used to embed or surround an object and then is allowed to harden". Thus it is by encasing an object within a hard layer that refracts light, an investment creates a new reality by simultaneously blocking the light and therefore one's sight from penetrating to the actual object. Now when one looks at the thing invested, one sees a simulacra – a general value in the place of a singular object.

25 See Žižek, *The Sublime Object of Ideology*, 11–13. As suggested by the references I have made to Marx, there are obvious parallels between Austin's analysis of "things" and Marx's analysis of "commodities". I have indicated some of these parallels in passing, although unfortunately the scope of this chapter does not allow for deeper exploration. However, one way of understanding the parallels might be that, as Marx observes, the economic relation between commodities is reflected in the juridical relation that facilitates their exchange; see Marx, *Capital*, 60. In other words, the legal representational framework through which objects become things, analysed by Austin, "is but the reflex of the real economic relation" analysed by Marx. If so, then what I am concerned with here is not the underlying or "originary" economic exchange relation but the *medium* through which this relation becomes operative through its reflection on the world, that is, in and through law. In this line, one might pursue Alfred Sohn-Rethel's argument that the abstract activity of commodity exchange informs not only the field of political economy, as Marx had shown, but the entire ideational fabric of society. In other words, the exchange abstraction that defines the logic of capital is *real*, impregnating the mind (that is, its forms of consciousness) through interactions that more and more occur according to the solipsism of the market. Thus, while Marx was concerned with how this real abstraction informs political economy, its effect is certainly not limited to this field but extends to the very "conceptual mode of thinking peculiar to societies based on commodity production". See Alfred Sohn-Rethel, *Intellectual and Manual Labour: A Critique of Epistemology* (Atlantic Highlands: Humanities Press, 1978), 19–23. Of course, this was also the driving concern of Adorno and many of his other Frankfurt School colleagues, who restlessly pursued the totalitarian effect of the exchange abstraction on life. On the Marxist drive in Adorno's work, see Jameson, *Late Marxism*, and of particular relevance here see at 9 and 23–24. For an overview of Adorno's "sociology of exchange society", see Matthias Benzer, *The Sociology of Theodor Adorno* (Cambridge: Cambridge University Press, 2011). For a sustained examination of how the smallest details of everyday life are informed by the exchange abstraction, see Theodor W Adorno, *Minima Moralia: Reflections from Damaged Life* (Dennis Redmond, members.efn.org, 2005).

representational framework and the first power of representation are the effect and power of presence instead of absence and death".[26] What Marin means is that representation can present anew what is absent or dead: "[s]omething that was present and is no longer is now represented".[27] As a result, when the thing moves on – when the representational framework ceases to be reflected onto the object – what is left in the place of the thing is absence, death, an object that remains to be seen, as the hotel on the hill, as a hollowed-out site. At least that is the case for an object such as the Ducor Hotel, which before acquiring its presence as a "real asset" was absent from the hill overlooking Monrovia. But what of an object that was not dead or absent before becoming animated as a thing? What of an object that was still present and is now re-presented? What are the consequences for *it* of this transformation?

On one hand, the process holds the promise of freeing an object from its immediate material circumstances, releasing it from the context that binds it and enabling it to circulate in new forms. This is a kind of Hegelian promise: to free the object from its empirical situation by realising its potential – a move that requires seeing not the actual object but the abstracted idea of it.[28] Of course, here the object is not limited to non-human matter. Despite Austin's positive-analytical heroicism, dividing persons from things with the formidable strokes of his pen, the logic is not so easily circumscribed. As Austin knew a human might become a thing if, or when, they are treated as "persons considered mere subjects of rights: that is to say, considered as the subjects of rights residing in other persons".[29] Such a person is not a human but a thing because, on this analysis, humans are considered rightful in themselves.[30] A slave is thus styled a thing as a mere subject of rights residing in another and not in themself. But then, what of other humans who are treated as empty vessels whose subjectivity can only be fulfilled through the investment of rights residing in an other? What, for instance, of an African man who is thought to be human only once invested with the rights thought to reside in an American man? Does this make him not human but thing, at least in his primal state? If a slave is a thing because he is not rightful in himself, in his immediate empirical situation, and might only be recognised as human if the rights residing in an other are invested in him, making him free, then what of the subject of rights who does not, in fact, already have those rights? The promise here is the very promise of human rights.[31] By reflecting this juristic logic onto

26 Marin, *Portrait of the King*, 6.

27 Ibid, 5.

28 See also Žižek, *The Sublime Object of Ideology*, 'Preface'.

29 Austin, *Lectures in Jurisprudence*, 802.

30 As Austin's forbear, John Locke, argued, "every man has a property in his own person; this nobody has any right to but himself": John Locke, *The Second Treatise of Government and a Letter Concerning Toleration* (New York: Dover, 2002), para 27.

31 For a different consideration of this, see Jacques Rancière, 'Who is the Subject of the Rights of Man?', *South Atlantic Quarterly*, vol 103, no 2/3 (2004); Emma Larking, *Refugees and the Myth of Human Rights: Life Outside the Pale of the Law* (Farnham: Ashgate, 2014).

such abject humans, as one might shine a light onto a dark face, they acquire their *real* humanity as persons of the law. As I will show in a moment, this was precisely the promise of "Liberia", as an idea that would liberate not only African-Americans from their abject existence in the United States, but the whole of Africa from its benighted condition.

Freedom might be the promise, but there is also what rests on the other hand. The consequence here can be seen in Marx's "general formula for capital", according to which one makes an investment by purchasing a commodity only in order to sell it again.[32] Such a transaction (buying in order to sell) is contrasted with its opposite, a transaction in which a commodity is sold to enable the purchase of another commodity. Whereas the purpose of the latter transaction is to satisfy different wants through the acquisition of different use-values, the purpose of the former – the capitalist transaction – is to acquire money. In this the commodity is reduced to a mere means of money-making; when the capitalist looks at the commodity in which they have invested they see only exchange-value and not an object of substance in itself. In other words, the object's real "potential", which previously was the promise of freedom – of being more and other than its immediate material self – is now fulfilled in its being wholly a thing of capital. No longer seeing anything of value in the object itself, and only value in its form as an exchangeable commodity, the object is freed into a universal form. But this is the very opposite of the liberation promised in the first place, which would free the object into a position to realise its singular potentialities. Stamped with the universal currency, the object's freedom now is to be what others make of it.

This also points to a more general meaning of "capital": *power*. Indeed, as an adjective, "capital" was first used to mean a quality of power, as in "standing at the head".[33] But more than just power: *power over life*. Thus "relating to the head", the term "capital" meant "of an enemy or enmity: deadly, mortal"; "involving loss of the head or life"; "that causes death, fatal".[34] This understanding of capital also goes back to Roman law, where:

> Of Public Judgments, some were 1. CAPITAL; in which the Punishment prescribed was Death; which Death was (1) Natural; such as took away the Life of the Criminal. (2) Civil; such as took away his Liberty, or his Citizenship.[35]

Thus one did not need to lose one's head literally to suffer capital punishment. "Civil death" (the loss of liberty) typically manifested in the form of "degradation to slavery", "superseded by condemnation to the mines", which included being "sent into the mines themselves" or "to some smelting-house or other works

32 See Marx, *Capital*, Chapter 4.

33 See 'capital, *adj.* and *n.2*', Oxford English Dictionary Online, September 2015.

34 Ibid.

35 Samuel Hallifax, *An Analysis of the Roman Civil Law, Compared with the Laws of England* (Cambridge: printed by J Archdeacon Printer to the University, 1774), 116–117.

connected with the mines".[36] It also included deprivation of citizenship. Civil death was thus the epitome of capital punishment, with the body kept alive – and put to work – while being stripped of its subjectivity by law. There could hardly be a better historical analogy for the logical consequences of being a thing of capital.

Land of the free'd

If there is, it is the history of Liberia. I now turn to examine how this logic informed the articulation of "Liberia", from its conception as an idea of liberty at the beginning of the nineteenth century, to its consolidation as a nation-state in the twentieth century.

The idea of Liberia

> But here the thing is impossible: a slave cannot be really emancipated. You cannot raise him from the abyss of his degradation. You may call him free, you may enact a statute book of laws to make him free, but you cannot bleach him into the enjoyment of freedom.[37]
>
> *Christian Spectator*, 1824

By the turn of the nineteenth century it was no longer possible to ignore the immanent problem of slavery in the United States of America, that is, freedom. Two versions of this problem in particular concerned the slave-holders who, in 1816, founded the American Society for Colonizing the Free People of Color of the United States, and who, eight years later, would name their colonial experiment in west Africa "Liberia".[38]

(1) With the abolition of the slave trade nationally, along with the abolition of the institution of slavery in an increasing number of states, humans who had once been styled a movable species of thing were gaining legal status as persons. Slavery, which always contains (holds within, and withholds from manifesting) a condition of freedom, was visibly giving rise to its opposite. For slave-holders this was problematic because it was making visible a contradiction in the concept of slavery that threatened to destabilise its institution. The presence of free people of colour

36 Patrick Mac Chombaich de Colquhoun, *A Summary of the Roman Civil Law: Volume 3* (London: V and R Stevens and Sons, 1849); see also Hallifax, *Analysis of the Roman Civil Law*, 117.

37 'Review of the Reports of the American Colonization Society, from the Christian Spectator', in American Colonization Society, *Seventh Annual Report of the American Society for Colonizing the Free People of Colour of the United States* (Washington, DC: printed by Davis and Force, 1824), 90.

38 For histories of the American Colonization Society, see Eric Burin, *Slavery and the Peculiar Solution: A History of the American Colonization Society* (Gainesville: University Press of Florida, 2005); Amos J Beyan, *The American Colonization Society and the Creation of the Liberian State: A Historical Perspective, 1822–1900* (Lanham: University Press of America, 1991); John Seh David, *The American Colonization Society and the Founding of the First African Republic* (Bloomington: iUniverse, 2014).

presented a possibility – the free African-American – which contradicted the norm – the enslaved African in America. Against the non-human characterisation of Africans in America that justified their enslavement in the language of the law, here were *African-Americans*. This was seen as a threat to the institution of slavery still foundational in many parts of the country because the appearance of this possibility threatened to awaken their slaves from docility, or worse, excite them to rebellion, with bloody consequences.[39] Securing the institution of slavery depended on keeping the slaves docile, which depended on maintaining a reality in which emancipation was impossible to imagine.

(2) At the same time, as persons, free people of colour in the United States suffered a form of civil death, "degraded", if not directly by law, then by effect. As the *Christian Spectator* observed in 1824: "A barrier more difficult to be surmounted than the institution of the *Caste*, cuts off, and while the present state of society continues must always cut off, the negro from all that is valuable in citizenship".[40] Although no longer legally things, the freedom of these free people of colour was being visibly contradicted by a virtual enslavement that operated, like a caste system, as a social rather than officially legal condition. The result, in the view of the *Christian Spectator*, was a form of slavery "never heard of [...] in any country, ancient or modern".[41] By "slavery" the *Christian Spectator* did not mean physical bondage: "We do not mean here to speak of slavery as a system of bonds and stripes and all kinds of bodily suffering".[42] What made slavery in the United States "more ominous in its character and tendency than any similar system which has ever existed" was that its condition did not cease with legal emancipation.[43] As a supporter of the American Colonization Society stated in 1833, free people of colour were "nominally free, it is true, but virtually slaves – a proscribed and degraded caste, whose liberty (if liberty it may be called) is but negative, giving them but little, and exacting from them every thing".[44]

In sum, these are the two main ways the problem of slavery was manifesting in the United States at the turn of the nineteenth century, as far as the American Colonization Society and its supporters were concerned. On one side, the presence of free people of colour contradicted the presence of unfree people of colour, destabilising the institution of slavery by making visible the contradiction that underwrites it. On the other side, the ongoing "virtual enslavement" of these free people of colour contradicted their presence as free people. Wherever one

39 See, e.g., the discussion at one of the first meetings of the American Colonization Society, in *A View of Exertions Lately Made for the Purpose of Colonizing the Free People of Color, in the United States, in Africa, or Elsewhere* (Washington, DC: printed by Jonathan Elliot, 1817), 4–11, and see in particular the statement of John Randolph at 9–10.

40 American Colonization Society, *Seventh Annual Report*, 87.

41 Ibid, 88–89.

42 Ibid.

43 Ibid, 90.

44 'Motion of Z C Lee, Esq, seconded by Hon J W Taylor', in American Colonization Society, *Sixteenth Annual Report of the American Society for Colonizing the Free People of Colour of the United States* (Washington, DC: printed by James C Dunn, 1833), x.

looked black people appeared simultaneously free and unfree, never wholly slaves and yet never wholly citizens – their degradation as things contradicted by the appearance of their freedom as humans; their freedom as humans undermined by their degradation as things.[45]

The founders of the American Colonization Society conceived of "Liberia" as the solution to this double-sided problem. Colonising these free people of colour in Africa (or elsewhere) was conceived as the solution because the problem was understood as the *appearance* of free black bodies in the United States. The institution of slavery, they argued, would remain insecure as long as the possibility of emancipation was made apparent by the presence of people of colour freely walking the streets. At the same time, they argued, emancipation itself would remain merely apparent as long as these free people of colour remained in the United States: here they would only ever experience the semblance of freedom and not *real* freedom; for "[h]ere the thing is impossible: a slave cannot really be emancipated".[46] In short, whether they walked free or laboured in bonds, a person of colour remained a thing in the United States, but *seeing* them walk free was both fanciful and dangerous because it gave the appearance of another, unreal reality, which threatened the real asset of slavery by revealing the crack in its logic.

If turning coloured skin white with a liberal dousing of bleach was not a Christian solution to the perceived problem of the appearance of these free people of colour,[47] then the next best solution was to make the black bodies disappear altogether, by colonising them in Africa (or elsewhere). Not only would this affirm the position of the United States as the land of the free but it would also establish a new "land of the free'd",[48] a home and country where people of colour could come to exhibit "not the semblance, but the reality of freedom".[49] To quote the slave-owning member of the American Colonization Society, General Harper, who coined the name in 1824:

> I have thought of a name that is peculiar, short, and familiar, and that expresses the object and nature of the establishment – it is the term LIBERIA; and denotes a settlement of persons *made free*: for our Colony may with truth

45 See also David, *The American Colonization Society*, Chapter 3.

46 American Colonization Society, *Seventh Annual Report*, 90; see also American Colonization Society, *Sixteenth Annual Report*, v, xvii.

47 See the passage from the *Christian Spectator* cited in note 37 above:

> But here the thing is impossible: a slave cannot be really emancipated. You cannot raise him from the abyss of his degradation. You may call him free, you may enact a statute book of laws to make him free, but you cannot bleach him into the enjoyment of freedom.

48 American Colonization Society, *Address of the Managers of the American Colonization Society, to the People of the United States* (Washington, DC: printed by James C Dunn, 1832), 11.

49 Ibid, 4.

> be called the home and country of freedmen, in contradistinction to the slaves of whom they once formed a part.[50]

Liberia would achieve in practice what Austin had sought to do in his *Lectures*: establish a clear distinction between a human person and a non-human thing. Liberia in Africa would be a place where people of colour would be wholly free; the United States of America would be a place where people of colour would be wholly things of capital; and the distinction would be kept in place by a vast ocean.

"Liberia" was thus born as an idea of liberty, conceived to make the free *positively* free (while, incidentally, making the unfree positively unfree). But there is also a third way in which "Liberia" was conceived as a force of liberty. Colonisation would provide a model of civilisation that would lead to the emancipation of *all* of Africa's peoples.

> Such is the history of the American Colonization Society. Its *design* is general – the benefit of the whole African race. Its plan of *operation* is specific, the establishment on the coast of Africa of a colony of *free* people of colour from America.[51]

This was the great humanitarian mission of the day: to make Africans free from enslavement to their traditional ways – or as one of the founders of the American Colonization Society proclaimed in an initial meeting of the organisation: "[i]t is the hope of redeeming many millions of people from the lowest state of ignorance and superstition".[52] Through this mission, "civilization and the Christian religion would be introduced into that benighted quarter of the world".[53] Or as another supporter wrote:

> When she shall have done the work, Sir, it will be seen that the new world will have sent back to the old, the most sublime empire of reason and law, ever known to mankind. She will have planted in a land, once illustrious, but long darkened by superstition and despotism, the institutions of civil and religious liberty; and savage men will feel their influence, and be converted to civilization and Christianity.[54]

This was the light that the American Colonization Society hoped to shine on the lands and peoples of Africa: *Liberia*, a beacon for the sublime object of logos and

50 American Colonization Society, *Seventh Annual Report*, 5–6 (italics in original).
51 Ibid, 86 (italics in original). See also Burin, *The Peculiar Solution*, 13–14.
52 Statement of Elias Caldwell, in *A View of Exertions Lately Made*, 7. See also James Ciment, *Another America: The Story of Liberia and the Former Slaves who Ruled it* (New York: Hill and Wang, 2013), 9.
53 Statement of Elias Caldwell, in *A View of Exertions Lately Made*, 7. On the aims of the colonisation mission, see also American Colonization Society, *Seventh Annual Report*, 7.
54 American Colonization Society, *Sixteenth Annual Report*, xvii.

law, enabling the growth of the institutions of liberty in a long-darkened land. "From them, under Heaven, the voice has gone forth – 'let there be light in Africa'".[55] *And savage men will feel their influence.*

Beyond the littoral

> I beg most respectfully to call Your Excellency's attention to this important and valuable section of country a primeval forest, heavily timbered and watered by the beautiful Manah River, brooks, rivulets, and creeks on all sides – just such a site as would be desirable for the building up of one or two good large towns and villages without the least molestation from any one. We should lose no time in taking possession of and occupying this point with as little delay as possible.[56]
>
> Report of the Special Commissioner for the Demarkation of the Anglo Liberian Boundary, 1903

In 1847 Liberia's African-American settlers declared the erstwhile colony a Free, Sovereign and Independent State,[57] making it the only independent African republic at the time and the only other "black republic" in the world after Haiti. One of the main reasons for the Declaration was to gain legal recognition as a member of the international community of states, to empower the government to collect customs duties from foreign merchants.[58] The problem was summarised by a British Commodore in a letter to the Americo-Liberian Governor in 1844:

> For the rights in question, those of imposing custom duties and limiting the trade of foreigners by restrictions, are sovereign rights, which can only be lawfully exercised by sovereign and independent states, within their own recognized borders and dominions. I need not remind your excellency that this description does not apply to "Liberia" which is not recognized as a subsisting state, even by the government of the country from which its settlers have immigrated.[59]

The settlers' Declaration three years later, that Liberia is a "Sovereign and Independent State", was their answer to the British Commodore. And the Declaration succeeded in bringing the desired status in international law of nation-statehood – although the European governments would have to be reminded from time to time that this description did apply to Liberia.

European recognition of Liberia's international personality remained qualified in two ways in particular. As the "scramble for Africa" intensified in the 1880s,

55 'Motion of Z C Lee, Esq, seconded by Hon J W Taylor', in ibid, x.

56 *Report of the Special Commissioner for the Demarkation of the Anglo Liberian Boundary* (Monrovia: 10 August 1903), 8–9.

57 Declaration of Independence of Liberia (1847).

58 See Yekutiel Gershoni, 'The Formation of Liberia's Boundaries, Part 1: Agreements', *Liberian Studies Journal*, vol 17, no 1 (1992).

59 'Letter dated September 9, 1844 sent by Commodore Jones of the HMS Penelope to Joseph Jenkins Roberts, governor of the Liberian commonwealth', cited in ibid, 25.

Britain and France made clear that, if Liberia was to subsist as a sovereign and independent state, and not be annexed to either of their colonial empires, it had to have recognised borders and exercise dominion over the peoples within that territory. The problem was that, since its inception, Liberia had remained an unbounded idea. As a beacon for logos and law in a long-darkened continent, "Liberia" was supposed to be without limit in Africa.[60] This was not just metaphorical; *physically* Liberia was supposed to reach "indefinitely into the interior" of Africa. As the American Colonization Society wrote in 1832 in its *Description of the Colony*: "The tract of country under the Colonial jurisdiction [...] extends from one hundred and fifty, to two hundred miles along the coast, and indefinitely into the interior".[61] Liberia's littoral reach might have been under pressure from the encroaching forces of Britain and France, but beyond the littoral Liberia's constitution was left entirely open.[62]

At least that was the idea. By the end of the nineteenth century Britain and France were forcefully circumscribing it, making clear that, if the Black Republic was to retain its international status, then it would have to define its territory and population and bring both under its rule. The process of demarcating the territory of "Liberia" (the first of these two requirements) can be seen in the following set of maps (Figure 3.1), adapted from Reed Stewart's study of Liberia's boundaries.[63] The first map, drawn in anticipation of Independence, shows the limited extent of Liberia's coastal settlement. Known as "littoral Liberia",[64] this thin coastal strip, reaching at its widest little more than 65 kilometres inland, was effectively the limits of Americo-Liberian dominion well into the twentieth century.

If Map 1 depicts the extent of the Republic on the ground at Independence, then Map 2 shows how Liberia nonetheless remained an unbounded idea. Despite the encroachment of the British on the Republic's north-western frontier and the French to the south-east, Liberia was still seen to reach indefinitely into the interior. Maps 3 and 4 then record the process of establishing Liberia as a bounded reality. Map 3 depicts the Republic's north-western boundary with Sierra Leone according to the 1885 Anglo-Liberian treaty. The result is a solid line that begins confidently before fading into the interior, the answer it is supposed to provide ending in a question mark. Likewise, Map 4, depicting the south-eastern

60 See also Gershoni, 'Liberia's Boundaries, Part 1', 26, 30–31.

61 American Colonization Society, *Address of the Managers*, 11; see also American Colonization Society, *A Few Facts Respecting the American Colonization Society and the Colony at Liberia* (Washington, DC: printed by Way and Gideon, 1830), 5; Gershoni, 'Liberia's Boundaries, Part 1', 26.

62 See, e.g., Constitution of the Commonwealth of Liberia (1839) and Constitution of the Republic of Liberia (1847). See also Gershoni, 'Liberia's Boundaries, Part 1', 26.

63 Reed F Stewart, 'Liberia's Boundaries: A Preliminary Study', *Conference on Social Science in Liberia* (Stanford, 1–2 August 1969). My "Map 1" is Stewart's "Map B"; "Map 2" is "Map C"; "Map 3" is "Map E"; "Map 4" is "Map H"; and "Map 5" is "Map J".

64 See, e.g., D Elwood Dunn and Svend E Holsoe, *Historical Dictionary of Liberia* (Metuchen: Scarecrow Press, 1985), 1.

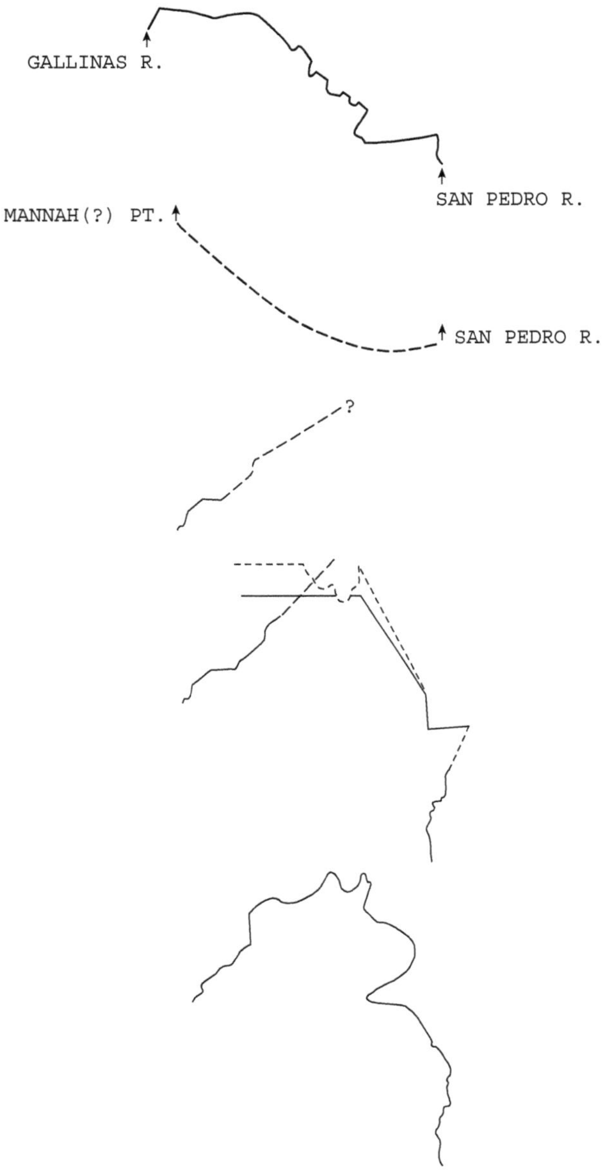

Figure 3.1 The territory of "Liberia"[65]

boundary with France's west African colonies, "tries to apply the provisions of the 1892 treaty to actuality"; and yet, as Stewart concludes, the result is "two sets of boundary descriptions [that] do not jibe".[66] While Maps 3 and 4 are an attempt

65 Adapted from Stewart, 'Liberia's Boundaries'.
66 Ibid, 'Map H'.

to depict the bounded reality of "Liberia", Map 5 is drawn as an imagined territory. Proposed in 1906 during negotiations between Liberia and France, it is the least realistic of the maps, in the sense that it did not correspond to "Liberia" as articulated by law, and yet it is also the most realistic, in the sense that it comes closest to the actual lay of the land.[67]

Taken together, this set of maps shows the high abstraction of the colonial framework that was projected onto the lands and peoples of "Liberia" in the attempt to consolidate the nation-state.[68] The lines crawling across the blank page suggest a movable species of thing capable of changing place without an essential change in its actual nature. At the same time, as a jurisdictional technology, these lines were cutting deep into an actual place, reflecting and facilitating the transformation of its lands and peoples into the territory and citizens of Liberia.[69] Thus as a kind of performance artwork, the map series shows the gradual overlay of "Liberia" upon the country over which it sought to extend its jurisdiction between 1847 and 1906; while as a work of surrealism the maps show just how indefinite the territory remained and how fantastic the process was of consolidating "Liberia".

The fantastical nature of this process can be read in the *Report of the Commissioner for the Demarkation of the Anglo Liberian Boundary*.[70] Written in 1903 as a record of the Commissioner's expedition to map the north-western boundary set down in the 1885 Anglo-Liberian treaty,[71] the report reads like the journal of a man exploring the realms of a mythical country that exists in name alone, as

67 Even after the boundaries had been finalised, the interior of Liberia remained indefinite. In Graham Greene's account of his 1936 walking tour through Liberia, he notes:

> I could find only two large-scale maps for sale. One, issued by the British General Staff, quite openly confesses ignorance; there is a large white space covering the greater part of the Republic, with a few dotted lines indicating the conjectured course of rivers (incorrectly, I usually found) […] The other map is issued by the United States War Department. There is a dashing quality about it; it shows a vigorous imagination. Where the English map is content to leave a blank space, the American in large letters fills it with the word "Cannibals". It has no use for dotted lines and confessions of ignorance; it is so inaccurate that it would be useless, perhaps even dangerous, to follow it, though there is something Elizabethan in its imagination. "Dense Forest"; "Cannibals": rivers which don't exist, at any rate anywhere near where they are put; one expects to find Eldorado, two-headed men and fabulous beasts represented in little pictures in the Gola Forest.
>
> Graham Greene, *Journey Without Maps* (London: Vintage, 2002), 45–46

68 For a more general discussion of mapping as a jurisdictional technology and the connection with colonialism, see Shaunnagh Dorsett, 'Mapping Territories', in Shaun McVeigh (ed), *Jurisprudence of Jurisdiction* (Abingdon: Routledge, 2007).

69 On jurisdictional technologies, see also Dorsett and McVeigh, *Jurisdiction*. On the connection between technologies of jurisdiction and colonialism, see also Olivia Barr, *A Jurisprudence of Movement: Common Law, Walking, Unsettling Place* (Abingdon: Routledge, 2016).

70 *Report of the Special Commissioner*.

71 On the demarcation process, see also Yekutiel Gershoni, 'The Formation of Liberia's Boundaries, Part 2: The Demarcation Process', *Liberian Studies Journal*, vol 17, no 2

"Liberia", but which has not yet been made conscious of itself as *Liberian*. Throughout the report there is a striking dissonance in how the Commissioner describes the places he passes through, as a kind of future-present Republic – present in the minds of the governing Americo-Liberians, only yet to be made present on the ground. At the same time as he describes these places as "our Republic" and advises his government to "lose no time in taking possession of and occupying" them, he notes the lack of the State's actual presence. Thus at one point, having presented the Liberian flag to some Chiefs, he notes: "For the first time had our flag been seen in this part of our Republic so they informed us".[72]

The Americo-Liberian vision of making citizens out of the African peoples living within the envisioned territory of the Republic can also be read in this report. At one point, on entering a town on the north-western frontier, the Commissioner notes that its "3000 or 4000 inhabitants" were "kindly disposed and friendly – in a word they are nice people and will make us good citizens by and by. But the imitation must come from us".[73] This reflects the view, shared by the government and its supporters, that the process of extending "Liberia" into the interior would be uni-directional and top-down: these people would be made into *our* citizens.[74] The sentence that follows – "but the imitation *must come from us*" – is remarkable, not only because it repeats the thought that the extension of "Liberia" into the interior would be uni-directional and top-down, but because of its apparent typographical error. Presumably the Commissioner meant "invitation" and not "imitation", in line with the European practice of establishing authority over an African people and their land through the signature of a treaty.[75] The "invitation" would be to enter into a treaty with the Liberian government, perhaps on the promise of military protection and the provision of infrastructure and schools, in return for recognising the sovereignty of Liberia and allowing the Republic to raise its flag over the town.[76] But the word "imitation" is equally, if not more appropriate, pointing to the implication of such an invitation. Becoming a Liberian citizen would involve not merely a change in legal status: it would involve, by and by, becoming "civilised". As the Commissioner writes early in his report, after

(1992); Nnamdi Azikiwe, *Liberia in World Politics* (Westport: Negro Universities Press, 1970), 101–105.

72 *Report of the Special Commissioner*, 9–10. In his study of the "pacification of the Liberian hinterland", Akingbade also notes how "there were many people in the interior who were totally untouched by the influence of the Americo-Liberians" and that "their first awareness began when they were required to pay taxes and recruit men of their number for public works or for work on the farms of individual Americo-Liberians": Harrison Akingbade, 'The Pacification of the Liberian Hinterland', *Journal of Negro History*, vol 79, no 3 (1994): 292–293.

73 *Report of the Special Commissioner*, 12.

74 As it turned out, these particular people and their land would be annexed to Sierra Leone by the British.

75 See Gershoni, 'Liberia's Boundaries, Part 1', 27.

76 See *Report of the Special Commissioner*, in particular the summary of the "political character" of the mission at 20–24. On the importance of the flag as a sign of the Republic's dominion in the interior, see, e.g., at 9–10, 13–14, 18, 20–21.

carrying out "an inspection of these stalwart sons of our forest": "[I was] proud to know that we had thousands of such good strong men that could be utilized as citizens, if civilized, in building up a strong commonwealth on our border and Interior".[77] Of course, to "utilise" means not simply to "use" but to use in a way that alters the object in use: it is to "render useful", to "convert to use".[78] To render these sons of the forest citizens would be to make them useful to the nation-state. Not only would they make useful soldiers for the Republic, as the Commissioner anticipated, but they would also be especially useful as labour.[79] However, as the Commissioner notes, to make these hinterland peoples useful first they would have to be made civilised, which was essentially a process of imitation involving conversion to Christianity and a proper "book education". In other words, their "use" was not a property belonging to them already, as self-possessed peoples (use-value in the Marxian sense), but a *potential* property that would be realised with their conversion into valuable citizens.

If the success of metonymy is the fusion of signifier and signified – so that a name such as "Liberia" is thought to correspond with the lands and peoples it circumscribes – then key to this success is the realism of the representational framework. This does not mean the representational framework must *actually* correspond with the given form of its object. The opposite: as an act of articulation, giving new form to what "is", the framework must be super-real. The more super-real, or surreal, the framework's articulated vision, the more able it will be to transform its object. This of course creates a dissonance between the representational framework and the object, but that is why the success of metonymy depends on the realism of the representation, which does not mean it has to be actually real but only *imagined* to be real. This is the genius of a metonym: its capacity to be simultaneously separate and inseparable from its object – inseparable in the sense that the framework and its object become all but indistinguishable (hence the realism); separate in the sense that the two are never quite identical (hence the realism is over-laid or super-imposed, that is, surreal). Thus for the Commissioner going out to map the interior of Liberia the task was not to describe the country "as is" but to overlay the territory articulated in the treaty onto the country. As visionaries, instead of seeing an existing country, the Americo-Liberians who set out to realise "Liberia" saw a fantasy world of primeval forests "heavily timbered and watered" by "brooks, rivulets, and creeks" and populated by primitive "sons of the forests" poised to become useful citizens. It is not necessarily that they did not see the dissonance between their vision and what they encountered on the ground; it is just that they saw their vision as *more* real. Any dissonance was just the reflection of the unrealised state of nature. After all, this was the light that would illuminate Africa's true potential and enable the transformation of its lands and peoples.

77 Ibid, 5.

78 'Utilize, *v.*', Oxford English Dictionary Online, September 2015.

79 I discuss this in the next section. See also Akingbade, 'The Pacification of the Liberian Hinterland', 279.

This can be understood as a case of "fetishistic misrecognition".[80] Thus to the Americo-Liberian nation-state-builders, the west Africans and their lands appeared as unrealised citizens and territory – as objects that *did* intrinsically possess these properties (as being *not-yet-citizens* and *not-yet-territory*) and that only needed to overcome their backwardness to achieve their proper mode of existence.[81] This was a case of "fetishistic misrecognition" in that the potential was of course not an *intrinsic* property of the west Africans and their lands but rather the property of a network of social relations that the Americo-Liberians were projecting onto them.[82] Specifically, the properties of "citizen" and "territory" derived from the legal framework of the so-called international community. Squeezed tight between the colonial empires of Britain and France, its survival dependent on international recognition, Liberia's agents were acting out this international-colonial fantasy by treating the west Africans and their lands *as if* they were naturally the things of the nation-state. But as such, it did not matter what individual Americo-Liberians actually thought – and it is clear that many did recognise the already-existing qualities of their west African neighbours.[83] What mattered is that these state-builders acted on the "misrecognition"; what mattered was that they were "fetishists in practice, not in theory".[84]

In sum, extending Liberia beyond the littoral was supposed to be a process of super-imposing the idea of it over the blank space of the hinterland to consolidate the nation-state. In the second half of the nineteenth century, littoral Liberia – the place of Americo-Liberian coastal settlements – was a place in flux, its north-western limits under pressure from the British, its south-western limits contested by the French, with both threatening to subsume the nascent Republic within their colonial empires.[85] Extending Liberia beyond the littoral was supposed to finally settle the uncertain, contested place of "Liberia" in west Africa by bringing the country – lands and peoples – under its dominion, as required by the international-colonial legal framework. And yet, as I now turn to show, super-imposing the idea of "Liberia" over the hinterland by means of this legal-representational framework did not place Liberia beyond the littoral, settling its place in west Africa and the world. Rather the effect was to extend littoral Liberia *into the interior.* Desmond Manderson and Honni van Rijswijk describe littoral spaces as

80 See Žižek, *The Sublime Object of Ideology*, 19–21.

81 In Hegelian terms this would be the negation of the negation. If the first negation involves negating an object's immediate mode of existence by seeing its potential (reflected here in the transformation from self-possessed west African into potential-citizen or not-yet-citizen), then the second negation involves overcoming the abstraction by realising the potential (reflected in the transformation from not-yet-citizen into actual citizen).

82 See Žižek, *The Sublime Object of Ideology*, 20; compare Pahuja, *Decolonising International Law*, 29.

83 See, e.g., James Fairhead, et al (eds), *African-American Exploration in West Africa: Four Nineteenth-Century Diaries* (Bloomington: Indiana University Press, 2003).

84 Žižek, *The Sublime Object of Ideology*, 28.

85 Nnamdi Azikiwe describes this in terms of "the claws of imperialism": Azikiwe, *Liberia in World Politics*, Chapter 7.

"heightened and active, places of contested imaginaries" – "an environment of flux and change *par excellence*".[86] Despite the attempt to settle "littoral Liberia" by defining its territory and population, what had been throughout the nineteenth century a largely open and indeterminate idea, with only "a narrow strip squeezed in between the twin perils of land and sea",[87] would become in the twentieth century a littoral space *par excellence.*

Civil death

> The genius of liberty shall go out from thence; the dominion of freedom shall be extended; tribe after tribe shall send in its adhesion, until the entire of long neglected – long injured Africa – no longer pillaged and plundered of her children, shall be crowned with all the blessings of civil liberty. And by the advancement of this cause shall commerce be advanced. The hidden treasures of another continent shall be developed and borne upon many a sea.
>
> The Rev Mr Hammet, Annual Meeting of the American Colonisation Society, 1833

The vision of making the African peoples over whom Liberia claimed jurisdiction into citizens was not formalised until 1904. Under the interior policy of President Arthur Barclay, the Constitution was amended to recognise Liberia's "indigenous peoples" as subjects of – rather than just subject to – the nation-state. The recognition of citizenship remained partial, however, with African-Liberians invested with the Constitutional status of "uncivilised citizens", with the proviso that they *could* become "civilised citizens", at which point they would be invested with the full body of rights residing in Americo-Liberians. Finally, this would be the realisation of the promise of "Liberia" as a beacon for the sublime object of logos and law in Africa: the possibility of becoming wholly rightful subjects, marked by graduation into civilization; this was the invitation (of citizenship) and the imitation (of civilization) that would render the sons of the forest useful to the nation-state.

If this vision was a violent one, its violence was felt most in its non-realisation. Failure to become a wholly rightful citizen meant suffering a form of civil death as an "uncivilised citizen", remaining suspended in the negative form of not-yet-citizen, of potential-citizen. This is precisely what happened to the vast majority of Liberia's citizens in the first half of the twentieth century. The African peoples over whom the government sought to exercise dominion remained "Liberian" in name alone, the two ("African" and "Liberian") being synonymous only in the language of the national law. To be African-Liberian at this time was like being African-American in the United States, as free people of colour who remained unfree as a result of

86 Desmond Manderson and Honni van Rijswick, 'Introduction to Littoral Readings: Representations of Land and Sea in Law, Literature, and Geography', *Law and Literature*, vol 27, no 2 (2015): 174. See also Desmond Manderson, *Kangaroo Courts and the Rule of Law* (Abingdon: Routledge, 2012), Chapter 10.

87 Manderson and van Rijswick, 'Littoral Readings', 174.

their degradation as second-class citizens. This experience of civil death is writ large in the history of twentieth-century Liberia.

In the first decade of the twentieth century the government was still struggling to establish effective occupation of the interior, in large part because it lacked the resources to extend its presence beyond its coastal settlements.[88] Without funds to build infrastructure and without security forces to deploy, the interior of Liberia remained "effectively unoccupied", according to the terms of the "declaration relative to the essential conditions to be observed in order that new occupations on the coasts of the African continent may be held to be effective", adopted by the *General Act of the Berlin Conference* in 1885.[89] In the attempt to effectively occupy the interior the Government had entered into an agreement with the British owned Liberian Development Company in 1904. The agreement was supposed to do two things: the Liberian Development Company would provide the Government with a loan, thus addressing its financial problems[90]; and the company would carry out commercial (rubber) operations in the interior, which would count towards "effective occupation".[91] In 1906 the government secured another large loan from British bankers with the assistance of the Liberian Development Company.[92] However, within a year – heavily indebted, unable to repay its loans, and still without control over the African peoples within its territory, to the frustration of the British and French – the government was forced to agree to

88 See Akingbade, 'Pacification of the Liberian Hinterland', 281.

89 *General Act of the Berlin Conference*, 26 February 1885, Chapter VI. On what would constitute "effective occupation", see also *General Act of the Brussels Conference Relative to the African Slave Trade*, 2 July 1890, in which "the Powers",

> [e]qually animated by the firm intention of putting an end to the crimes and devastations engendered by the traffic in African slaves, of effectively protecting the aboriginal populations of Africa, and of assuring to that vast continent the benefits of peace and civilization; [...] have adopted the following provisions:
>
> ARTICLE 1. The Powers declare that the most effective means for counteracting the Slave Trade in the interior of Africa are the following: – 1. Progressive organization of the administrative, judicial, religious, and military services in the African territories [...] 2. The gradual establishment in the interior by the responsible Power in each territory of strongly occupied stations in such a way as to make their protective or repressive action effectively felt [...] 3. The construction of roads, and in particular of railways, connecting the advanced stations with the coast [...] 6. Organization of expeditions and flying columns to keep up the communication of the stations with each other and with the coast, to support repressive action, and to assure the security of roadways. 7. Restriction of the importation of fire-arms, at least of modern pattern, and of ammunition, throughout the entire extent of the territories infected by the Slave Trade.

90 On Liberia's financial problems, see Nnamdi Azikiwe's discussion of Liberia's loans from 1871 through to the 1930s as "one of the latest phases of imperialism": Azikiwe, *Liberia in World Politics*, Chapter 8.

91 See Akingbade, 'The Pacification of the Liberian Hinterland', 280. See also *Brussels Conference Act* (1890), Art 1.

92 See also Gershoni, 'Liberia's Boundaries, Part 1', 36–37.

a set of reforms. As the British Consul-General in Monrovia put it threateningly, Liberia would have to "put her house in order, or be prepared, at no distant date, to disappear from the catalogue of independent countries".[93] Or, as the US Secretary of State put it in a letter to a delegation appointed to investigate the situation in Liberia two years later:

> owing to the inability of the Liberian Government properly to control the native tribes and its consequent failure to maintain order upon the border, there is reason to apprehend the temporary and eventually the permanent occupation of Liberian territory by her more powerful neighbors [Britain and France] on the ground of the necessity of assuring order and safety in their own colimiting territories.[94]

"Putting her house in order" meant establishing a Frontier Police Force, reforming its Judiciary and Treasury, under the supervision of Western advisors, appointing three more British customs officials, and granting the British Inspector-General of Customs a seat in the Cabinet of the Liberian Government "with a plenary power of veto over all expenditures".[95] Complying with the first of these demands, the Liberian government established the Frontier Force in 1908,[96] putting it under the command of British army Major McKay Cadell with the assistance of two other British officers, and within a few years under US supervision and command.[97] Officially mandated "for the maintenance of law and order throughout the republic and for the prevention and detection of crimes on the frontier and in the interior of the country",[98] the Frontier Force quickly gained a

93 Cited in Monday B Abasiattai, 'European Intervention in Liberia with Special Reference to the "Cadell Incident" of 1908–1909', *Liberian Studies Journal*, vol 14, no 1 (1989).

94 'The Secretary of State to the Commissioners of Liberia', US Department of State, Washington, DC, 13 April 1909.

95 Azikiwe, *Liberia in World Politics*, 114; Abasiattai, 'European Intervention in Liberia', 79.

96 'Joint Resolution Providing for the Pay and Formation of a Frontier Police Force', in *Acts Passed by the Legislature of the Republic of Liberia during the Session 1907–1908* (Monrovia: Government Printing Office, 1908), 23, cited in Akingbade, 'The Pacification of the Liberian Hinterland', 281–284. See also Azikiwe, *Liberia in World Politics*, 115. According to Azikiwe, Major Cadell, transferring from Sierra Leone, "brought with him about one-third of his soldiers from Sierra Leone, all uniformed in suits and caps stamped with the emblem of 'His Britannic Majesty's Service'", and upon arrival in Liberia "immediately he requested the Municipality of Monrovia to recognise him as the Inspector-General of Police", before taking over "the positions of Street Commissioner, Tax Collector and Municipal Treasurer".

97 See Abasiattai, 'European Intervention in Liberia', 79–85; Akingbade, 'The Pacification of the Liberian Hinterland', 281; Azikiwe, *Liberia in World Politics*, 114–117. On the involvement of US officers in the Liberian Frontier Force between 1912 and 1927, see Timothy A Rainey, 'Buffalo Soldiers in Africa: The US Army and the Liberian Frontier Force, 1912–1927', *Liberian Studies Journal*, vol 21, no 2 (1996).

98 *Frontier Force Manual*, Article 2, Section 5, cited in Akingbade, 'The Pacification of the Liberian Hinterland', 286.

reputation for "wanton cruelty, harassment, indiscipline, and rapine".[99] The government's justification for the Frontier Force's oppressive conduct was its necessity in realising the vision of "Liberia". Not only would this Force assist in establishing the authority of the Republic in the interior, thereby securing Liberia's international citizenship, but it would also accelerate the development of Liberia's uncivilized citizens. As the Liberian Secretary of State, Charles King, wrote in 1916, through the Frontier Force Liberia "strikes at the very root of [...] political, religious and social institutions which are uncompromisingly antagonistic to the laws of humanity and civilisation".[100]

King would go on to become President of Liberia from 1920 to 1930, before being forced from office upon the release of a report by the League of Nations International Commission of Enquiry into "the existence of slavery and forced labour in the Republic of Liberia".[101] The Enquiry had found that forced labour was being used extensively in Liberia, "frequently under conditions involving systematic intimidation and ill-treatment on the part of Government officials, messengers and Frontier Force soldiers".[102] Moreover, the Enquiry found that officials had "condoned" the use of this Force "for the intimidation of villagers, for the humiliation and degradation of chiefs, for the imprisonment of inhabitants, and for the convoying of gangs of captured natives to the coast, there guarding them till the time of shipment" to islands such as the Spanish colony of Fernando Pó.[103] A further effect of this use of force, the Enquiry found, was the abandonment of villages by people who had fled into exile.[104] In the Commission's summation, "[t]he words development and social progress are unknown, servitude and slavery have taken their place".[105]

99 Ibid.

100 'Secretary of State CDB King to James L Curtis, American Minister Resident', 26 May 1916, RDSL 882.00/540, cited in Martin Ford, *Ethnic Relations and the Transformation of Leadership among the Dan of Nimba, Liberia (ca. 1900–1940)* (Dissertation, State University of New York at Binghamton, 1990), 93.

101 League of Nations, *Report of the International Commission of Enquiry into the Existence of Slavery and Forced Labour in the Republic of Liberia*, Monrovia, Liberia, August 1930 (Geneva: League of Nations, 1930). The findings and recommendations are reprinted in ICE, 'The 1930 Enquiry Commission to Liberia', *Journal of the Royal African Society*, vol 30, no 120 (1931): 277–290.

102 Ibid, 279, see also at 280, 289.

103 Ibid, 280.

104 Ibid, 284.

105 Ibid. Cf Azikiwe, *Liberia in World Politics*, Chapter 12. According to Azikiwe (94):

> A critical analysis of the report of the findings of the Commission reveals to the unbiased student of Liberian affairs the fact that, out of seven counts, Liberia is guilty of only three. These three counts are (a) the use of forced labour for public and private purposes, (b) the compulsory method employed in recruiting labourers to Fernando Po and Gabun, and (c) its *vicarious responsibility* for the acts of the Liberian Frontier Force.

Thus, for the Africans who had been made Liberian the experience was an abject one: denied full rightful citizenship, subjected to forms of enslavement,[106] forced labour, and exile, amongst other degradation.[107] This was the opposite of "making free" the peoples of Africa. Indeed, it was the repetition of the very problem "Liberia" was meant to resolve. Having set out to emancipate all of Africa, the Liberian government had reduced the vast majority of its population to the status of "uncivilised citizens", with terrible consequences. And yet, rather than see these results as a logical function of the colonisation mission, they were seen as a failure to properly implement the colonial vision. "The now obvious fact", the International Commission of Enquiry observed in prelude to its recommendations, is "that tropical Africa can never be developed, its agricultural, mineral, and other sources utilised, nor surplus Government funds be hoped for, without the willing co-operation and assistance of the indigenous population".[108] In a continuation of the nineteenth-century policy of enlightening the dark continent, the Commission recommended gaining that "co-operation and assistance" by finally making civilized the uncivilized citizens of Liberia by investing them with full rights of citizenship under the Constitution. "We believe that the sooner class distinction between civilised and uncivilised is broken, and the indigenous native allowed an equal status with the coast dweller, the better for all concerned".[109] This would be "better for all concerned" because civilisation would make the native ***truly useful.*** "It is now becoming everywhere recognised by tropical African administrators that the first considerations towards financial competence must include provision for the civilisation, education, and the gaining of the confidence of the native".[110]

> Schools are of the first importance, not merely for the purpose of teaching reading and writing, but for improving the native's sociological conditions; and specialist instructors invaluable for broadening his ideas, teaching him market values, and the use he can make of the innumerable economic

106 Importantly, the International Commission of Enquiry found that "classic slavery carrying the idea of slave markets and slave dealers no longer exists as such in the Republic of Liberia", although it did find that "slavery as defined by the (1926) Anti-Slavery Convention does exist in so far as inter- and intra-tribal domestic slavery exists"; however see the rebuttal of this finding of "slavery" in Azikiwe, *Liberia in World Politics*, 191–193.

107 According to the findings of the Commission of Enquiry,

> intimidation has apparently been and is the keyword of the Government's native policy. Not only have the native village classes been intimidated and terrorised by a display of force, cruelty and suppression, but the chiefs themselves, men whom the people not so many years ago looked up to, were glad to serve, and relied upon for protection [...] have been so systematically humiliated, degraded and robbed of their power, that now they are mere go-betweens, paid by the Government to rob the people.
>
> ICE, '1930 Enquiry Commission', 284

108 Ibid, 281.

109 Ibid, 282.

110 Ibid, 281.

> products and raw materials around him. The unsophisticated native learns something of the outside world, and his wants are increased. The missionary, the school teacher, and the trader teach him what he may buy for money, and he then wants to learn what he can grow, what he should do, or where he should work to make some money, with the result that trade increases, the coast merchant flourishes, the revenues of Government expand, and money is forthcoming.[111]

The alternative, the Commission cautioned, is a situation where "the native must continue his harried existence with a feeling that he is really and truly a slave",[112] before issuing a warning – echoing the warnings of Britain and France in previous decades – that if the Liberian government failed to act on its recommendations, "Liberia may discover that its place in the community of civilised nations is jeopardised".[113]

The International Commission of Enquiry has been convincingly critiqued as an attempt to undermine the Black Republic as a model of African self-rule at a time of anti-colonial revolution across the continent.[114] Whether or not the indirect aim was to make it a protectorate,[115] however, more insidious was the Commission's direct goal as expressed in its recommendations for reform: Liberia would keep its international citizenship as long as it demonstrated progress in making its population "useful", by which it meant economically productive. At the time there was a shortage of labour in Europe's West African colonies, leading colonial administrations to erect barriers to keep their domestic labourers within the

111 Ibid.

112 Ibid.

113 Ibid, 288.

114 As Nnamdi Azikiwe wrote in 1932 in response to the Enquiry and the coverage of its findings: "Liberia today is a winter resort for any artist who is interested in caricaturing Negro statehood": Nnamdi Azikiwe, 'In Defense of Liberia', *Journal of Negro History*, vol 17, no 1 (1932): 45. Azikiwe goes on to critique the:

> systematically organized propaganda that Liberia, Haiti, and Abyssinia are failures, and that they furnish evidence to prove the incapacity of the Negro for self-government in the tropical regions. Discarding all problems which sovereign states must face in order to maintain their *de jure* existence, most of the writers on Liberia, excepting Benjamin Brawley, McPherson, Froude, Jore, Cuthbert Christy, and Buell, have delighted themselves in seeing chaos, disorder, hopeless anarchy and failure of the Liberian "experiment" whenever her case is before the bar of international opinion. Even Emmett J Scott, of Howard University, holds that the usual charges of official corruption are not always true. This is generally done to take advantage of the people and pave way for economic exploitation.
>
> Ibid, 46–47

See also Azikiwe, *Liberia in World Politics*, Chapter 12.

115 See Azikiwe, *Liberia in World Politics*, Chapters 14–17. In sum, Azikiwe writes, having "invite[d] the world to make a healthy criticism of its [Liberia's] labour policy", "instead of lauding it for its sincerity and moral courage, all avenues and institutions of public opinion have been utilized to vilify it and to pave way for its extermination from the family of nations": 305–306.

territories of their colonies. Against this policy the Liberian government was committing two offences: not only was it failing to realise the value of its human resources by transforming them into productive citizens, but it was also "leaking" labourers from its neighbouring colonies, especially Sierra Leone, by acting as a conduit for recruiters to ship them to the island of Fernando Pó.[116]

The intervention by the League of Nations in the form of the Enquiry succeeded in stopping that leak, to the satisfaction of British interests in Sierra Leone. But it also satisfied US interests by putting international pressure on Liberia to create a domestic labour market.[117] In 1926, four years before the finalisation of the report of the International Commission of Enquiry, and around the time of the Enquiry's establishment "at the instigation of the United States Government",[118] the US-owned Firestone Tire and Rubber Company had signed a planting agreement with the Liberian government to lease more than 1 million acres for its planned rubber plantations, requiring a projected 350,000 labourers – labourers which, the Company reminded the government, it had promised to make available.[119] As Harvey Firestone Jr stated in a letter to President King in 1926: "We desire to point out to the Government again that the success of our development in Liberia is largely dependent upon the organization of a permanent and contented labour force".[120] What Firestone needed was a mass of bodies to transform Liberia's primeval forest into a productive rubber plantation.[121] If Liberia's already scarce human resources were being shipped to Fernando Pó, Firestone's investment would fail.[122]

116 See I K Sundiata, 'Prelude to Scandal: Liberia and Fernando Po, 1880–1930', *Journal of African History*, vol 15, no 1 (1974): 110.

117 See also Azikiwe, 'In Defense of Liberia', 30. On the connection between the League of Nations International Commission of Enquiry into Liberia and the Firestone company/United States interests, see also W E B Du Bois, 'Liberia, the League and the United States', *Foreign Affairs*, vol 11, no 4 (1933); Azikiwe, *Liberia in World Politics*, 195–196.

118 ICE, '1930 Enquiry Commission', 277. Although the Liberian Government "requested" the League of Nations to conduct the International Commission of Enquiry, "in order to remove all doubts with respect to the existence of slavery as defined in the Slavery Conventions of 1926": Azikiwe, *Liberia in World Politics*, 189.

119 Sundiata, 'Liberia and Fernando Po', 108; Azikiwe, *Liberia in World Politics*, 150.

120 Firestone Plantations Company, *Liberia and Firestone: The Development of a Rubber Industry, a Story of Friendship and Progress* (Akron: Firestone, 1956), 7. See also Sundiata, 'Liberia and Fernando Po', 108; Azikiwe, *Liberia in World Politics*, 153.

121 For a discussion of the requirement of labour and the use of "forced labour" by the Firestone Company, see Azikiwe, *Liberia in World Politics*, Chapter 10.

122 In a letter to the US Secretary of State in 1931, Harvey S Firestone Sr also noted his:

> appreciation of the firm stand which our [US] Government is taking in demanding that Liberia take effective measures to abolish enforced labor [...] As you know [... this] has seriously interfered with our obtaining free labor [...] I cannot urge upon you too strongly that whatever steps are necessary to bring about the correction of the conditions outlined in the report [of the International Commission of Enquiry], should be taken with the least possible delay.
>
> Quoted in ibid, 206–207

The International Commission of Enquiry into slavery and forced labour marked a turning point in the history of the Republic.[123] In 1944 the new government of President William V S Tubman launched its National Unification Policy, according to which the Liberian government would "strive with all our might to agglutinate and unify our populations and political adherents composing the body politics [...] to make our country a united nation with LIBERTY and JUSTICE for all".[124] This was to be achieved through a programme that would seek, in line with the International Commission of Enquiry's recommendations, to finally realise the vision of liberating African-Liberians by overcoming the division between "civilised" and "uncivilised" citizens and ensuring equal economic development for all.[125] The Unification Program would finally invest full rights of citizenship in all Liberians, including voting rights for women; it would abolish the distinction between the "Americo-Liberian" and "tribal" jurisdictions, along with the parallel administrative division between coastal "Counties" and hinterland "Provinces"; and it would extend education and employment opportunities to Liberia's "indigenous" peoples. As one of President Tubman's admirers wrote in 1967 in commemoration of the Unification Policy: "In the mid 1940s, a great event occurred in the history of the indigenous population of Liberia. This was the coming into power of the Great Emancipator of the Liberian Hinterland, William V S Tubman".[126]

And yet, as I have sought to show through this chapter, at each point in the history of Liberia, the representational framework that promised to liberate its object – human and land – resulted in the opposite. African-Americans in the United States at the beginning of the nineteenth century suffered a form of civil death as a result of their non-recognition as wholly rightful persons in the United States. The idea of "Liberia" promised to overcome that condition, making the free *really* free; and yet Americo-Liberians suffered another form of civil death at the turn of the nineteenth century and into the twentieth as a result of their non-recognition as wholly rightful persons in the "international community". The

123 On the "reconstruction of Liberia", undertaken by the Government in response to the International Commission of Enquiry, see ibid, Chapter 15. The "changes" made, summarised in a 1933 memorandum from the Liberian Government to the League of Nations, included reform of the "native policy [...] in so far as criticism was justified", including removal of "barriers between civilized and uncivilized Liberians": quoted in ibid, 282–283.

124 Tubman, quoted in Varney J Fahnbulleh, 'A Concise Synopsis of the Tubman National Unification Policy', *William V S Tubman Papers*, Department of Internal Affairs, Republic of Liberia, 1967 (Bloomington: Liberian Collections, Indiana University Libraries, 2008), 2–3.

125 On the National Unification Policy, see also Yekutiel Gershoni, 'Liberia's Unification Policy and Decolonization in Africa: A Parallel Process', *Asian and African Studies*, vol 16 (1982).

126 Fahnbulleh, 'Tubman National Unification Policy', 5. The subtitle reads: 'A Special Literary Work done for DR WILLIAM V S TUBMAN And presented during his 72nd Birthday Celebration in Gbarnga, Bong County, on November 29, 1967 as A Birthday Presentation by Varney Jakema Fahnbulleh, Liason Officer-General, Department of Internal Affairs'.

consolidation of Liberia as a nation-state promised to overcome that condition, finally making the Americo-Liberian people Sovereign and Independent; and yet African-Liberians suffered as degraded citizens throughout the twentieth century as a consequence. At each point, having been denied their own particular value as self-possessed humans, but never fully possessed of the general value, the result was a form of capital punishment – being abject before the law, suspended in a state of civil death.

Rather than presenting a radical departure from this history, Tubman's National Unification Policy represented the last great attempt of the twentieth century to realise the idea of Liberia. The interior ("tribal") Provinces were made the same as the coastal ("Americo-Liberian") Counties as a matter of territorial jurisdiction, while African-Liberians were finally invested with all the rights possessed by Americo-Liberians. Thus, the identity of "Americo-Liberian" could be done away with, as President Tubman advocated, because there would no longer be anyone within Liberia who did not fit its description. As a nation of civilised citizens all would be effectively Americo-Liberian, and so the distinction would be redundant. In short, the end of Unification, or "oneness",[127] would be the absolute triumph of "Liberia". And yet, informed by the same logic, this still treated African-Liberians as objects to be liberated into subjecthood. The ideal end of "oneness" – a state in which subject and object would merge indistinguishably, with every body possessed of the same subjectivity – was based on the logical separation of subject and object, with the bodies denied their own particular subjectivities.

Little surprise then that Unification erupted in its opposite. In the 1970s Liberia underwent a revolution led by young African-Liberians that culminated in a massive demonstration in 1979. A year later, the Americo-Liberian Republic was brought to a bloody end with a *coup d'état* led by the "indigenous" man, Master-Sergeant Samuel Doe, who would become Liberia's first "African-Liberian" President. The *coup* also precipitated the civil wars of the 1990s and early 2000s that killed a quarter of a million people, displaced many more, and destroyed the institutions and infrastructure of the state of Liberia.

Vision 2030

Having emerged from nearly 150 years under a colonial framework, and almost 25 years of civil conflict and armed warfare, the question remains whether the same logic of capital will inform the remaking of Liberia in the twenty-first century. The evidence points to the further institutionalisation of this logic. The Government's primary policy documents for its state-building and development strategy read like a neoliberal manifesto,[128] which is not surprising given that they were developed

127 Ibid, 1–2.

128 See Republic of Liberia, *Interim Poverty Reduction Strategy (2006–2008)* (Washington, DC: International Monetary Fund, 2007); Republic of Liberia, *Poverty Reduction Strategy (2008–2011)* (Monrovia: Republic of Liberia, 2008); Republic of Liberia, *Agenda for Transformation: Steps toward Liberia Rising 2030 – Liberia's Medium*

according to the framework of the International Monetary Fund and World Bank standard "poverty reduction strategy". Thus Pillar II of the Government's overarching five-year plan for 2012–2017 (also referred to as Liberia's "development framework") is "economic transformation", with the "*Goal*: To transform the economy so that it meets the demands of Liberians through development of the domestic private sector".[129] "Essential to this economic transformation", the strategy states, "is the growth of employment and output in agriculture, small-scale mining and forestry, agro-processing and other industries".[130] The strategy continues:

> Ideally, households and individuals will have more opportunity to work or engage in their own enterprises, leading to improved income and the opportunity to purchase desired consumption. To support provision of public services and infrastructure, the private economy and concessions will generate tax and royalty revenue for the public sector.[131]

On one hand, there is nothing remarkable about this strategy. Indeed, it is part of the standard economic system modelled by advanced-capitalist economies and pursued by "developing countries" globally. On the other hand, that it would go without remark, remaining overlooked as a source of violence, would be remarkable. Also remarkable is how similar the language in this paragraph of the strategy is to the language in the International Commission of Enquiry's report into slavery and forced labour in Liberia, where it recommended developing the labour and consumption capacity of its citizens:

> teach him what he may buy for money, and he then wants to learn what he can grow, what he should do, or where he should work to make some money, with the result that trade increases, the coast merchant flourishes, the revenues of Government expand, and money is forthcoming.[132]

The repetition, or continuation, does not end there. Central to achieving the primary goal of Pillar II is "private sector development", and central to achieving this is "property rights and contract enforcement".[133] However, two fundamental problems arise at this point: one, the necessary land rights regime is practically non-existent in Liberia; and two, the state legal system is dysfunctional. I examine the second problem – the condition of the state legal system – in Chapter 6. Of interest here is the non-existence of the land rights regime, and the Government's framework that promises to make land rightful.[134]

Term Economic and Development Strategy (2012–2017) (Monrovia: Republic of Liberia, 2012).

129 Republic of Liberia, *Agenda for Transformation*, 54 (italics in original).

130 Ibid.

131 Ibid.

132 See note 111 above.

133 See Republic of Liberia, *Agenda for Transformation*, Chapter 9.

134 Republic of Liberia, *Land Rights Policy* (Monrovia: Land Commission, 2013).

In 2013 the government published a new *Land Rights Policy.* [135] The policy sets out a framework for creating four categories of land rights: "public land", "government land", "private land", and "customary land". The last of these is the most radical proposition.

> Rights to Customary Land, including ownership rights, must be secured by ensuring that these rights are equally protected as private land rights. Rights to Customary Land include rights of the community as a collective land owner and rights of groups, families, and individuals within the community.[136]

With the overlay of this framework, "customary land" will be invested with the character of private land, capable of alienation, although the rights will be possessed by "the community as a collective land owner", with "groups, families, and individuals within the community" also possessed of certain rights.[137] However, in order to implement this policy – that is, to invest "a community" and "its customary land" with these rights – two criteria must be met: "the community" must be clearly defined ("community ownership of Customary Land will be formalized by the issuance of a deed to a legal entity, bearing the name of the community"),[138] as must the boundaries of "its land".[139] The problem is that there are no such clear distinctions on the ground. These communities and their lands have littoral identities. Extending this development framework over them will not put them "beyond the littoral", rather it will extend the littoral back over Liberia. That is, the attempt to define these communities by identifying their precise corporate membership along with the boundaries of their land will create more conflict, not less. The Government is aware of this, indeed "the policy recommendations recognize this diversity".[140] That is why the Government has created a parallel policy for "land conflict management",[141] while at the same time ensuring that the communities self-define their membership, lead the process of demarcating their boundaries, and have a large degree of regulatory autonomy over "Customary Land management, use, and allocation decisions [...] within a framework of shared responsibility with the Government".[142]

This scheme might grant the communities autonomy over the content of the new regime, and yet in its *form* it is a continuation, if not an intensification, of the

135 Ibid. The Policy was yet to be enacted into law at the time of writing (June 2017); see also UN Doc S/2017/510 (16 June 2017), *Thirty-Third Progress Report of the Secretary-General on the United Nations Mission in Liberia*, para 18.
136 Republic of Liberia, *Land Rights Policy*, 15.
137 Ibid, 18.
138 Ibid.
139 Ibid, 19.
140 Ibid, 15.
141 Author interviews with officers of the Liberian Land Commission in Monrovia, 14 August 2013 (MG5, MG7, and MG8); in Zorzor, 29 August 2013 (Li18); and in Harper, 27 September 2013 (Li39). See also Liberian Land Commission, *2014 Annual Report* (Monrovia: Land Commission, 2014).
142 Republic of Liberia, *Land Rights Policy*, 19.

logic of capital. It represents a twenty-first-century attempt to transform the lands and peoples of Liberia into productive things through the overlay of the same logical framework that has operated parasitically in this country since its colonial settlement. Granting autonomy over the content of the regime might appear to be a liberating move, but if this history of Liberia shows anything, it is that such a promise is never one-sided. The question for the Government is how it will deal with this: how it will consolidate its envisioned state of peace given the violence of the logic that informs it.

4 A peace formidable to any eye

Peace through Justice

Standing in the entrance hall of the Peace Palace in The Hague is a marble statue entitled "Peace through Justice".[1] The statue depicts a figure who appears at once female and male, merging feminine and masculine types. This is the figure of a "modern Lady Justice",[2] of *Justitia* bulging with strength. Resembling Michelangelo's marble statue of David poised for battle against Goliath – and as the very embodiment of Pascal's *pensée* – this image poses a disturbing truth: *peace requires a forceful justice.*

> *Justice, force.* – [...] Justice without force is impotent; force without justice is tyrannical. Justice without force is contradictory, as there are always the wicked; force without justice is accused of wrong. And so it is necessary to put justice and force together; and, for this, to make sure that what is just be strong, or what is strong be just.[3]

Why is this image, and what it poses, disturbing? How does it differ from the conventional figure of Lady Justice brandishing a sword? In both, justice and force together constitute the image of *Justitia*, leaving no doubt about the capacity of justice for violence. There is a terrible difference. In the conventional image *Justitia* holds a sword; she has picked up the sword and she wields it as her instrument – an animate justice in control of an inanimate force. What is so disturbing about the statue in the Peace Palace is the ambiguity it introduces. Force is no longer a mere object at the disposal and under the control of Lady

1 Created by Andrew O'Connor. For a photograph of the statue, see The Hague, 'Piece of the Palace', http://pointsoflight.pieceofthepalace.com/PTJvert.pdf

2 US Department of State, 'Sites relating to US history in the Netherlands', 20 August 2013: http://photos.state.gov/libraries/netherlands/328666/pdfs/Sites%20of%20memory%20Ranked%20by%20Theme%202013-8.pdf, 35

3 Blaise Pascal, *Pascal's Pensées* (New York: E P Dutton & Co, 1958), 85. This translation is from Jacques Derrida, 'Force of Law: The "Mystical Foundation of Authority"', *Cardozo Law Review*, vol 11 (1989–1990), 937. See also Marin's discussion in Louis Marin, *Portrait of the King* (Minneapolis: University of Minnesota Press, 1988), 17–23.

Justice; force *ripples through her limbs*, force *pulses through her veins*. The wind blowing aside her gown reveals not the typically feminine legs of justice but brute trunks of force.

The experience of aporia in seeing this figure of *Justitia* is the impossibility of distinguishing justice from force, as one might distinguish the Lady from her sword. Here is justice and force embodied as one; and this, we are told, is *necessary* for peace. This is "Peace through Justice". Here justice is a force that is not only capable of great violence in itself, but depends on this self-defining capacity for violence to function in the service of peace.

Securing peace

A vision of security

A growing body of United Nations policy literature represents justice and force as mutually constitutive conditions *for* and *of* peace. As the UN Secretary-General has made clear, peace must be secured: "the most fundamental lesson for the United Nations is that security is a precondition for sustainable peace"[4]; and it must be secured through the UN's peace operations by assisting in the reform of a state's "security sector".[5] As the Secretary-General has also made clear, this vision of security combines force with justice:

> The United Nations has devoted considerable attention to articulating a common understanding of security. The United Nations Millennium Declaration (General Assembly resolution 55/2) captures the principle that lies at the core of this vision: that men and women have the right to live their lives and raise their children in dignity, free from hunger and the fear of violence, oppression or injustice.[6]

Thus at the core of the UN's vision of security is a principle of justice; but make no mistake that this vision is not a forceful one. "Security" may be presented as a

4 UN Doc A/62/659–S/2008/39 (23 January 2008), *Report of the Secretary General: Securing Peace and Development: The Role of the United Nations in Supporting Security Sector Reform* ('Securing Peace'), para 35. See also UN Doc A/47/277–S/2411 (17 June 1992), *Report of the Secretary-General Pursuant to the Statement Adopted by the Summit Meeting of the Security Council on 31 January 1992: An Agenda for Peace: Preventive Diplomacy, Peacemaking and Peace-Keeping*, para 22, where it states that the UN's peace operations, "taken together, and carried out with the backing of all Members, offer a coherent contribution towards securing peace in the spirit of the Charter".

5 See also the UN Secretary-General's second report on security sector reform: UN Doc A/67/970–S/2013/480 (13 August 2013), *Report of the Secretary General: Securing States and Societies: Strengthening the United Nations Comprehensive Support to Security Sector Reform* ('Securing States and Societies').

6 UN, 'Securing Peace', para 5.

heart-warming vision of justice, in which children are free to play,[7] but look over the children's shoulders at the sector that secures this vision and one will see "the structures, institutions and personnel responsible for the management, provision and oversight of security in a country" including "defence, law enforcement, corrections, intelligence services and institutions responsible for border management, customs and civil emergencies" as well as "elements of the judicial sector responsible for the adjudication of cases of alleged criminal conduct and misuse of force" along with "actors that play a role in managing and overseeing the design and implementation of security, such as ministries, legislative bodies and civil society groups" not to mention "the other non-State actors that could be considered part of the security sector" such as "customary or informal authorities and private security services".[8] The security sector is as vast as justice is core.

So, when the UN says security is a precondition for peace, it is also saying, justice and force brought together in a single mould – the security sector – is a precondition for peace, which is to say, *peace requires a forceful justice.* In this discourse, however, security is not just a precondition *for* peace: it is also a condition *of* peace. The UN Secretary-General highlights this foundational nature of security when he emphasises the role of the security sector in "preventing countries from relapsing into conflict and in laying the foundations for sustainable peace".[9] Indeed security is so foundational of peace that the two – peace and security – have become indistinguishable in UN discourse on security sector reform. Thus five years after the Secretary-General's initial report on security sector reform in 2008, the Secretary-General published a second report in 2013, with its central message: "The security of the State and the state of security (of individuals and communities) are mutually interdependent; in other words, we have learned that when populations are not secure, neither is the State".[10]

If the Secretary-General's first report on security sector reform set out a vision for the UN to strengthen its capacity to "secure peace" (as that report is titled) – emphasising security as a precondition for peace – then this second report extends the vision to see security, and the State's security sector in particular, as a necessary condition of this state of peace.[11] In this report on "securing States and societies"

7 Or at least where they might grow up "free from hunger and the fear of violence, oppression or injustice": ibid.

8 Ibid, para 14. This is the UN's definition of "security sector".

9 Ibid, para 3.

10 UN, 'Securing States and Societies', para 9.

11 That justice and force are considered within UN discourse as inseparable, coming together in a concept of security that constitutes a condition of peace, is recognised in the academic literature. See, e.g., the contributions to the 'Special Issue on Rule of Law and Security Sector Reform', *Hague Journal on the Rule of Law*, vol 4, no 1 (2012). For instance, Schröder and Kode discuss how the UN defines "justice" and "security" as inseparable conditions of peace, constituting (in the words of the UN Development Programme) a "comprehensive and integrated whole": Ursula C Schröder and Johannes Kode, 'Rule of Law and Security Sector Reform in International State-building: Dilemmas of Converging Agendas', *Hague Journal on the Rule of Law*, vol 4, no 1 (2012): 32. See also Till Blume, 'Review Essay: Security, Justice

(as it is titled), "State" and "society" merge in a singular peace-and-security complex: when a "population" (itself a category of governmental control) is secure, the State is secure, and the result is a state/State of peace.

In sum, the two reports together present a vision of peace as secured only when security becomes indistinguishable from the state of the State. Recalling that the UN's "common understanding of security" merges justice and force in the single concept, this vision of securing a state/State of peace thus resembles the figure of "Peace through Justice", with justice and force conjoined as conditions *for* and *of* peace.

The logic of security

This vision of securing peace is held together by a configuration of three antagonistic propositions: peace contains the force of war; law contains the force of peace; and justice contains the force of law. Each of these propositions is an unstable, internally combustible arrangement, with force – the very thing that is their generative essence – threatening to explode each in turn. When brought together the three propositions are supposed to be sustainable, securing a state/State of peace by containing force through a just rule of law. However, the antagonisms that bind this arrangement become its combined logic – the logic of security.[12]

(i) Peace contains the force of war

The first proposition is that peace contains the force of war. This means two things. First, peace "contains" force in the sense that peace "withholds" force from its violent manifestation. Second, peace "contains" force in the sense that peace "holds within it" the very force that would manifest violently. This is in keeping with how peace is imagined throughout the Peace Palace in the Hague, as a violent character that overpowers war, posing peace as the forceful opposition to the manifest violence of war. This can be seen most strikingly in the stained-glass windows of the International Court of Justice where the figure of Peace is depicted stomping mercilessly on the head of War even while War is down.[13] In this peace

and the Rule of Law in Peace Operations', *International Peacekeeping*, vol 15, no 5 (2008).

12 In implicit ways, and at times explicitly, the discussion here is in conversation with the study of law and force in Walter Benjamin, 'Critique of Violence', in Marcus Bullock and Michael W Jennings (eds), *Walter Benjamin: Selected Writings, Volume 1, 1913–1926* (Cambridge: Belknap Press, 2002). In line with this, I use the word "force" in the multiple senses of the word *Gewalt*, as used by Benjamin, which carries the meanings "violence", "(public) force", and "(legitimate) power"; on this see Derrida, 'Force of Law', 927. To retain the unsettling sense of connection between these meanings I have retained the ambiguity in the word "force" rather than attempt to specify the most fitting meaning in each instance.

13 This recalls the Biblical image of David standing on the head of Goliath: see, e.g., Donatello's bronze figure of David (with thanks to Desmond Manderson for drawing my attention to this).

is not the absence of violence but its *containment*.[14] Peace *withholds* force from its violent manifestation by *holding within it* overwhelming force. Peace as such is "made", "kept", and "built" through the forceful containment of violence, erecting a barrier to the manifestation of violent conflict by subsuming its potential within a state/State of peaceful violence.

This is *peace through force*, and the result is a combustible proposition: a state/State of peaceful violence. The combination of "peace" and "force" within a single mould makes this peace antagonistic. If "peace contains force", in the sense that peace forcefully opposes the manifestation of violent conflict by subsuming its potential as its own condition, then what contains the force of peace? What keeps the forces of this peaceful State from manifesting violently, as is its condition? What keeps this State of peace from being tyrannical? The difficulty is this: peace, we are told, must be secured against the manifestation of violent conflict, but what secures this peace *against itself*? What secures this state/State from becoming the manifestation of violence in the name of "peace and stability"?

(ii) Law contains the force of peace

The first proposition (peace contains the force of war) is therefore unstable in itself, containing the potential to destroy the very state of peace it seeks to establish, requiring a second proposition to secure its peaceful intent. The second proposition is that law contains the force of peace. This is often formulated in the more specific proposition of "the rule of law", that is, the rule of law contains the force of peace by guarding against its arbitrary exercise.[15] Thus "law contains force" by subsuming the violence that is the condition of peace within a legal framework that regulates its exercise and makes it "accountable" and "legitimate".[16] Under the rule of law, the force of peace might be exercised in the interests of its state/State.

14 Compare Michael Howard, 'The Concept of Peace', *Encounter*, vol 61, no 4 (1983). For discussion of Howard's approach as part of a "minimalist approach to peace", see William Maley, 'Peace, Needs and Utopia', *Political Studies*, vol 33, no 4 (1985): 579. See also Johan Galtung, 'Twenty-Five Years of Peace Research: Ten Challenges and Some Responses', *Journal of Peace Research*, vol 22, no 2 (1985).

15 Or, as the UN Development Programme puts it: "From a conflict prevention & recovery perspective, the notion of 'the rule of law' represents a situation that is diametrically opposed to 'the rule by force'". UNDP, *Strengthening the Rule of Law in Conflict- and Post-conflict Situations: A Global UNDP Programme for Justice and Security 2008–2011* (New York: United Nations), 30.

16 For reasons that will become clear in the following discussion, this resembles Benjamin's argument in his 'Critique of Violence', which might be summed up in his observation that:

> one might perhaps consider the surprising possibility that the law's interest in a monopoly of violence vis-à-vis individuals is explained not by the intention of preserving legal ends but, rather, by the intention of preserving the law itself; that violence, when not in the hands of the law, threatens it not by the end that it may pursue but by its mere existence outside the law.
>
> Benjamin, 'Critique of Violence', 239

This proposition is central to the UN's discourse according to which a State's security sector must be contained "within a framework of the rule of law".[17] As the UN Secretary-General emphasises in his 2008 report on security sector reform, if the first lesson the UN has learnt in its 60-year "search for effective responses to address insecurity based on its Charter" is that security is a condition for and of peace, then the second lesson is that this "can be achieved only within a broad framework of the rule of law".[18] Above all this means ensuring "accountability to law".[19] The UN thus qualifies its support for strengthening a State's capacity for peaceful violence with the proviso that security sector reform must seek to enhance the "accountability" of the security sector.[20] And, as the 2008 report emphasises, the first common feature of "accountable security sectors" is a "legal and/or constitutional framework providing for the legitimate and accountable use of force".[21] That is, if security is a condition for/of peace, then accountability to law is a condition for/of the security sector as the domain of legitimate violence. This is the UN's "vision of security based on the rule of law".[22]

And yet this vision of securing peace through the institution of a legally accountable security sector does not overcome the antagonism of peaceful violence. Rather the proposition that law contains the force of peace by making that force "legitimate and accountable" takes over this antagonism as its own condition. *The force of peace becomes the force of law.* Law "contains" the force of peace by "holding within it" a monopoly on legitimate violence in order to "withhold it from" any unlawful manifestation. This makes the rule of law fundamentally arbitrary at the same time as it guards against the arbitrary exercise of power. To serve the interests of peace, the fundament, or condition, of law's rule must be its monopoly on violence: peace requires law to contain force, and to contain force,

17 UN, 'Securing States and Societies', para 8.

18 UN, 'Securing Peace', paras 1 and 2. The same line is repeated by the UN Security Council in its first resolution on "security sector reform" (SSR), in "recalling that SSR must take place within a broad framework of the rule of law": UN Doc S/Res/2151 (28 April 2014), preambular para 15. As indicated above, the point is also repeated in the UN Secretary-General's report when he writes that the objective of security sector reform is "enhanced effectiveness and accountability of security institutions operating under civilian control within a framework of the rule of law": UN, 'Securing States and Societies', para 8.

19 UN, 'Securing Peace', para 12, citing the definition of the rule of law set out in UN Doc S/2004/616 (23 August 2004), para 6. The definition is reproduced in note 28 below. On the discursive relation between "the rule of law" and "accountability" in the context of UN peace operations, see Jeremy Matam Farrall, 'Rule of Accountability or Rule of law? Regulating the UN Security Council's Accountability Deficits', *Journal of Conflict and Security Law*, vol 19 (2014).

20 See, e.g., UN, 'Securing Peace', paras 3, 12, 15, 17, 35 and 45. That the "objective of SSR is to help ensure that people are safer through the enhanced effectiveness and accountability of security institutions operating under civilian control within a framework of the rule of law" is reaffirmed in the Secretary-General's second report; see, e.g., UN, 'Securing States and Societies', para 8.

21 UN, 'Securing Peace', para 15.

22 Ibid, para 4.

law must become *its* monopoly.[23] Force, in other words, defines this rule of law: law secures the state/State of "peaceful violence" by making violence coincidental with itself.[24] In the same way that justice and force must inhabit the same body in the figure of "Peace through Justice", law and force must merge indistinguishably in the rule of law in order to sustain this arrangement of "peace through law". This is arbitrary because it means that the rule of law is ultimately directed at securing *itself*. The end of the rule of law becomes the rule of law – an absurd tautology that is nonetheless necessary to sustain the telos of "peace".[25] To secure peace through law, the law of this state/State of peace must become the absolute arbiter of force; but in this force becomes the arbiter of law. Hence the antagonism that enlivens this second proposition: "law contains the force of peace" means that law and force must be conjoined indistinguishably. This is arbitrary in the precise meaning of the word: the use of force must be according to law (law must be its arbiter), but force *is* law, and so the force of law becomes its own arbiter.

(iii) Justice contains the force of law

The second proposition of "peace through law" is thus as unsustainable as the first proposition of "peace through force" that it is supposed to secure. If the rule of law is concerned with the stability of this state/State of peace, and must legitimately, according to its concept, exercise violence at will in order to uphold the peace, what ensures law's rule does not become endlessly tyrannical? What makes this state/State of peace under the rule of law bearable? To recall Pascal: justice without force might be impotent, but force without justice is tyrannical. And arbitrariness is by definition tyrannical: "unrestrained in the exercise of will; of uncontrolled power or authority, absolute; *hence*, despotic, tyrannical".[26]

The two propositions just considered (peace contains the force of war, and law contains the force of peace) say little about justice and both risk becoming tyrannical. This vision of peace thus requires a third proposition to ensure that its antagonistic arrangement does not go up in flames. The third proposition is that justice contains the force of law.[27] Justice must contain the force of law if the rule

23 See also Benjamin's argument that the thing most threatening to the rule of law is the manifestation of a force that is outside itself: Benjamin, 'Critique of Violence'.

24 This is also how I read Benjamin's argument on the self-constituting and self-preserving force of law: ibid. See also the reading of Benjamin's essay in Derrida, 'Force of Law'.

25 See also Slaughter's examination of how an "impossible tautological-teleological developmental complex" animates the "formal, paradoxical structure of international human rights law and the narrative of human personality development that it charters": Joseph Slaughter, 'Enabling fictions and novel subjects: The Bildungsroman and international human rights law', *PMLA*, vol 121, no 5 (2006): 1412.

26 'Arbitrary, *adj.* and *n.*', Oxford English Dictionary Online, December 2015.

27 Or again, as the UN Development Programme emphasises after noting that:

> from a conflict prevention & recovery perspective, the notion of "the rule of law" represents a situation that is diametrically opposed to "the rule by force". Without

of law is not to become tyrannical, which means the force of law must be indistinguishable from justice, held within the body of *Justitia* in order that law's violence is withheld from its unjust exercise. Or to put this another way, force, as law, must be a means for and of justice if its rule is not to threaten the state/State of peace that it exists to secure. Finally, *this* is what is meant by "peace through justice".

This proposition is also apparent in the UN's vision of security. While the UN Secretary-General's reports on security sector reform tell us that security must be accountable to law for peace to prevail, they say very little explicitly about justice. The implication is there, of course; as noted earlier a principle of justice is said to be at the core of the UN's concept of security. However one has to turn to the Secretary-General's 2004 report on "the rule of law and transitional justice in conflict and post-conflict societies" to read that the full definition of the rule of law also requires "fairness in the application of the law".[28] It is also in this report on the rule of law that we learn that "for the United Nations, 'justice' is an ideal of accountability and fairness",[29] and that the "consolidation of peace in the immediate post-conflict period, as well as the maintenance of peace in the long term" requires "legitimate structures for the peaceful settlement of disputes and the fair administration of justice".[30] Even more explicitly, for the UN Development Programme's work in "strengthening the rule of law in conflict and post-conflict societies", the rule of law is "based on two pillars, i.e. justice and security", and further, "that: (b) 'justice and security' are interdependent and require a *holistic approach*".[31]

(iv) Peace through justice

Drawing these three antagonistic propositions together, the logic of security can be summarised as follows: peace contains the force of war, and yet this gives rise to

> physical security, the most basic premises for peace remain absent. And, without access to justice and empowered rule of law institutions, no peace will last long enough to lay the ground for sustainable development.
>
> UNDP, *Programme for Justice and Security 2008–2011*, 30

28 UN Doc S/2004/616 (23 August 2004), para 6:

> The "rule of law" is a concept at the very heart of the Organization's mission. It refers to a principle of governance in which all persons, institutions and entities, public and private, including the State itself, are accountable to laws that are publicly promulgated, equally enforced and independently adjudicated, and which are consistent with international human rights norms and standards. It requires, as well, measures to ensure adherence to the principles of supremacy of law, equality before the law, accountability to the law, fairness in the application of the law, separation of powers, participation in decision-making, legal certainty, avoidance of arbitrariness and procedural and legal transparency.

29 Ibid, para 7.

30 Ibid, para 2, and see also para 4.

31 UNDP, *Programme for Justice and Security 2008–2011*, 30 (emphasis in original).

a state/State of peaceful violence that is highly combustible; therefore peace requires the rule of law to contain the exercise of peaceful violence, and yet the forcefulness of law makes it fundamentally arbitrary; therefore peace requires justice to contain the force of law – or in other words, peace requires a forceful justice. Without justice containing the force of law, the arbitrariness of the rule of law would turn the exercise of peaceful violence against peace itself.

And yet: just as the antagonism of peaceful violence that is the condition for/of a state/State of peace is not resolved by the rule of law, so the antagonism of lawful (legitimate and accountable) violence that is the condition for/of a state/State of peace under the rule of law is not resolved by the inclusion of a principle of justice at the core of security. Rather, justice and force merge in this state/State of security. In short, a state of peace might be maintained only as long as the State's violence is just. This is the residual antagonism – a just violence – that holds the whole arrangement together; *this* is what "secures peace".

Securing peace in Liberia

At the end of the preceding chapter I considered the Liberian Government's post-war vision for the country – a vision that suggests a continuation, if not an intensification, of the logic of capital. This raises a question, which I posed in closing: how will the Government realise its envisioned state of peace given the violence of the logic that informs it? My aim now is to answer that question by examining what is taking place in the attempt to consolidate a state/State of peace in Liberia post-war.

The peace framework

In 2012 the Government of Liberia launched a "long-term national vision" for the country to pursue between 2012 and 2030.[32] The vision is introduced in the Government's overarching development framework, the *Agenda for Transformation: Steps Toward Liberia Rising 2030*,[33] which provides an "action plan" for the first five years (2012–2017).[34] The Government describes its national vision in Chapter 2 of the *Agenda for Transformation*. In a passage that evokes the Liberian Commissioner's 1903 report on the demarcation of the hinterland,[35] the description switches to the present tense in presenting its vision of the future, creating the sense of a truly future-present Liberia:

> The goal is to have a vibrant economy; one in which more than half of the workforce is employed in the formal sector. This is led – but not dominated

32 See Republic of Liberia, *Agenda for Transformation: Steps Toward Liberia Rising 2030* (Monrovia: Republic of Liberia, 2012), 29.
33 Ibid, Chapter 2.
34 Ibid, 29.
35 Discussed in Chapter 3 of this book.

> by – the [natural resource] concessions economy, which is integrated into a prosperous Liberian economy. Liberians are successful managers and are entrepreneurs by choice. People trust that contracts and business agreements will be honored, all of which are supported by transparent, fair and efficient Commercial Courts. [...] A special economic zone in Buchanan permits complex activities to service the extractive sector in the sub-region, while also acting as a staging ground for institutional reforms at the national level. [...] Smaller commercial zones on the borders with Guinea, Sierra Leone and Ivory Coast serve as bridges of peace and prosperity, backstopping a broader regional integration of tariffs and infrastructure.[36]

The vision continues in much the same way before ending with a note on the future beyond this future-present: "Liberians are saving, confidently, for their own futures and average incomes have reached the middle-income threshold".[37]

The *Agenda for Transformation* sets out a development framework for realising this national vision based on four "pillars" that combine a capitalist-economic regime (Pillar II) with institutions of democratic governance (Pillar IV), concern for human rights and development (Pillar III), secured through the rule of law (Pillar I).[38] I briefly discussed "Pillar II – Economic Transformation" at the end of the previous chapter. My focus now is on "Pillar I – Peace, Justice, Security and Rule of Law",[39] the overarching goal of which is to establish the conditions for and of the envisioned peace.[40] To achieve this overarching goal the Pillar has four "sector goals": (1) "security"; (2) "peace and reconciliation"; (3) "justice and rule of law"; and (4) "judicial reform". The latter two sector goals are explicitly concerned with law, while "peace and reconciliation" is concerned with social justice. Along with the sector goal of "security", which is concerned with the institutionalisation of force, these four sector goals thus constitute three propositions, which together provide a peace framework for realising the new, post-war idea of Liberia.

As the following diagram (Figure 4.1) indicates, the Government's "idea of Liberia" – the vision that will guide the remaking of the nation-state – is set out in *Vision 2030: Liberia Rising*; the Government's "development framework" for realising this vision is set out in the *Agenda for Transformation*; while the "peace framework" that is supposed to secure the entire edifice is set out in Pillar I of the *Agenda for Transformation.* As I now turn to show, the elements of this peace framework (the "sector goals") are informed by the same three propositions considered above, that is, the logic of security.

36 Republic of Liberia, *Agenda for Transformation*, 9–10.
37 Ibid, 10.
38 A fifth pillar includes "cross-cutting themes": ibid.
39 Ibid, Chapter 8.
40 As the government writes, the *Agenda for Transformation* will "coordinate all activities for peace and security into one development framework": ibid, 41.

idea of Liberia
(*Vision 2030: Liberia Rising*)

development framework
(*Agenda for Transformation*)

peace framework
(Pillar I: Peace, Justice, Security and Rule of Law)

peace contains the force of war
(Sector Goal 1: Security)

law contains the force of peace
(Sector Goal 3: Justice and Rule of Law; Sector Goal 4: Judicial Reform)

justice contains the force of law
(Sector Goal 2: Peace and Reconciliation)

Figure 4.1 The framework for remaking Liberia

(i) Peace contains the force of war

The Government provides the following narrative in introducing the first sector goal ("security"):

> Ten years ago, security forces intimidated and terrorized the population, intervened in political processes and disregarded the rule of law. Today, the police force, armed forces and all other security forces are being restored into professional and capable institutions.[41]

These first two sentences in the Government's narrative set out the transition from a state of war to a state of peace. In 2002 ("ten years ago") Liberia was experiencing its second civil war and some of the worst violence of the 14-year conflict; in 2012 ("today") the same forces that had "intimidated and terrorized the population" "are being restored into professional and capable institutions". The narrative then emphasises how the Government has "exerted immense efforts to effectively address the negative attributes of the security sector" and how it plans to continue "building on these efforts" with a focus "on sustaining and augmenting progress made in creating a secure environment".[42] As it states in summary: "*Goal:* Maintain a secure and safe environment to enable sustainable socio-economic growth and development".[43]

The primary "strategic objective" for achieving this sector goal is to "maintain security nation-wide and protect territorial integrity" after the withdrawal of the UN's peace operation in Liberia, UNMIL, by "consolidating [...] the new Liberian security architecture".[44] In other words, having brought the forces of war under the control of the Government and transformed them into forces of peace, the goal of security will be achieved through the consolidation of force within the State's "security sector" (*peace will contain the force of war*). However, the action

41 Ibid, section 8.1.
42 Ibid.
43 Ibid.
44 Ibid.

plan also includes two other strategic objectives for achieving the sector goal of security. The first of these is "increasing operational effectiveness"; the second is "increasing the accountability and legitimacy of national security institutions and the public's confidence in them", to be achieved in part by "building synergies" between the security sector and the state legal system.[45] Thus, while the primary goal of "security" is to ensure peace contains the force of war, the action plan recognises that this is a combustible proposition requiring more than just "operational effectiveness". To ensure the forces of peace do not become tyrannical there must be "oversight, accountability, professionalization, and legitimacy of the security sector".[46]

(ii) Law contains the force of peace

The Government sets out two "ends" in its discussion of "Sector Goal 3: Justice and Rule of Law".[47] One is to provide a medium for the capitalist-economic regime: "an effective justice system [is] essential to economic revitalization because it can provide a framework for resolving contractual and property disputes, increasing commercial certainty and promoting private sector growth".[48] The other is to secure this regime: "an effective justice system is vital to addressing Liberia's most significant security threat – the growth in crime".[49] By "justice system" the Government means the institutions of the State legal system,[50] while "extending the rule of law" is meant to strengthen these institutions, to achieve these two goals. At the same time, however, the Government is clearly concerned about the justice of its legal system. Thus the overarching sector goal is not only "to build the effectiveness and integrity of legal institutions" but also "to increase equitable access to justice and to strengthen the rule of law for the social and economic benefit of all Liberians".[51] That is, while the Government's goal of "extending the rule of law" is to strengthen the institutions of the State legal system, to ensure law contains the force of peace, the Government also recognises that more is needed than institutional "effectiveness and integrity". The rule of law must be as *just* as it is forceful.

(iii) Justice contains the force of law

The Government addresses the question of justice in the sector goal of "Peace and Reconciliation", beginning with the following passage:

45 Ibid.
46 Ibid.
47 Ibid, section 8.3.
48 Ibid.
49 Ibid.
50 Ibid.
51 Republic of Liberia, *Agenda for Transformation*, section 8.3. As I examine in Chapter 6, the justice of the Government's vision of what is "for the benefit of all Liberians" is questionable. The point here is not to evaluate the Government's vision of justice, however, and only to highlight its awareness that the proposition of "peace through law" is a combustible one.

> Reconciliation remains an indispensable goal for cultivating and protecting Liberia's still-fragile peace. The civil war opened and exacerbated social cleavages that must be bridged – inter-tribal tensions must be resolved and economic, social and political exclusion and marginalization must be addressed. The goal of this development strategy is to increase the equity and fairness necessary to build prolonged peace.[52]

The Government then summarises the sector goal:

> To ensure long-term peace and stability through (1) managing tensions in society to reduce the risk of future conflict; (2) increasing social cohesion; and (3) ensuring that the principles of human rights are upheld.[53]

Thus the concern here is to ensure peace through justice. In this "justice" is framed primarily in terms of social cohesion – mending social cleavages, resolving tensions, and generally reducing marginalisation and exclusion. "Justice" is therefore directed above all at overcoming the separation of subjects in society. This recalls the UN's global policy on security sector reform, which is directed at achieving a singular peace-and-security complex in which "State" and "society" merge in a state/State of peace. To achieve this state/State of peace, society must first be reconciled with itself. Having achieved this reconciliation, the national legal system will be "legitimate" and "equitable" to the extent that all will be equally before the law of the nation-state. As the Government writes, the goal is to ensure peace and stability by "increasing social, economic and legal justice" as well as "political reconciliation and procedural justice" in State governance.[54]

(iv) Peace through justice

Pillar I of the *Agenda for Transformation* thus sets out a peace framework for realising its national vision that brings together the three propositions that constitute "the logic of security". The configuration of these propositions is seen most clearly in the introduction to Pillar I:

> The government will continue to address the key sources of conflict and insecurity, protecting the citizens of Liberia from violence and crime; delivering justice and upholding the rule of law; reconciling all Liberian people and together building a more peaceful and more secure nation.[55]

In other words, the overall goal of this Pillar is to achieve a state/State in which "the government"/"all Liberian people" together constitute "a more peaceful and

52 Ibid, section 8.2.
53 Ibid.
54 Ibid.
55 Ibid.

more secure nation", and this peace will be achieved by: "address[ing] the key sources of conflict and insecurity" and "protecting the citizens of Liberia from violence and crime" (*peace containing the force of war*); "upholding the rule of law" (*law containing the force of peace*); and "reconciling all Liberian people" and "delivering justice" (*justice containing the force of law*). Thus the Government's envisioned state/State of peace will be secured by containing force through a just rule of law. In the next three sections I examine how the Government, with the support of the UN's peace operation, is working to consolidate this vision, beginning with the UN's operational vision for building this state of peace in Liberia post-war.

Peace-building

In September 1997, in his final report to the UN Security Council on the United Nations Observer Mission in Liberia (UNOMIL), the UN Secretary-General observed:

> The conflict in Liberia was essentially a power struggle with some ethnic elements, but the command and control exercised by faction leaders over their commanders and troops in the field was often loose. The central government, law and order and physical infrastructure of Liberia had been either seriously degraded or had disappeared altogether. As a result, the fighting was characterized by widespread lawlessness, the easy availability of small arms and gross violations of human rights by all factions against innocent civilians.[56]

Forming part of the epilogue (the "Observations and Conclusions") of the ultimate report on a Mission that had reached its "successful conclusion",[57] this passage offers an account of the situation in Liberia at a moment of peace. The paragraphs that precede and succeed it in this part of the report recount a short history of the UN Observer Mission's establishment.[58] They recall the devastating facts that the war had taken as many as 150,000 civilian lives and driven 700,000 people to flee.[59] They retrace the failed attempts since 1993 to resolve the conflict,[60] before the "turning of the tide" in 1996,[61] which saw "the restoration of a climate of security" that was "crucial" to the "successful organization and conduct of the elections".[62] The human rights activities of the Mission receive special mention for their "important role in the peace process",[63] as does the "successful completion

56 UN Doc S/1997/712 (12 September 1997), para 23.
57 Words of the UN Secretary-General: ibid, paras 21 and 31.
58 Ibid, paras 21–34.
59 Ibid, para 22.
60 Ibid, paras 24 and 25.
61 Ibid, para 25.
62 Ibid, paras 28–30. That the elections were seen as a core benchmark of success is made clear in UN Doc S/1997/643 (13 August 1997), para 45, where the UN Secretary-General writes: "With the establishment of a democratically elected government in Liberia, the principal objective of UNOMIL has now been achieved".
63 UN Doc S/1997/712 (12 September 1997), para 31.

of the disarmament and demobilization exercise" and the "initial reintegration programs" which were "crucial in providing useful employment to thousands of former fighters and war-affected populations as a means both of restoring social stability and of rehabilitating some of the country's basic infrastructure".[64]

These themes – violent conflict; humanitarian relief, disarmament and demobilisation and reintegration; democratic elections, national reconciliation, human rights; the country's physical infrastructure – characterise the focus of the first UN peace operation in Liberia that had begun in 1993 and culminated in 1997 in the election of Charles Taylor to the presidency.[65] These themes also characterise the subsequent UN peace operations in Liberia, from the UN Peace-building Support Office (UNOL) that replaced the Observer Mission in 1997, to the Multilateral Force that oversaw the transition with the signing of the Comprehensive Peace Agreement in 2003 and the arrival of the UN Mission in Liberia (UNMIL).[66] What is missing from the UN's characterisation of the situation in Liberia between 1993 and 1997 and the mandate of the UN Observer Mission is the expression that this has anything to do with "the rule of law".

The term "rule of law" only entered the Security Council's lexicon with respect to the UN's peace operations in Liberia in September 2000, when it was used by the UN Secretary-General in a letter to the Council to justify the extension of UNOL's mandate for another 12 months.[67] In November 2002, in what appears to be the first use of the term by the Council itself with respect to Liberia, the President of the Council directed UNOL to "[offer] assistance to the Liberian authorities and to the public for strengthening democratic institutions and the rule of law".[68] However, it was only with the establishment of UNMIL in 2003 that the Council began to use the term "rule of law" more prominently and frequently in its resolutions on the UN's peace operation. Even then the Council used the term sparingly at first. In Resolution 1509 (2003) establishing UNMIL, the

64 Ibid, para 27.

65 This can be read in the UN Security Council resolutions creating and adjusting the mandate of UNOMIL: UN Doc S/Res/866 (22 September 1993) and UN Doc S/Res/1020 (10 November 1995). It can also be read in the rest of the Security Council resolutions extending the mandate of UNOMIL: UN Doc S/Res/911 (21 April 1994); UN Doc S/Res/950 (21 October 1995); UN Doc S/Res/972 (13 January 1995); UN Doc S/Res/985 (13 April 1995); UN Doc S/Res/1001 (30 June 1995); UN Doc S/Res/1014 (15 September 1995); UN Doc S/Res/1041 (29 January 1996); UN Doc S/Res/1059 (31 May 1996); UN Doc S/Res/1071 (30 August 1996); UN Doc S/Res/1083 (27 November 1996); UN Doc S/Res/1100 (27 March 1997); UN Doc S/Res/1116 (27 June 1997).

66 For the text of the Comprehensive Peace Agreement, see UN Doc S/2003/850 (29 August 2003), annex. For discussion and evaluation of the activities and performance of UNMIL during the transitional period, see Jeremy Matam Farrall, 'Recurring Dilemmas in a Recurring Conflict: Evaluating the UN Mission in Liberia (2003–2006)', *Journal of International Peacekeeping*, vol 16 (2012).

67 UN Doc S/2000/945 (3 October 2000).

68 UN Doc S/2002/1305 (29 November 2002), 1. This direction was reinforced two weeks later in a presidential statement: UN Doc S/PRST/2002/36 (13 December 2002), 3.

Council "urged" the transitional government of Liberia to prioritise "the establishment of a State based on the rule of law".[69] The Council did not mention the priority of establishing the rule of law in its resolutions extending UNMIL's mandate in 2004,[70] 2005,[71] or 2006,[72] and only returned to it in 2007, in "[r]ecognizing that significant challenges remain in the consolidation of Liberia's post-conflict transition, including [...] extension of the rule of law throughout the country".[73] In 2008 the Council again "recognized" the need for "extension of the rule of law throughout the country".[74]

The Security Council's language on the rule of law then shifted in 2009. In a preambular paragraph of its 2009 resolution extending UNMIL's mandate, the Council "recognized" that "lasting stability" in Liberia and the subregion would require "well-functioning and sustainable security and rule of law sectors".[75] A second reference to the rule of law in the same resolution "called upon" the Government and UN "to redouble efforts to develop national security and rule of law institutions".[76] This language, coupling "security" and "the rule of law" and framing them as technical matters for development, is repeated in the Council's resolutions extending UNMIL's mandate in 2010,[77] 2011,[78] and 2012.[79] By that

69 UN Doc S/Res/1509 (19 September 2003), preambular para 7.
70 UN Doc S/Res/1561 (17 September 2004).
71 UN Doc S/Res/1626 (19 September 2005); UN Doc S/Res/1638 (11 November 2005).
72 UN Doc S/Res/1667 (31 March 2006); UN Doc S/Res/1694 (13 July 2006); UN Doc S/Res/1712 (29 September 2006).
73 UN Doc S/Res/1750 (30 March 2007), preambular para 8. The same language is used in UN Doc S/Res/1777 (20 September 2007).
74 The only difference in 2008 is the additional emphasis on developing the Liberian National Police as part of the security architecture, and the note "that crimes of corruption and violence, in particular with regard to exploitation of Liberia's natural resources, threaten to undermine progress towards those ends": UN Doc S/Res/1836 (29 September 2008).
75 UN Doc S/Res/1885 (15 September 2009), preambular para 5.
76 Ibid, para 10.
77 UN Doc S/Res/1938 (15 September 2010), preambular paras 5 and 10.
78 UN Doc S/Res/2008 (16 September 2011), preambular paras 4 and 11.
79 UN Doc S/Res/2066 (17 September 2012), preambular paras 7 and 18. On the technocratic turn, Veronica Taylor notes:

> Formulations of rule-of-law programming, such as "law and justice reform", "security sector reform' (SSR), and "rule-of-law promotion" itself, all display a tension between technocratic and substantive justice concerns. For instance, in SSR discourse, "justice" denotes a technical "sector" and is an analogue for criminal law, procedure, adjudication, sanctions and corrections, regardless of whether the processes and outcomes of these are just. The potential slippage between the externally funded justice "fix" and the substantive realisation of justice locally varies with each rule-of-law intervention, but it is not unusual for the formal, technical face of the rule of law to dominate the more complex, indeterminate negotiation of "justice".
>
> Veronica L Taylor, 'Big Rule of Law©®SMTM (pat. pending): Branding and Certifying the Business of the Rule of Law', in Jeremy Matam Farrall and Hilary Charlesworth (eds), *Strengthening the Rule of Law through the United Nations Security Council* (Abingdon: Routledge, 2016), 29

point reference to "the rule of law" had become commonplace in the Council's characterisation of UNMIL. In addition to its usage already noted, the Council included the term an additional three times in the operative paragraphs of Resolution 2066 (2012): to refer to the "goal of increasing the capacity of the Government of Liberia, particularly the LNP [Liberian National Police], to implement sustainable rule of law, justice, governance and SSR programs"[80]; to "emphasize" that "in order to be sustainable, the transition planning process should take into account broad challenges, including governance and the rule of law as well as the political context"[81]; and to "call upon" UNMIL to enhance "its support for security sector and rule of law reforms".[82] Only one of these references was dropped from the 2013 resolution.

This account shows three things. One: it shows *continuity* in how the Security Council has characterised the UN's peace operations in Liberia from 1993 to 2013, concerned above all with security and stability ("peace through force"). Two: it shows a *shift* in language to the rule of law as the peace operation transitioned from peace-keeping to peace-building ("peace through law"). But three: it shows that the shift in language to "the rule of law" does not change the characterisation of the peace operation; rather, "the rule of law" enters the Council's resolutions only to be coupled with "security" and brought within its logic. This is remarkable because it shows how "the rule of law" emerges not as a break from the logic of security but as a concept of security. It leaves little doubt that "establishing the rule of law" is supposed to *contain* (hold within, to withhold from manifesting) the force of peace.

These findings are not surprising, indeed they are in keeping with the Security Council's primary responsibility for the maintenance of international peace and security under the UN Charter.[83] Yet no matter how obvious it might be that Council resolutions would characterise a UN peace operation as being fundamentally about stabilising a state of conflict and securing that stability, the point is nonetheless important. Its importance lies in the fact that "security" ultimately frames the UN's peace operation in Liberia. Nothing enters the peace operation through the Council without becoming securitised.[84] Peace becomes a matter of "stability"; law becomes a matter of "order" (to pacify the population) and

80 UN Doc S/Res/2066 (17 September 2012), para 7, repeated in UN Doc S/Res/2116 (18 September 2013), para 8.
81 UN Doc S/Res/2066 (17 September 2012), para 8, not repeated in UN Doc S/Res/2116 (18 September 2013).
82 UN Doc S/Res/2066 (17 September 2012), para 8, repeated in UN Doc S/Res/2116 (18 September 2013), para 8.
83 See Article 24 and Chapter VII of the Charter of the United Nations (adopted 26 June 1945, entered into force 24 October 1945) 1 *UNTS* 16.
84 On securitisation, see Luckham and Kirk's analysis of the "evolving concept of security" in Robin Luckham and Tom Kirk, 'The Two Faces of Security in Hybrid Political Orders: A Framework for Analysis and Research', *Stability: International Journal of Security and Development*, vol 2, no 2 (2013); Robin Luckham and Tom Kirk, 'Security in Hybrid Political Contexts: An End-User Approach', *Justice and Security Research Program* (Paper 2, 2012).

"accountability" (to pacify the government and its armed forces); and justice becomes a matter of the injustices resulting from armed conflict and addressing them in the interests of "securing stability", or else a matter of criminal justice and therefore a matter of "law and order". This, in other words, is the UN's vision of peace in Liberia: a reconciled state/State with a strong security sector capable of maintaining stability and order.

Establishing a state based on the rule of law

I began the account in the previous section by quoting a passage from the final report of the UN Secretary-General on the UN Observer Mission in Liberia. Written at a moment of peace in 1997 and looking back on the first civil war in Liberia, the passage reflects on how the state/State of peace in Liberia had broken down ("the central government, law and order and physical infrastructure of Liberia had been either seriously degraded or had disappeared altogether"). This state/State of non-peace was characterised by three elements in particular. One: the conflict was defined by a lack of control over the use of force ("command and control exercised by faction leaders over their commanders and troops in the field was often loose", combined with "the easy availability of small arms"). This was the opposite of the proposition "peace contains force": this was a state in which force was *uncontained*. Two: the conflict was defined by a lack of law ("the fighting was characterized by widespread lawlessness"). This was the opposite of the proposition "law contains force": this was a state in which force was wielded *lawlessly*. And three: the conflict was defined by injustice ("gross violations of human rights by all factions against innocent civilians"). This was the opposite of the proposition "justice contains force": this was a state in which violence was inflicted on civilians *unjustly*.

In short, the passage presented an image of the state/State that the first UN peace operation in Liberia had confronted, and it was the very opposite of "peace". Or rather, because this passage was written as a reflection on what had supposedly been overcome, the state/State of peace that the UN was celebrating in its 1997 report was the opposite of this image of war. *This* was the "peace" that had to be secured, defined in opposition to a state of *uncontained, lawless, unjust violence*.

Before the rule of law entered Security Council discourse with respect to the UN's peace operations in Liberia, its concern was with "law and order", or its absence, "lawlessness". This is not the same as a concern for the rule of law. As Nick Cheesman has persuasively shown in his study of Myanmar, the two concepts are "asymmetrically opposed".[85] By this Cheesman means that "law and order" is in an antagonistic relation with "the rule of law", not as its negation (its symmetrical

85 See Nick Cheesman, 'Law and Order as Asymmetrical Opposite to the Rule of Law', *Hague Journal on the Rule of Law*, vol 6, no 1 (2014). See further Nick Cheesman, *Opposing the Rule of Law: How Myanmar's Courts Make Law and Order* (Cambridge: Cambridge University Press, 2015).

opposite, as in "non-rule of law") but as a positive concept with its own contents that make it inherently antagonistic to the concept of the rule of law.[86] Following Michel Foucault, Cheesman highlights how "law and order" is concerned above all with a police-like "concern to maintain order, to abolish disorder, through good use of the state's forces".[87] The rule of law, by contrast, "does not aim to eliminate disorder" nor does it "purposefully design and pursue activities for the obtaining and maintenance of order".[88] Rather the rule of law seeks order in itself – or as Cheesman puts it, "the rule of law is orderly".[89] Cheesman does not elaborate on what he means by this, beyond saying that the rule of law is "characterized by an inherent type of order [...] it is orderly".[90] I agree to the extent that the rule of law is characterised by its relation to force, which, as discussed above, seeks to make law and force coincidental. In this sense, the rule of law is an ordering of force in itself. Whereas "law and order" is concerned with maintaining an orderly population through the use of force (and, therefore, maintaining order *exogenously*, in others), "the rule of law" is concerned with maintaining its monopoly of legitimate force (and, therefore, maintaining order *endogenously*, in itself).[91]

The distinction is important here because it assists in seeing how the two propositions – "law and order" and "rule of law" – merge in this account of the attempt to secure the state/State of Liberia against a return to uncontained, lawless, unjust violence. Thus in 2003, when the Security Council decided to establish UNMIL, "the stabilization force called for in Resolution 1497 (2003)", it further decided that this "stabilization force" would "consist of up to 15,000 UN military personnel [...] and up to 1,115 civilian police officers, including formed units to assist in the maintenance of law and order throughout Liberia".[92] At the same time, one of the "key priorities" of this stabilisation force was to support "the establishment of a state based on the rule of law".[93] So from the outset the peace operation was defined as a stabilisation mission with a primary objective of maintaining "law and order" (to assist in securing the State of Liberia from a return to a state of uncontained, lawless, unjust violence), but within the broader framework of the rule of law. The preambular position of the reference to the rule of law in the mandate is important here, setting it up as a threshold term of the peace operation.[94] However, in bringing the two propositions together in the same discourse of securing peace, "the rule of law" becomes conjoined with "law and order". As a threshold term its contents (what is meant by "the establishment of a state based on the rule of law") become concrete through the operative

86 Cheesman, 'Law and Order', 111.
87 Ibid, 108.
88 Ibid, 111.
89 Ibid.
90 Ibid.
91 Compare ibid.
92 UN Doc S/Res/1509 (19 September 2003), para 1.
93 Ibid, preambular para 1.
94 On the preamble to law, see Shane Chalmers, 'The Beginning of Human Rights: The Ritual of the Preamble to Law', *Humanity*, vol 9, no 1 (2018).

paragraphs that direct UNMIL's work. And there is no doubt that maintaining order and stability is the dominant concern of the operative paragraphs of UNMIL's mandate, making the Mission's core tasks to assist in monitoring and restructuring the police force of Liberia and to develop a civilian police training programme,[95] as well as to assist in developing a strategy to consolidate governmental institutions, including the national legal framework and judicial and correctional institutions.[96] UNMIL's rule-of-law mandate thus faithfully pursues the UN Department of Peacekeeping Operation's operational concept of the rule of law, focusing on the so-called "justice-chain institutions" of police, prisons, and courts, with the preambular goal of "establishing a state based on the rule of law" acquiring its core operative meaning in relation to this overarching objective. As such, "establishing a state based on the rule of law" comes to require, according to the implementation of UNMIL's mandate, bringing Liberia's forces of law and order – its police, prisons, and courts – within the concept of "the rule of law". On one hand this means ensuring Liberia's security sector is accountable to law, with appropriate democratic oversight and civilian control. On the other hand this means making "building and strengthening the security sector" the focus of work to establish a State based on the rule of law.

In sum, the task of establishing "a State based on the rule of law" was initially included in UNMIL's mandate as a preambular concern to the operative objective of securing the state/State of peace in Liberia. At this point the term was included as an aspirational vision, an ideal on the horizon of the peace operation. The timing of this mandate (2003) also coincided with the entry of "the rule of law" as a discrete item on the Security Council's agenda and in the lead-up to the publication of the Secretary-General's definitional report on the rule of law in 2004.[97] This was a time of high aspiration for promoting "the rule of law" through the UN and the Security Council in particular.[98] As UNMIL became more established, however, and especially as it began to transition from a peace-keeping to a peace-building operation after the 2006 presidential elections, "the rule of law" was brought increasingly within UNMIL's mandate as an operative term and coupled with its security objectives. From 2009 the vision of establishing a State based on the rule of law became a reminder that "lasting stability in Liberia and the subregion requires well-functioning and sustainable security and rule of law sectors" and "re-doubled efforts" "to develop national security and rule of law institutions".[99]

The justice-and-security complex

Thus by 2013 a securitised rule of law had become definitive of the UN's operation to assist the Government of Liberia to secure its vision of peace. If in 2003 it

95 UN Doc S/Res/1509 (19 September 2003), para 3(n).
96 Ibid, para 3(q).
97 See note 28 above.
98 See Jeremy Matam Farrall and Hilary Charlesworth (eds), *Strengthening the Rule of Law through the United Nations Security Council* (Abingdon: Routledge, 2016).
99 See notes 75 and 76 above.

was implicit that the aim of establishing a State based on the rule of law contained the peace operation's objectives of securing stability and order, then by 2013 the contingent relation of "the rule of law" and "security" could not have been more explicit. So far this is in keeping with the first two propositions in the logic of security. As I have shown, the UN's peace operations in Liberia have been directed first and foremost at ensuring peace contains the force of war. I have also shown how UNMIL's mandate became increasingly concerned with consolidating this State by ensuring law contains the force of peace. But this raises the question: what about the third proposition, of securing this State of peace by ensuring justice contains the force of law?

In 2013, as the withdrawal of UNMIL became an increasingly unavoidable reality, with UN troops leaving the country in large numbers and a complete exit anticipated by 2018,[100] building the capacity of Liberia's security sector had become the main priority for the first time since the peace operation began in 2003.[101] Up until 2012 UNMIL's main security focus had been to provide operational support to the Liberian National Police and the Bureau of Immigration and Naturalization as part of its peacekeeping strategy, rather than to develop the capacity of these agencies.[102] At the same time, with UNMIL providing security under its peacekeeping mandate, the Government had been reluctant to commit resources from its limited budget to develop the capacity of its security agencies.[103] This meant that in 2013 the police and immigration forces lacked the capacity to take control of domestic security in Liberia. Fearful that this would lead to a "security vacuum" that would allow non-government actors to challenge the Government's monopoly on the use of force, especially in the interior, the

100 In 2013 UNMIL was in "the first phase of the second military draw down": author interview with United Nations Department of Peacekeeping Operations official, New York City, 22 June 2013 (NY7). See also UN Doc S/Res/2215 (2 April 2015), para 1, in which the Security Council "reaffirmed" "its expectation that the Government of Liberia will assume fully its complete security responsibilities from UNMIL no later than 30 June 2016 and also reaffirms its intention to consider the continued and future reconfiguration of UNMIL accordingly": para 3. This transfer of security responsibilities from UNMIL to Liberia's security services was completed on 30 June 2016, and a complete withdrawal of UNMIL is at the time of writing scheduled for the end of April 2018: UN Doc S/Res/2333 (23 December 2016), para 10.

101 Author interview with NY7.

102 Ibid.

103 Ibid. The reason for this reluctance is unclear but a common interpretation within UNMIL is that it was at least partly a form of strategic dependence intended to prolong the UN Mission in Liberia. Once Liberia could maintain peace and stability on its own, UNMIL would no longer be necessary. As one UN official put it:

> In terms of political will [...] the Government of Liberia would like the UN Mission to be there forever. That is unusual – we have been literally kicked out of other countries, such as Chad recently – but in Liberia the Government feels very comfortable with the Mission. And you know, maybe the budget is part of the overall strategy of the Government in order to prolong the presence of the Mission – that is kind of a conspiracy theory.

Ibid

Liberian Government began to focus on building the capacity of the police and immigration.[104]

A few years before, in 2010, the Government had submitted a request to the UN Peacebuilding Commission to be placed on its agenda, which would open up access to international resources through the UN Peacebuilding Fund. The request was granted, and a Statement of Mutual Commitments between the Government and the Peacebuilding Commission identified three core commitments in the areas of "security sector reform", "rule of law", and "national reconciliation".[105] As its "centrepiece" the Statement of Mutual Commitments envisioned a network of five Regional Justice and Security Hubs covering the interior of Liberia. The promise was a new "peacebuilding technology"[106]: a decentralised network of fortified government complexes that would draw together the rule of law and security sector priorities in a way that would address both the feared "security vacuum" and the perceived "justice vacuum".[107] The vision is set out in a report published by the Government in early 2013 to update international stakeholders on the status of the project:

> The Justice and Security Regional Hubs are designed to extend security and justice services to all Liberians throughout the country. The Regional Hubs seek to promote a comprehensive approach to address justice and security problems through co-location of the regional Liberian National Police headquarters (including a robust Police Support Unit (PSU) element), as well as a Bureau of Immigration and Naturalization (BIN) Patrol Unit and elements of the justice system such as county attorneys, city solicitors, public defends, magistrates and judges.[108]

104 Ibid. See also UN Doc S/2013/124 (28 February 2013); UN Doc S/2013/479 (12 August 2013); UN Doc S/2014/123 (18 February 2014); UN Doc S/2014/598 (15 August 2014); UN Doc S/2015/275 (23 April 2015). See also Rory Keane, 'Reviewing the Justice and Security Hub Modality as Piloted in Liberia', *Stability: International Journal of Security and Development*, vol 1, no 1 (2012). Keane (87) notes:

> The strategic focus on SSR and rule of law is based on the fact that the UN Peacekeeping Mission in the country, known as UNMIL, will gradually reduce troop numbers between 2012 and 2015 by up to 50%. In order to ensure that there is no security vacuum during or after this drawdown process, it is critical to build up and support Liberian security and justice services.

105 UN Doc PBC/4/LBR/2 (16 November 2010). The Statement of Mutual Commitments was revised in 2012 as set out in UN Doc PBC/6/LBR/2 (9 May 2012).

106 See Keane, 'Justice and Security Hub Modality', 87. However, as Veronica Taylor pointed out to me, these Hubs resemble the Provincial Reconstruction Teams previously designed and implemented in Afghanistan and then in Iraq.

107 Ibid, 88.

108 Justice and Security Joint Program, 'Introduction', *Gbarnga Regional Justice and Security Hub January 2012 – January 2013 Report*, 3.

The first Hub, completed in 2013, was built just outside of Gbarnga to serve Region 3, the north-western security bloc comprising the interior Counties of Bong, Lofa, and Nimba. At least three reasons stand out for why Gbarnga was chosen for the location of the first Hub. One: Gbarnga was the capital of Charles Taylor's "Greater Liberia", the area he had controlled during the civil war, and it remained a stronghold for his supporters, many of whom were still occupying Taylor's farm just south of the city. Two: the social cleavages that hold the greatest potential to return Liberia to war run through Lofa and Nimba Counties. Three: Nimba County is the centre of the mining industry and economic activity outside of Monrovia.

From the perspective of the Government and its international partners, these are all good reasons to build the first Hub in Gbarnga, before extending the model to the other four security blocs in the country. And yet, the vision is for these Hubs to enhance *access to justice* in the process of strengthening security in the interior. Given this, the fact that the Gbarnga Hub stands as a fortified complex beyond the outskirts of town, and well beyond the physical access of the vast majority of the people it is supposed to serve, is perplexing. If the intention is to bring the law closer to the people, the only sense in which this is achieved is by reducing the time needed for police to respond to security threats in the region.

Figure 4.2 Gbarnga Regional Justice and Security Hub[109]

109 Attribution: Shane Chalmers (2013).

The obvious implication is that the Regional Justice and Security Hub in Gbarnga is directed at strengthening the police and immigration forces in the interior. Indeed, the Government originally conceived of the Hubs as regional command centres for the Liberian National Police to have "forward operating bases" in the interior,[110] and, as the Government states in its 2013 report, "this is precisely one of the reasons why the hub was established, as a rapid response forward operational base".[111] Thus brought together within the same complex in the Government's leading justice initiative, "security" and "justice" would complement each other exactly as the Government and the UN hoped they would: a new police force deployed in the interior, with courthouses and lawyers co-located on-site for processing offenders of the national law.

Justice to come

> Light appeared in the horizon: a triumph was before this Society such as the wisest man might envy, and the most virtuous man long to realize. They would triumph, not as conquerors, binding bleeding nations to their chariot wheels; but as liberators, who came not to destroy but to save. [...] their march would be surrounded by the songs of the grateful, the blessings of the free; their triumph would be recorded in two hemispheres, and its lasting memorial would be written in heaven.[112]
>
> George Washington Parke Custis, Address to the Annual Meeting of the American Colonization Society, 1824

Imagine this. The year is 1821, the season is winter, and the day is stretched out radially between the unbroken circumference of the horizon as the US brig the *Nautilus* courses across the Atlantic Ocean in the direction of Africa. Aboard are 33 free black women, men, and children under the command of two white officers of the US Government and two white agents of the American Colonization Society.[113] The *Nautilus* is bound for the British colony of Sierra Leone where it is to join another group of black colonists who departed the United States a year

110 Author interview with NY7. The design was "scaled up" to include legal services with the intervention of the UN Peacebuilding Commission. See also Keane, 'Justice and Security Hub Modality', 88.

111 Justice and Security Joint Program, *Gbarnga Regional Justice and Security Hub Report*, 11.

112 George Washington Parke Custis, Address to the Annual Meeting of the American Colonization Society in support of their colonisation mission, in American Colonization Society, *Seventh Annual Report* (Washington, DC: printed by Davis and Force, 1824), 15–16.

113 See Charles Henry Huberich, *The Political and Legislative History of Liberia: Volume 1* (New York: Central Book Company, 1947), 143. See also Frederick Starr, *Liberia: Description, History, Problems* (Chicago: publisher not identified, 1913), 57; Amos J Beyan, *The American Colonization Society and the Creation of the Liberian State: A Historical Perspective, 1822–1900* (Lanham: University Press of America, 1991), 62.

earlier aboard the *Elizabeth* before continuing to search for their promised land along the Windward Coast. But all of that is to come. Out at sea for now, there they are: coursing across the Atlantic, gazing beyond the railings of the *Nautilus* at an apparently limitless expanse of sky and ocean, cut only by the horizon. And the light on the horizon holds out a promise: *imagine*, Africa ahead! A land of justice to come!

To begin with, the American Colonization Society was dominated by slaveholders, and there is little doubt about their motivations in organising the colonisation mission that would establish Liberia in Africa: to secure the institution of slavery still foundational in the south of the country as well as the whiteness of the United States. The answer to a visible contradiction was to make it less visible, in this case by deporting the free people of colour of the United States, whose presence threatened the security and purity of whites and the docility of their slaves. However, the idea of colonising these free people of colour in Africa (or elsewhere) was also seen by some, both white and black, as a promise of liberty, equality, and fraternity.[114] Colonisation would, it was said, make black people free in a way they could never be in the United States. What is more, the establishment of an African-American colony in Africa would, it was said, provide a model of African civilisation that would lead to the emancipation of all of Africa's peoples. This was the colour of justice to come with the realisation of "Liberia": the flourishing of the United States as a white homeland and the flourishing of Africa as a black homeland. On one side this vision was propagated by slaveholders and white supremacists; on another side it was championed by radical black nationalists, along with pragmatists black and white; while the views of the Africans who were to be made civilised were nowhere to be seen. And this troubled vision underwrote Liberia. The colony, which had been referred to simply by its geographical indicator – Cape Montserado – and therefore by a name that "meant nothing", by a name that signified no more than the outcrop of rubble that history had piled at the place where the settlers now stood, was named "LIBERIA", expressing the "object and nature" of the American Colonization Society's vision, not simply of liberty, but of the kind of liberty that comes with being made free. *This* was the justice to come, just over the horizon.

A peace formidable to any eye

> Cape Montserado, November 26th, 1822, (morning.) Sir: I had the honour of writing you by the Shark, on the 9th ultimo, and, subsequently, by the "Strong", in a very weak and sickly condition. We are now engaged in a bloody and perilous war with all the native tribes around us. On the morning of the 11th, were attacked by eight hundred, who were repulsed, after doing us some injury, with the loss of nearly one hundred killed on the spot. Subsequently, we have been employed in a negotiation for

114 See also Eric Burin, *Slavery and the Peculiar Solution: A History of the American Colonization Society* (Gainesville: University Press of Florida, 2005), Chapter 1.

> peace, which I fear will fail. We expect another assault to be made on us in two or three days. [...] I have the honour, sir, to be, your most obedient servant,
>
> J. ASHMUN,
>
> *Acting Agent for liberated Africans.*
>
> November 26th, (evening.) Sir: Our negotiation with our perfidious enemies seems to have entirely failed of its object. They are bent on our ruin.[115]

Now imagine this. It is December 1822, mere months after the *Nautilus* was at sea, and the tiny colony erected on Cape Montserado is on the brink of ruin. Without food or adequate shelter, its 50-odd residents, sick and dying from disease, are under attack from an alliance led by the Dey, who are demanding the return of land "purchased" from them by the two white American agents (with the assistance of a cocked pistol).[116] Two battles ensue. The first, in late November, is described by the American Colonization Society's "Acting Agent for liberated Africans" in the letter to the Secretary of the US Navy quoted above. The second assault, foreseen by the Agent in his letter, occurs five days later. During this battle an estimated 1,500 soldiers led by the Dey attack the American settlers. The settlement barely avoids destruction. Its survival is attributed to cannon fire, forcing the Dey to retreat.

This war will be memorialised as the Providential beginning of Liberia. Half a century later the first President of the Republic, Joseph Jenkins Roberts, will recall it as "that signal triumph of freedom over the implacable enemies of human progress and the rights of man" – a triumph "which permanently established on this hill the foundations of our present political fabric".[117] Or, in the words of President William V S Tubman (the Great Emancipator of the Liberian Hinterland), addressing the legislature a century later: "If the defenders of the Commonwealth had lost the day in the Battle of Fort Hill there would have been no Liberia".[118]

But there is more to this scene. Shortly after the second battle a US Navy ship arrives at the Cape, having heard the cannon fire. The Captain offers his assistance in constructing a fort – or as he describes it later, "a tower of strength". This, the Captain notes, "I conceived well suited to effect the object in view", to make an "impression on the minds" of those who might threaten the colony and its just claims.[119] He describes the construction of this tower of strength in a letter to the Secretary of the US Navy:

115 Letter from the acting Agent of the American Colonization Society at Cape Montserado, J Ashmun, to the Secretary of the US Navy, in American Colonization Society, *Seventh Annual Report*, 49–50.

116 See, e.g., 'Extract of a letter from Captain Robert T Spence to the Secretary of the US Navy', in American Colonization Society, *Seventh Annual Report*, 58–59.

117 Cited in Svend E Holsoe, 'Matilda Newport: The Power of a Liberian-Invented Tradition', *Liberian Studies Journal*, vol 32, no 2 (2007): 30.

118 William V S Tubman, 'Annual Message to the Legislature, November 16, 1965', in D Elwood Dunn (ed), *The Annual Messages of the Presidents of Liberia 1848–2010: Volume 1* (Gottingen: De Gruyter, 2011), 1348.

119 American Colonization Society, *Seventh Annual Report*, 55 and 60 (my italics).

> In fifteen days, a circular massive work of stone, measuring one hundred and twelve feet in circumference, eight feet in thickness, and ten feet in elevation, was seen to tower above the surrounding heights, commanding the site for the town, and a wide range of the circumjacent country.[120]

The result, he writes, is "formidable to any eye". And indeed, the Captain is left with no doubt about:

> its effect in neutralizing, in no small degree, the menacing designs of the natives. Every day brought me additional proof of a change in their intentions [...] I was happy in perceiving this revolution in their sentiments, this change in their designs.[121]

Not long after the settlers declared Liberia a Free, Sovereign and Independent Republic in 1847, accounts began to circulate that it was a young settler woman, Matilda Newport, who had fired the cannon that saved the colony during the Providential battle of Fort Hill.[122] Whether she did or not is unknown, but that fact is insignificant to this history. What is significant is that she came to be represented as if she had. What is significant is that this image of "Matilda Newport" substituted for a woman whose trace in history is little more than the name that would give birth to "Liberia" as a republic. As another Liberian woman proclaimed admiringly almost a century later:

> It was [...] our noble Matilda, seeing the handful of men dispirited, observing the shattered condition of affairs and the gloom which the menacing advance of the natives had cast upon the lives of the pioneers, stepped forth, lighted the cannon [...] and the existence of the Republic became a possibility.[123]

120 Ibid, 60.
121 Ibid (my italics).
122 See Holsoe, 'Matilda Newport'. For an example of the repetition of this account, see 'The Looking-Glass: Being a True Report and Narrative of the Life, Travels, and Labors of the Rev Daniel H Peterson, a Colored Clergyman; Embracing a Period of Time from the Year 1812 to 1854, and Including His Visit to Western Africa', in Wilson Jeremiah Moses (ed), *Liberian Dreams: Back-to-Africa Narratives from the 1850s* (University Park: Pennsylvania State University Press, 1998), 51–52. According to this account:

> Liberia would never have been the home of the immigrants, had it not been for a woman. When the first settlers were preparing themselves resting-places, the natives came upon them with hostile intent. One woman only remained in her house, the other inhabitants having fled. She fired upon the natives until she had succeeded in killing quite a number of them. The survivors fled. The name of the woman was Mrs Newport; and she secured a *new port* for the colored people. The natives never returned.

123 Holsoe, 'Matilda Newport', 34.

Figure 4.3 Part of a relief depicting the origin myth of Liberia, set at the base of a monument on Cape Montserrado[124]

And the existence of the Republic became a possibility. There she stands: on public monuments and commemorative stamps, in children's school books,[125] in poems, parades,[126] and civic names,[127] her heroism retold and re-enacted – Lady Newport, always behind the cannon with a hand to the fuse, a figure both just and *formidable to any eye.*

The timing of the emergence of the myth of Matilda Newport is important. In the second half of the nineteenth century the European "scramble for Africa" was intensifying and the government of the Black Republic was under great pressure to secure both its external sovereignty against the incursions of France and Britain and its internal sovereignty against the African peoples who were rebelling against, or simply ignoring, the claims of the Americo-Liberian government. In this situation of colonial state-building the name of Matilda Newport was given to a company of the Republic's first militia.[128] Around the same time, December 1 was proclaimed a public holiday – to be named Matilda Newport Day – in honour of the 1822 battle

124 Attribution: Shane Chalmers (2013).

125 Holsoe, 'Matilda Newport', 38.

126 'The Story of Matilda Newport – Liberian Heroine', *AFRO Magazine*, 3 February 1953, 8.

127 A main street and a school in central Monrovia are named after Matilda Newport. An Act to establish a township named "in honor of the heroine Matilda Newport" was also passed in 1854: see American Colonization Society, *The African Repository*, vol 30 (Washington, DC: ACS, 1854), 241.

128 Holsoe, 'Matilda Newport', 33.

Figure 4.4 Stamp issued in 1947[129]

of Fort Hill and the birth of the nation. In this way, and very importantly at this time, when the existence of the Republic was once again imperilled by its "perfidious enemies",[130] both the militia created to secure Liberia's future presence and the holiday created to commemorate the battle that secured Liberia's past presence were drawn together in the figure of Matilda Newport.[131]

Matilda Newport thus emerged as an image in and of this history, connecting what was behind – the providential battle for Liberia's past – with what was ahead – the promise of Liberia's future – through an image that legitimated and propagated the legality and force of this history.[132] Where "Liberia" remained an abstraction even after its declaration as a Republic in 1847 – with an uncertain presence in international law and an uncertain presence on the ground in west Africa – the figure of Matilda Newport came to sediment a place for Liberia both

129 Attribution: Manfred Beier, *Philately of Liberia*, philib.org

130 See note 115 above.

131 Thus an historian, writing in 1926, claimed that Matilda Newport's heroic deeds contributed to securing Liberia's independence from external powers, France and Britain: see Siahyonkron Nyanseor, 'Putting to Rest the Matilda Newport Myth – Part 2', *The Perspective*, 7 January 2004: www.theperspective.org/2004/jan/matildanewportmyth.htm

132 For a theoretical framework for thinking about images "in" and "of" history, see Shane Chalmers, 'The Visual Force of Justice in the Making of Liberia', in Desmond Manderson (ed), *Law and the Visual: Representations, Technologies, and Critique* (Toronto: University of Toronto Press, 2017).

as an image of justice and as an historical reality. Thus the body of the settler woman, now the body of the Republic, gave birth to "Liberia" in two ways. As an origin myth, Matilda Newport came to signify the history of Liberia, visualising – making visible – its providence as a settlement of pioneers under a banner of liberty; and as a technology of colonial state-building, the image of Matilda Newport deployed to *make* this history.[133] In these two ways, not only did Matilda Newport come to represent the past and future of Liberia in west Africa – and thus a narrative of history that placed Liberia in history – but she also combined the justice of "Liberia" with the force that *had* and *would* secure its presence as a Republic in Africa and the world. Conjugating woman and cannon in the act that gave birth to the nation-state, the image unites feminine justice with phallic force to make its vision of "Liberia" manifest. There is nothing rigid, nothing timeless, nothing placeless, about Matilda Newport. Like Bernini's version of David, she is tensed in action, a bandana keeping her hair and sweat from blinding her vision, the barrel of the cannon directed in no uncertain way at whatever would deny her place in the promised land.[134] This is not an anaemic figure of *Justitia* for all times and for all places; she is active, determined, *forceful.*

And that is precisely why the image of Matilda Newport was eventually condemned as a representation of "Liberia". Following the revolution that culminated in 1980 with the overthrow of the Americo-Liberian regime, the celebration of Matilda Newport Day was swept away and the image publicly denounced for glorifying "the defeat of one group of citizens by another group of citizens".[135] The image that had represented and that had been deployed to achieve the consolidation of Liberia as a nation-state, through the forceful seizure of the lands and the institution of control over the peoples of this place, was condemned along with a government that had failed to see the problem with the state/State of peace secured through Matilda Newport.[136]

The idea of "Liberia" survived the revolution that swept the country in the second half of the twentieth century as well as the wars of the 1990s and early 2000s. Whereas the figure of Matilda Newport, as a representation of "Liberia", sank too deeply into a specific colonial history to remain viable as a dynamic image of a revised post-colonial Republic, the idea of "Liberia" as a nation-state remains wholly acceptable today. But the very floating quality that has kept the idea of Liberia from sinking into history along with Matilda Newport has also kept it from providing a solid basis for remaking the nation-state in the twenty-first century.

133 On the image as "interpretive resource" and "technology", see the introduction to Desmond Manderson (ed), *Law and the Visual: Representations, Technologies, and Critique* (Toronto: University of Toronto Press, 2017).

134 With thanks to Desmond Manderson for drawing my attention to the comparison.

135 Holsoe, 'Matilda Newport', 37–38.

136 As President Tubman (that Great Emancipator of the Hinterland) stated in 1965: "Adverse comments on the Celebration of Mathilda Newport Day are being made but I see no objections to the celebration", indeed "a day dedicated to her would appear to be most appropriate": Tubman, 'Annual Message to the Legislature, November 16, 1965', in Dunn (ed), *Annual Messages of the Presidents*, 1348.

The abstract idea of "Liberia" that required the figure of Matilda Newport for its realisation keeps it on the surface of history. What it means to "be" Liberian in the second decade of the twenty-first century remains as fluid and plural as the peoples who inhabit its lands. Liberia remains a state without a nation, and more than that, a state without a definite *image* of itself as a nation. Like the figure of Matilda Newport, the official symbols of the Republic – its flag, patterned on the US flag, its coat of arms, with its colonial motifs, and its motto, "the love of liberty brought us here" – are of a vision that was, a vision that a violent history submerged. Thus "Liberia" remains an unsettled and disembodied ideal, *still* a promise of justice to come, just over the horizon.

5 Talking drums, talking back

Law at sea

Now reimagine. The year is 1821, the month is winter, and the day is stretched out radially between the unbroken circumference of the horizon, as the US brig the *Nautilus* courses across the Atlantic Ocean in the direction of Africa. The *Nautilus* is sailing in the wake of another vessel, carrying a *Constitution For the Government of the African Settlement at* . "At": like the 33 free black children, women, and men aboard the *Nautilus*, this is an unsettled law; defined by a blank space, imaginatively conceived so that it might take form elsewhere and otherwise, this is a law to come – the light on the horizon.

The first iteration of Liberia's national law was inscribed in this sea-borne Constitution, adopted in 1820 by the United States-based Board of Managers of the American Colonization Society at the request of one of its Agents.[1] Along with this Constitution the Board of Managers also provided a code of laws in Instructions to its Agents.[2] What is remarkable about these legal texts is that they were adopted in anticipation of the creation of a settlement on the west coast of Africa, while the ship that would eventually deliver the first emigrants to the shores of Liberia was still anchored off the coast of Sierra Leone. The initial lack of a territorial basis for this law – and therefore, according to the intentions of the American Colonization Society, the fact that it was not yet law when it was set down in 1820[3] – appears as two blank spaces in the text of this Constitution, like a call that is waiting to be answered:

Constitution
For the
Government of the African Settlement at
ARTICLE 1ST.

1 See Charles Henry Huberich, *The Political and Legislative History of Liberia: Volume 1* (New York: Central Book Company, 1947), 145–146.

2 Reproduced in ibid, 95–96, 103–105, 146–148.

3 Ibid, 148.

> All persons born within the limits of the territory held by the American Colonization Society in or removing there to reside, shall be free, and entitled to all the rights and privileges of the free people of the United States.

The answer that would be inscribed in the blank space is of course "Liberia", but even that would remain more an open question than an answer.

Despite Liberia's formative shifts throughout the nineteenth and twentieth centuries – from Colony to Commonwealth to Republic, through revolution and war – the law under the 1820 Constitution has continued to inform the subsequent manifestations of Liberia's national law. This includes both what was posited in the 1820 Constitution and what was left blank. What was posited as the law that would apply at settlement was most clearly expressed in Article 6 of the 1820 Constitution: "The common law as in force and modified in the United States, and applicable to the situation of the people, shall be in force in the Settlement" – a provision that was essentially replaced in each of Liberia's subsequent Constitutions.[4] At the same time, the blank space that signified the law's groundlessness in west Africa has also allowed it to become grounded there. From 1847, at least, when Liberia declared itself a Free, Sovereign and Independent State, Americo-Liberians could speak of this law, as the national law of a sovereign republic, as the law of the land. From this point the unsettled nature of the law that marked the Constitution in 1820 was history.

And yet, the question lingers. Precisely because it was history, the initial fact of *terra nullius* – of being "without settled law" – has continued to underlie the Constitution of Liberia, as a law that was on first encounter empty of its new land, as a law that had to have inscribed upon it this land.[5] The blank space that marked the first iteration of the Constitution of Liberia could not be filled in simply by printing over it the name of this settled land, especially when that name itself signified an idea without any immediate grounding. "Liberia": an imaginary land of liberty to come, for emigrants to come, in Africa (or elsewhere).

The problem of our laws

The blank space is one dimension of the contradictory form of law, undermining every grounded expression of the law. This blank space is what leaves law open to being an oppressive conceit, but it also points to the possibilities of law as a medium of justice. I examined the violent consequences of law's conceptual blankness in the previous two chapters. Thus I showed in Chapter 3 how the blank space that separates law from its subjects enables the super-imposition of a

4 For example, Article 17 of the Constitution of the Commonwealth of Liberia (1839); Article V(1) of the Constitution of the Republic of Liberia (1847); and generally the Constitution of the Republic of Liberia (1984).

5 Or, as Farrall writes, "Liberia began its existence as a constitution in search of a country": Jeremy Matam Farrall, 'Recurring Dilemmas in a Recurring Conflict: Evaluating the UN Mission in Liberia (2003–2006)', *Journal of International Peacekeeping*, vol 16 (2012), 313.

legal framework over lands and humans that transforms them into fungible things. Likewise, the separation of law from its subjects is at the core of the logic of security that I examined in the preceding chapter. As I showed there, the proposition "peace through justice" requires the institution of a rule of law that is both forceful and just for the very reason that law remains disconnected from its subjects. The difference between the two is that, whereas the logic of capital exploits the separation, the logic of security seeks to overcome it. Having examined the violent consequences of these two "responses" to the contradiction in law (reifying the separation in the case of capital, enforcing unity in the case of security), I now continue the analysis by examining how this contradiction in law is also for the better, leaving law open to its subjects as a medium of justice. This involves examining how the national law is taking form on the ground in Liberia post-war in an "illogical" way. But before I get to that, I need to say something more about the "problem of our laws" in the case of Liberia.

Talking drums

On the threshold of the national museum of Liberia, set down between the curated expression of history contained within the building and the normality of everyday life taking place on the streets of Monrovia below, is a drum standing two and a half meters tall. An official sign introduces the artefact as a "Dukpa drum", and in brackets "communication drum". The sign then continues with the following description:

> This communication drum was used in time past to disseminate information by beating it and using various rhythms for different signals or messages such as declaring war, fire outbreak, danger, emergency, marriage, death, selecting a leader and receiving guests.

I had heard about the talking drums of west Africa before I arrived in Liberia, and I asked the museum guide (once a glimpse of the drum from the street drew me in) if this was one of them. The official laughed. Pointing through the door to the street below, he said "talking drum" is what it is normally called. I asked if Liberians would know it as a "communication drum". He laughed again. No, he said, they would call it a "talking drum". Why then, I asked, does the museum call it a "communication drum". Because, he said, "communication drum" better explains what the drum is used for. It *disseminates information*; it does not talk. And he laughed again.[6]

Several weeks later, in the interior of Liberia, a man in a teashop said to me in response to a question about the rule of law: "The rule of law? How can you have the rule of law when we don't even know our own laws?"[7] Unlike the museum official this man was not laughing, and yet the irony was there. For him the

6 Conversation with author, Monrovia, Liberia, 28 March 2013.
7 Conversation with author, Zorzor, Liberia, 2 August 2013.

national law of Liberia *is* law – he spoke of it in terms of "our own laws" – and there is no doubt it could be enforced against him, that he would feel it as one can only feel the law. At the same time, it is not law, not *his* law. How could it be when its laws are unknown to him? Like in the museum, in this man's response was a finger pointing past the official signs that hold up the national law of Liberia as "the organic law of the land",[8] to law in a form that is also not law. Like the museum's drum, the law in this form might "disseminate information" but it does not talk. Set down on the threshold of curated expression and the normativity of everyday life, it lacks the connection that would ground it and make it law; and yet it is the law of the nation.

Talking back

There is a Kafkaesque quality to the response of the man in the teashop to my enquiry about the rule of law, although Franz Kafka would not have been the first to reflect on how "it is an extremely painful thing to be ruled by laws that one does not know".[9] By "not knowing", Kafka was clear that he did not mean a simple lack of information about the laws,[10] as if disseminating information would be sufficient to overcome the problem. What is so painful about being ruled by laws that one does not know is the pain of not knowing "the very existence of these laws".[11] Existing entirely otherwise, no more than a secret code, the essence of which is pure mystery – to be ruled by such laws is the very definition of arbitrariness: it is "whatever the nobles do".[12] It is to be ruled in a way that denies you the possibility of talking back because the law does not talk to you. Left speechless, one option is to laugh at the absurdity; another is to, as Kafka put it, "repudiate the nobility" in a more forceful manner.[13]

The First Republic of Liberia was brought to a bloody end in 1980. Led by Master-Sergeant Samuel Doe, a 25-year-old African-Liberian man, the *coup d'état* was the culmination of a revolution that had been building since the 1960s (if not earlier) against the oligarchic Americo-Liberian regime that had ruled Liberia since 1847. The revolution's driving force was the pain experienced by the vast majority of African-Liberians, whose ancestors had known the lands of Liberia long before it was an idea, and who were reduced to a state of abjection, of civil death, as the idea was consolidated into a nation-state.[14] For African-Liberians, the pain that

8 This is how Liberians often refer to the national law of Liberia, as "the organic law of the land".

9 Franz Kafka, 'The Problem of Our Laws', in *The Collected Short Stories of Franz Kafka* (London: Penguin, 1988), 437–438.

10 Ibid.

11 Ibid.

12 Ibid.

13 Ibid.

14 The Liberian Truth and Reconciliation Commission also highlighted the connection between the unjust rule of the Americo-Liberian regime and the civil conflict in its final report: Republic of Liberia, *Truth and Reconciliation Commission: Consolidated Final Report: Volume 2* (2009), Part V.

drove the revolution and ultimately manifested in the bloody overthrow of the Americo-Liberian regime, precipitating the civil wars that engulfed Liberia in the 1990s and early 2000s, was the pain of being left speechless by the law of this regime, the existence of which was known to them through the ways in which it was enforced against them.

Kafka ends his parable on "the problem of our laws" not with the repudiation of the nobility, however, but with a paradox:

> Any party which would repudiate, not only all belief in the law, but in the nobility as well, would have the whole people behind it; yet no such party can come into existence, for nobody would dare to repudiate the nobility.[15]

Kafka summarizes the problem in a final line: "The sole visible and indubitable law that is imposed upon us is the nobility, and must we ourselves deprive ourselves of that one law?"[16]

Having dared to repudiate the nobility in the bloodiest fashion, with the overthrow of the Americo-Liberian oligarchy, Liberians are now facing a reversal of Kafka's paradox. With the national law opened up to the whole people, the "sole visible and indubitable law" has been broken. The one law that provided absolute certainty, in that its existence might be known at least in its enforcement against them, in "whatever the nobles do", has been shattered by a quarter-century of civil conflict that has left the State of Liberia in fragments. The question now is: how can law rule in Liberia when there is no longer a sole visible and indubitable authority to signify its existence? Existing entirely otherwise, the arbitrariness of the national law is no longer "whatever the nobles do" but whatever Liberia's different peoples do, in as much as they talk and talk back in so many different ways. For the Liberian man in the teashop, the pain of not knowing the very existence of "our laws" is now the pain of having to know the national law in its non-existence as a wholly given form. This is the pain of having to know a law that exists otherwise, as an unsettled concept that is substantial only to the extent that it takes form on the ground – which is also the pain of speech, of having to recognise that every act of articulation is only ever substantiated through the acts of others talking back.[17]

The national law of Liberia

In 2013 a coalition of civil society groups led by young aspiring political leaders threatened to orchestrate a massive day of protest on April 12, unless the Government of Liberia met its list of demands. Two grievances in particular were used to rally the masses in support of the protest: the failure to improve the economic

15 Kafka, 'The Problem of Our Laws', 437–438.

16 Ibid.

17 On the notion of talking back as a kind of "call and answer", see Desmond Manderson, *Kangaroo Courts and the Rule of Law* (Abingdon: Routledge, 2012), Chapter 9.

situation for the majority of Liberians, despite "ten good years of peace",[18] and the impunity with which the country's ruling class has continued to enrich itself through corruption.[19]

The significance of the chosen date for this rally – April 12 – was not lost on Liberians. It was on 12 April 1980 that the last Americo-Liberian government was overthrown in a revolutionary *coup* that brought to power Liberia's first "indigenous" government. More hauntingly, a year before the 1980 *coup*, almost to the day – 14 April 1979 – the capital was thrown into violent chaos as a similar planned demonstration descended into deadly riots and looting. The same two grievances had fuelled that protest, which became known as the 1979 Rice Riots: impoverishment of the majority and corruption of the ruling class. With this in mind, and with the civil wars of the 1990s and early 2000s still a living memory, there is little wonder that Monrovians saw in the proposed demonstrations of 12 April 2013, the spectre of violence and war. A passionate counter-campaign by a representative cross-section of Liberian civil society sought to persuade the organisers to call off the protest, for the sake of peace and stability[20]; which they finally did, but not without allegations and a widespread perception that the protest leaders had been "bought off" by the Government,[21] reflecting a profound distrust of people in authority.

What made this cynical view of political leadership striking was its juxtaposition with an apparent universal belief in the good of "the rule of law". All sides to the debate framed their arguments using the language of law and stressed how their actions were within the limits of the Constitution of Liberia. The Government's public position was that the protest would be permissible so long as the organisers followed "the rules and procedures allowing protests",[22] which in effect meant obtaining a permit from the Government. With such permission, "Government would not obstruct its citizens from exercising their rights as provided by the Constitution of Liberia".[23] The protest leaders refused to apply for a permit, arguing as a matter of constitutional law that they did not need one. "Peaceful

18 A number of times during my fieldwork I heard this phrase used by Liberians when critiquing the (in)action of the government.

19 In the words of one of the organisers, the protest was intended to give voice:

> to the cries of thousands of Liberians that are subjected to poverty in the midst of abundant resources [...] to champion the cause of the downtrodden masses for a better living condition and for an equitable distribution of our resources.
>
> 'The Storm Passes Over – April 12 Demonstration Suspended', *The Analyst*, Monrovia, 9 April 2013: http://allafrica.com/stories/201304090983.html?viewall=1

20 Ibid.

21 'Government Admits Bribing "April 12" Protesters', *The New Dawn*, Monrovia, 18 April 2013: http://allafrica.com/stories/201304180788.html

22 'Observing the Law in Protest', *New Democrat*, Monrovia, 1 April 2013: http://allafrica.com/stories/201304011077.html%3fviewall=1

23 Ibid.

assembly" – which is how they characterised the proposed demonstration – is protected under the Constitution and therefore, they argued, could be held lawfully without a permit. The Government rejected this argument and repeated its demand, eliciting from the organisers a blunt reply: "we are going to oppose it in the full concept of the rule of law of the Republic of Liberia".[24]

The national law, accepted

It seems clear that most, if not all, Liberians accept the national law of Liberia as the predominant form of law in the country today. What that acceptance means, and how deeply it resonates in everyday life, is much less clear. At least Liberians appear united in a common acceptance of the national law as a political ideal, as much as they accept the idea of Liberia as a nation-state. During the fervent and divisive debate that played out on the radio, in newspapers, and on the streets in response to the planned April 12 protest, which threatened to return Liberia to civil war, the single point of agreement was the need to "respect the rule of law", which meant ensuring the Constitution of Liberia and its law was upheld and not threatened by the actions of any group.[25] In this situation the common acceptance of the national law appeared to reflect a commitment to the idea of Liberia itself.

In line with this idealistic commitment, however, to some extent acceptance of the national law also appears to reflect resignation to what is seen as the inevitability of "modernity". Human rights – one of the core aspects of the concept of the rule of law promoted by national and international actors in Liberia – is exemplary in this regard. When I asked a Liberian scholar who researches in the field of legal anthropology in the country about how Liberians tend to perceive human rights, his response was to point out that "human rights are not going anywhere", that they are here to stay.[26] In other words, my question – premised on the notion that human rights is something that might be accepted or rejected – naively missed the point. According to him, for people in Liberia it is not a question of whether human rights might be, or ought to be, accepted or rejected; the question is *how* to accept it as part of their future. The same view was expressed to me by another Liberian scholar researching at the community level in the field of land rights. In a conversation about the shift that is currently taking place to a formalised system of land rights under a proposed national law that would require communities to precisely define their membership and the boundaries of their land, he did not see any reason to resist the change. Again, for him the question is not whether this shift *should* take place, because it *is* taking place. The question for him is *how* it takes place – and critically, whether those leading the change are "now *sincere* in trying to transform the society for the better".[27] "To me, that is more important as a question

24 'Planned Rally Invokes Violent Past', *New Democrat*, Monrovia, 9 April 2013: http://allafrica.com/stories/201304091169.html%3fviewall=1
25 For example, see newspaper articles in the previous footnotes.
26 Author interview, May 2013 (MC2).
27 Author interview, 15 August 2013 (MN5). The contrast he appears to have had in mind here is with the previous attempt at social transformation, following the

than the fact that the society will be transformed from what it was originally, because it's not like that anymore. Things have changed. You can't go back".[28]

It is not just university-educated Liberians in Monrovia who are resigned to a modernity defined by the nation-state and its law. There is a similar view amongst traditional leaders concerning changes to traditional practices considered repugnant to a modern nation, such as the use of magic to determine violations of traditional law and the cutting of girls' genitals as part of their initiation into womanhood. A female head *zoe*,[29] and "one of the most powerful traditional leaders in Liberia", is quoted as saying in response to a national push to abolish the traditional *sande* society:

> We know the country has changed. We are in modern days. So we are changing the system small small until we reach to the end. But it can't be the way they want it to happen, as quickly as they want it to happen. We're not ready for people to say, "No more Sande".[30]

revolution of 1980 (although he did not say this). From the Doe Government to Charles Taylor to the array of faction leaders and financiers living abroad, the consensus amongst historians and Liberians is that the people who led Liberia into war were acting out of self-interest rather than being "sincere" in trying to transform the society as a whole for the better. See also William Reno, 'Predatory Rebellions and Governance: The National Patriotic Front of Liberia, 1989–1992', in Ana Arjona, Nelson Kasfir, and Zachariah Mampilly (eds), *Rebel Governance in Civil War* (New York: Cambridge University Press, 2015).

28 Author interview with MN5.

29 Also spelt *zo*. The term, as noted in the *Historical Dictionary of Liberia*, is "used in Central and Western Liberia to refer to an individual, male or female, who is a respected elder. Often these individuals are considered to have medical and spiritual powers, as well". D Elwood Dunn and Svend E Holsoe, *Historical Dictionary of Liberia* (Metuchen: Scarecrow Press, 1985), 192.

30 'Female Circumcision Temporarily Stopped in Liberia', *PRI's The World*, 29 March 2012: www.pri.org/stories/2012-03-29/female-circumcision-temporarily-stopped-liberia. The terms *sande* and *poro* refer to institutions of "traditional society" in central and western Liberia, often called "secret societies". See, e.g., the entry for *sande* in Dunn and Holsoe, *Historical Dictionary of Liberia*, 153:

> A female sodality found among various peoples located in central and western Liberia. […] The main function of the Sande is to serve as an enculturative institution and to make the transition of girls to women. The Sande sessions in the past have lasted for three years. Among some groups, particularly the Vai, Gola and Mende, the main spirit of the society is represented by a helmet-masked figure which makes its appearance at important social events, such as the death of a prominent female. The male counterpart of this institution is the Poro.

See also the entry for *poro* in Dunn and Holsoe, *Historical Dictionary of Liberia*, 140:

> A male sodality found among several groups in central and western Liberia […] The society serves two primary functions. It is the main institution to enculturate young males and to formally carry them through the rite of passage from child to adult. In addition, the elders of the Poro serve as the intermediaries between the ancestors and the living, and thus act as the ultimate arbitors of asocial actions which affect the society. The female counterpart of this organization is the Sande society.

Liberians might be resigned to the idea of the national law under the Constitution as an abstract reality, but as the *zoe's* comment indicates, they are also contesting its implications. Far from accepting the changes as given, they are deeply engaged in how this new Liberia, and its law, takes form. In making the question of change a matter of *how* change takes place, rather than whether it takes place at all, Liberians are including their resistance within the process of transformation. "Resignation" as such is not the same as passive acceptance of, or absolute submission to, a given state. From this perspective "to resign" has a much more dynamic meaning than its popular definition suggests ("to give up" or "to yield" to the will of another). From this perspective "to resign" is not only to accept the given situation but also to "sign again", which is to reject what is given as something that signifies itself. Thus it is to accept the nation-state and the rule of its law as a modern reality *and* to have a hand in signifying what that means. Resignation to the national law of Liberia, in other words, can be seen as no less than an act of writing the land of Liberia into its given constitution.

The vast majority of Liberians appear to accept the national law as such for this very reason: because it represents an abstract expression of how they ought to be, as an idea, as a gesture, as a future state. At this moment in history – a moment when Liberia is beginning again as a nation post-war – law holds out a possibility of being together under the Constitution of Liberia. Whether for a Liberian on the street, a stakeholder in the political status quo, or a traditional leader, the national law is therefore acceptable because it is seen as a process of becoming, a change that is taking place, rather than an immediate order of things. Without doubt some Liberians accept the national law in a more grounded way, as a form of law that already more or less reflects and informs everyday life. However, for the vast majority the opposite appears to be the case: the national law is acceptable for the very reason that it is still *not yet law*. The blank space that was written into the Constitution in 1820 by the American Colonization Society, on the basis that it was an unsettled law, still underlies the Constitution of Liberia; and so it is as an idea with no grounding, with no settled content to speak of, that the national law is acceptable today.

Acceptance as such – as a commitment to an idea of how things ought to be, without conforming to how that idea ought to take form in practice (according to the conceptual schema of those who are promoting it as given) – is transgressive. It is to undermine what is given; to accept *and* to reject it at the same time. And indeed, for many Liberians, especially those who stand to lose power as the national law is strengthened, that is no doubt the point. For many traditional leaders, chiefs, and government officials more generally, acceptance of the national law is little more than a political gesture necessary to satisfy a system of patronage that is structured according to the model of the modern nation-state and the rule of its law. Certainly whenever I spoke with legal authorities in Liberia, whether "traditional", "customary", or "statutory", they were careful to repeat to me the official government position about the rule of law: chiefs are administrative and not judicial actors in accordance with the doctrine of the separation of powers; all criminal matters are to be dealt with by the national legal system; rape and other instances of sexual and gender-based violence must be apprehended as criminal conduct and not treated as "family matters"; communities are permitted to articulate their own laws as long as they are consistent with the national law as set out in the Constitution of the Republic; and so on. These messages were repeated to me precisely and formulaically in interviews, which is not surprising as they were the current focus of workshops, training sessions, and civic education campaigns being run by the government and international and national organisations to disseminate information about "the law". The messages were also widely contradicted in practice, however, leaving the distinct impression that the acceptance exhibited by these legal authorities was little more than a line expressed for the satisfaction of Western donors, the Government of Liberia, the UN Mission, and a researcher who might as well be an informant for those authorities.

The national law, subverted

On the periphery of the administrative square of a small town in Liberia's north-western foothills, on a slope leading down to a residential quarter, its zinc-panelled roof and flagpole only just visible from the other administrative buildings, I find the Chief's Office. The Office is similar in layout to the Magisterial Court located on the opposite side of the administrative square, except that the main room of the Chief's Office – its hearing room – is enclosed only by lattice with wide gaps in the woodwork opening it to the outside. Rows of wooden-plank benches in the middle of the hearing room lead up to where the chief and clerks sit under a Liberian flag pinned high on the wall. Columns of manila folders containing the Office's files are arranged on the only table in the room. Each column of folders contains files for the different areas of Office work, including a column of four folders containing Case Documents. The arrangement of these files, elevated on the desk next to the Chief's chair, is striking in a room with few other objects, with the exception of a large United States Agency for International Development poster on the wall below the flag illustrating the concept of "Alternative Dispute Resolution".

I am meeting with the Chiefdom Clerk to learn about the role of the Chief's Office. In the middle of describing the difference between the Chief's Office and the Magisterial Court – how the latter "deals directly with the Constitution" while the function of the Chief's Office is to "bring people together" and is not about "the law"[31] – a small group of women enter. I ask the Clerk if the women, who are sitting behind us, are waiting to speak with him. They are, and I offer to sit to the side while he hears from them. Two young women come forward and sit at the bench before the Clerk. One of them explains that she has come to see the Chief because her ex-husband is no longer abiding by their divorce settlement. The woman has made a complaint to another official, but the official said there is

31 Author interview with Paramount Chiefdom Clerk, 4 September 2013 (Li19). As a condition of my research I promised participants that I would not disclose identifying information, which includes specifying exact locations.

nothing he can do: he does not have the power to enforce the settlement. And so she has come to the Chief's Office. The Clerk then addresses the women. They should come back the next day with the other party and "all the papers" so the Chief will be able to assess the complaint. The Office has a record of the divorce on file setting out the settlement, he says, as evidence of the agreement. He appears to say this in order to assure the woman that enforcement will not be a problem. The two women thank the Clerk and promise to come back the next day.

Following this meeting with the Chiefdom Clerk I meet with a magistrate on the opposite side of the administrative square. The entry to the Magistrate's office is inside the small concrete-block building that houses the Magisterial Court, through the courtroom, past the bailiff and clerk, the rows of wooden benches leading up to the bar, under the Liberian flag spread above the Magistrate's courtroom desk and the door behind it, which is the door to the Magistrate's office. Sitting in the enclosure of this small room the Magistrate explains to me, in answer to a question about the kinds of matters that come before the Court, how the Magisterial Court has trial jurisdiction for minor criminal matters and that any case exceeding its jurisdiction is referred to the superior court located in the County capital. Having said this, he then explains how he usually seeks a compromise between parties out of court. To be clear, I ask if he conducts these out-of-court proceedings in criminal matters. He says he does. He then adds that he is well respected in town as a community leader and people trust him to help resolve their disputes. At the time of our meeting a young man and an older woman are also sitting in the Magistrate's office. To illustrate his point, the magistrate introduces them to me and explains that they are there to reach an understanding so they can return to the community. The young man is said to have assaulted the older woman, a neighbour in town.[32]

One of the most important rule-of-law messages being promoted during the time of my fieldwork was that chiefs, who are officers of the Ministry of Internal Affairs, and therefore part of the executive branch of government, perform an administrative and not a judicial function, in accordance with the doctrine of separation of powers.[33] As the Chiefdom Clerk said to me, in describing the difference between the Chief's Office and the Magisterial Court, the latter "deals directly with the Constitution" whereas the function of the Chief's Office is to "bring people together" and is *not*, he was careful to emphasise, about "the law". My point in describing the scene in the Chief's Office is not to suggest that the officials are wrong when they say – as they repeatedly did to me – that what chiefs do is "not law". From one perspective, the official perspective, it is no doubt true that what they are doing is not law. In hearing and resolving disputes in their

32 Author interview with Magistrate, 4 September 2013 (Li22).

33 For a summary of rule-of-law reform initiatives in Liberia, including the need for separation of powers, see Amanda C Rawls, 'Policy Proposals for Justice Reform in Liberia: Opportunities under the Current Legal Framework to Expand Access to Justice', *Traditional Justice: Practitioner's Perspectives* (IDLO Working Paper Series, 2011).

Offices, chiefs are conducting "alternative dispute resolution", they are dealing with "customary matters", they are doing "peace-building", and they are not performing a judicial function properly so called. At the same time, it certainly appears to be law, albeit in a confused form, combining different sources of authority in a way that leaves its conceptual definition open as to whether it is "the law" or otherwise.

One of the other important rule-of-law messages being promoted at the time was that all criminal matters are to be dealt with through the national legal system and not "informally" by community leaders. This message was being promoted in response to the fact that the vast majority of criminal matters – like almost all civil matters – are still dealt with at the local community level.[34] This is especially the case in north-west Liberia where traditional leaders are still powerful legal authorities, as well as in the south-east where traditional society remains strong.[35] In the Mandingo district of Quardugboni in Lofa County, for instance, only one matter – a murder case – had come to the superior court from Quardugboni in the past six or so years, according to an officer of the superior court in Voinjama, the capital of Lofa County. The reason, he thought, was "because of their beliefs", meaning they dealt with offensive conduct by community members under Islamic law.

This might undermine the national law, which is supposed to have exclusive jurisdiction over criminal matters, but it is not surprising in the case of Liberia that local legal authorities are continuing to enforce their communities' laws rather than refer violations to the national legal system. What is more surprising is that officials of the national legal system, including members of the police and judiciary, are *also* contradicting the official refrain that criminal matters are to be referred to the police and dealt with by the judiciary. This is more remarkable, and perplexing, because it is here, the point at which the national law is enlivened by its authorities on the ground, that the line separating what is "the law" and what is "not law" again dissolves. The result is an understandable confusion: the national law, in a form that both reflects and informs local law; the national law, in a form that is also not the national law and a local law.

Thus national legal officials, such as the magistrate in the small town in Liberia's north-western foothills, are dealing with criminal matters unofficially, in ways that might be said to pervert the course of justice by violating rule-of-law principles such as due process. At the same time, the unofficial treatment of criminal matters is taking place under the authority of the national law. Just as the columns of manila folders containing Case Documents could be seen to represent and thereby enhance the legal authority of the Chief's Office (despite not being, officially, an office of law), the symbolism of being a Court officer no doubt enhances the

34 See, e.g., Deborah H Isser, Stephen C Lubkemann, and Saah N'Tow, *Looking for Justice: Liberian Experiences with and Perceptions of Local Justice Options* (Washington, DC: USIP Peaceworks, 2009).

35 According to a prominent legal aid worker with a long history working in communities in the south-east of Liberia, traditional leaders are still the predominant legal authorities in all community-level disputes, including criminal matters: author interview with civil society actor, 26 September 2013 (Li35).

authority of the magistrate as a respected community leader. Just as what was taking place in the Chief's court under the sign of Alternative Dispute Resolution was "not law", and yet law in a certain form, what was taking place in the Magistrate's office under the sign of the Court was also not law, not officially, and yet surely law in a form for those whose disputes were dealt with in his office.[36]

Resolving disputes in the shadow of a courthouse, with and without the intervention of a judge who might order a first round of alternative dispute resolution, is not necessarily perverse. Nor is an out-of-court deal between the prosecution and an accused with the purpose of avoiding trial. However, something else was taking place here: it was clear that the Magistrate was acting as a mediator to resolve disputes, civil and criminal, through a process that was not the official one but that nonetheless derives its authority, like the Magistrate's reputation in town, from the national legal system. On one hand the criminal matters that are referred to the Magistrate are being dealt with "informally", in a way that might be said to pervert the course of justice by violating the principles of due process, the rights of the defendant, and the duty of the state to uphold the rights of the victim. On the other hand, the "informal" out-of-court proceedings are taking place with the authority of the national law. These matters must cross through the court to be resolved by the Magistrate, and yet they are resolved based on an approach that prioritises "peace" in the community over "the law" under the Constitution.

This magistrate was not alone in taking this approach. When discussing with two other magistrates in another district about the referral of criminal matters to the courts, they repeated the line to me that "all criminal matters are heard by the judiciary", before pointing out that some of these matters nonetheless "must be resolved at the community level" because "law doesn't necessarily mean peace".[37] Of six magistrates I spoke with in four Counties across the country, four emphasised this difference between "law" and "peace" and expressed a preference for taking a "restorative" or "peace-building" approach, while the other two commented on the value of out-of-court "mediation" without comparing it to the court process. The same view was shared by a prominent legal service provider whose profession is to promote the national law in communities through the provision of legal aid and education. Despite his obvious commitment to the national law he still held the view that only "serious" matters that cannot be handled by community leaders should be dealt with through the national legal system, such as violent crimes, otherwise disputes should be handled "informally", in a way that "brings the parties together". Taking these matters to court, he said, "only causes bitterness in the community".[38]

Subversion of the national law is not only occurring in the process of resolving disputes but also prior to that in the criminal justice system, at the point of police

36 See also Harry Arthurs, *'Without the Law': Administrative Justice and Legal Pluralism in Nineteenth-Century England* (Toronto: University of Toronto Press, 1985); Robert Mnookin and Lewis Kornhauser, 'Bargaining in the Shadow of the Law: the Case of Divorce', *Yale Law Journal*, vol 88, no 5 (1979).

37 Author interview with Magistrates, 12 September 2013 (Li7 and Li8).

38 Author interview with Li35.

apprehension. A Human Rights Officer with UNMIL told me about a case that had perplexed their Field Office.[39] The case involved a police investigation into conduct relating to female genital cutting. While the ritual cutting of girls' genitals was not a crime under the Criminal Code of Liberia, it was alleged that crimes had been committed in connection with this particular instance. The Liberian National Police, initially reluctant to investigate, eventually carried out an investigation under the supervision of UN Police and Human Rights monitors. The matter was referred to the County Attorney (as prosecutor) along with a brief of evidence; however, the case failed to progress through the court system and was eventually dropped. According to the Human Rights Officer it was clear that there was an unwillingness to prosecute these particular crimes. Despite being offences under the Liberian Criminal Code there was apparently "no shared understanding" about the imperative to prosecute. I asked whether the Human Rights Officer thought this reflected different understandings of what "the law" is in Liberia. The Officer responded by pointing out that the crux of the problem in this case was probably the fact that the prosecution and judicial officers did not see the crimes as "crimes".

However, on the assumption that the case had failed because the police and judiciary were operating incoherently, UNMIL facilitated a workshop with the aim of bringing together the local Liberian police and judicial officers to enhance their professional and institutional coordination and cooperation. The outcomes of the workshop included proposed reforms to the standard operating procedures for dealing with the transition from investigation to prosecution in general, and in particular for dealing with sexual offences, as well as the proposed creation of a liaison mechanism to coordinate and strengthen the relationship between the police and the judiciary. Thus the response was to treat the different understandings of the law as an information asymmetry, to be overcome with more and better information sharing.

It may be the case that the failed prosecution was a matter of inadequate institutional coordination between the Liberian police and judiciary. There is no doubt that the "justice-chain institutions" in Liberia are dysfunctional and can be improved with better operating procedures and mechanisms.[40] Even so, the issue here appears to have been fundamentally normative. It seems clear that the crimes were not prosecuted because they were also not crimes, as the Human Rights Officer observed, and as UNMIL appeared to recognise. From what the Human Rights Officer told me, and what I was told by other UN officers about the way the UN Police and Liberian National Police operate together, it seems that the matter in this case was only investigated and referred to the County Attorney for prosecution in the first place because of the intervention by the UN, both through the co-location of UN police with Liberian police and the watchful gaze of UN Human Rights Officers. The problem, in other words, was probably not the lack of institutional coordination or shared understanding between Liberian National Police and the judiciary, but precisely the shared understanding that, as a matter of

39 Author interview with UN officer, 21 June 2013 (NY8).
40 See, e.g., Isser, Lubkemann, and N'Tow, *Looking for Justice*.

local law, the case had no grounds. The practice of cutting girls' genitals is part of an initiation rite into *sande* society in many parts of Liberia and, as such, it comes under the authority of the female *zoes*. Any conduct carried out in the course of *sande* business would likewise come under the authority of the *zoes*. Subjects and authorities of this local law – including members of the police and judiciary – would have known that the conduct in question was within the jurisdiction of the *sande* society, and that the question of whether the conduct constituted a crime would have been decided under this law. What is more, given the law of secrecy that regulates traditional society, it is unlikely that this information would have been shared with the UN officers, as uninitiated outsiders. The incoherence, in other words, would not have been between the Liberian police and judiciary but between the UN officers and their Liberian counterparts.

It became clear in the course of my fieldwork that officers of the Liberian National Police tend not to intervene in traditional society, unless a dispute arises between communities or threatens the peace more broadly. This contradicts both the official role of the Liberian police as officers of the national law, as well as the refrain that all criminal matters are referred to the national courts. The police have this power as officers of the national law, and they do exercise it; the prisons are not vacant. Yet at the same time there are no grounds for the police, who are also subjects of local law, to investigate ritual killings and other forms of violence that are lawful under that law, even if there are grounds to do so under the Criminal Code of Liberia. The authority of the national law is still subject to the authority of local law, with officers of the judiciary and executive also subjects of local law.

The national law, ignored

Official authorities are not alone in undermining how the national law is taking form. Its subjects are also rejecting the national law, turning instead to "local" law in the resolution of disputes. In 2009 the United States Institute of Peace conducted the first extensive post-war study of "Liberian experiences with and perceptions of local justice options".[41] One of the study's most significant findings was a clear preference by Liberians across the country to use "customary dispute resolution processes" rather than resort to the "formal" legal system. The researchers identified a number of structural problems with the national legal system as reasons for this preference: it is considered unaffordable, inaccessible, untimely, non-transparent, un-accountable, corrupt, and simply ineffective in delivering "justice".[42] Underneath this structural dysfunction,[43] however, the researchers also identified a deeper normative problem: the national law articulates a fundamentally different approach to justice.

41 Ibid.

42 Ibid, 3.

43 I address the problems of structural dysfunction in the national legal system in Chapter 6.

> One of the most striking findings of our research is that most Liberians would still be unsatisfied with the justice meted out by the formal system, even if it were able to deliver on the basics discussed earlier [the structural problems]. This is because the core principles of justice that underlie Liberia's formal system, which is based on individual rights, adversarialism, and punitive sanctions, differ considerably from those valued by most Liberians.[44]

The perceived inappropriateness of the national legal system as a medium for resolving disputes was also a consistent theme in my conversations with Liberians. The reason for this is well-known and widely discussed in Liberia: the national law, based on the Anglo-American common law tradition of dispute resolution, is fundamentally at odds with the "restorative" approach that informs the African legal traditions in Liberia.[45] Unlike the national legal system, which seeks a determination of individualised cause and remedy through an oppositional trial process concerned with a temporally limited set of facts, the African legal systems in Liberia tend to be based on compromise and community well-being and a deep concern for the past and future.[46]

This is about more than what Liberians "value" as "core legal principles".[47] It is about a normative disposition that informs and reflects how Liberians tend to see the world. It is therefore unsurprising that this understanding of law and justice grounds the dispute resolution processes in communities throughout Liberia. This is certainly true of the "traditional" legal systems that still function in many parts of the country, but it is also true of "modern" dispute resolution processes being used by community peace-builders who are working to repair relationships fractured during the civil wars.[48] It is also true of how government officials, including national legal authorities, understand what is "appropriate" dispute resolution. This should not be surprising given the deep social roots of this approach in the world-views of Liberians. What makes this remarkable is that the difference in approach underlies one of the most perplexing dilemmas that rule-of-law promoters face in the country: the fact that traditional leaders, chiefs, magistrates, as well as the police and the population in general, are not engaging with the national law as they ought to, according to its official concept; and when they do engage with the national law, they do so in ways that undermine its conceptual schema.

This dilemma is a contemporary manifestation of the blank space that was written into the Constitution in 1820, reflecting the remaining groundlessness of the national law. One critical implication is that Liberians' repudiation of the national law has to be seen *in light* of its acceptance and not *in spite* of it. If the problem is seen in terms of the national law being rejected in spite of its

44 Isser, Lubkemann, and N'Tow, *Looking for Justice*, 3.

45 See also ibid, 69.

46 This was how a Liberian elder described the difference to me: author interview with civil society actor, 16 September 2013 (Li25). I consider these different approaches in more detail in Chapter 6.

47 See note 44 above.

48 See discussion of "community peace-builders" in Chapter 6.

acceptance, doubt is cast on its acceptance. If the law is rejected, then it cannot *really* be accepted, as it appears to be. The acceptance as such must be only apparent and not actual; it must be empty rhetoric, a political gesture, and nothing more. On this equation the solution that follows is to find ways to make "the law" more acceptable. Only then might the rule of law exist. If Liberians' repudiation of the national law is seen *in light* of its acceptance, however, rejection is not equated with a lack of acceptance but is seen as a *form* of acceptance. From this perspective, acceptance as such – as a rhetorical commitment to a groundless idea, as resignation, as a political gesture – is not merely "apparent", without "actual" substance, but a productive enactment. The law may not be taking form as expected, according to its concept, but it is nonetheless taking form. The dilemma, then – although now it begins to look less like a dilemma and more like an answer – is that acceptance of the national law is taking place in the form of repudiation.

This is no doubt frustrating for those who are attempting to institute the rule of law according to their own conceptual schema. For them, instituting the rule of law is not about supporting acceptance of the national law *as such*, but fundamentally about promoting *proper* acceptance, relegating any other form of acceptance to non-acceptance (rejection). Framing the intervention in terms of increasing rates of acceptance and decreasing rates of rejection may make the process seem more neutral, scientific – and therefore more legitimate – but it does not overcome the fact that what is taking place is an attempt to dictate the grounds of law according to a particular idea of it. This can be seen in the increasing use of "civic education" as a tool for developing the rule of law.[49] Recognising the subjectivity of law, interveners are using a range of media, including workshops and more general public awareness-raising campaigns, to teach Liberians law's "proper" conceptual schema.[50] The assumption underpinning these programmes is that the national law is not taking form on the ground as it ought to, because Liberians at large do not know how it ought to take form. The mistake, however, is in thinking that this ignorance – this not knowing – is simply a matter of a lack of information, to be resolved through the dissemination of more information about the concept of law. This is fundamentally about Liberians being out-of-order in their knowledge. To those who know "this" *is* the law, to know *this* otherwise becomes a negative infraction: it is to not know the law at all. But as a negative infraction, not

49 On the increasing use of "legal awareness" in United Nations rule-of-law assistance, see Richard Zajac Sannerholm and Frida Wall, 'Rule-of-Law Assistance in UN Peace Operations: Securitisation, Sectorisation and Goal Displacement', in Jeremy Matam Farrall and Hilary Charlesworth (eds), *Strengthening the Rule of Law through the United Nations Security Council* (Abingdon: Routledge, 2016). See also Richard Zajac Sannerholm, et al, *UN Peace Operations and Rule of Law Assistance in Africa 1989–2010: Data, Patterns and Questions for the Future* (Stockholm: Folke Bernadotte Academy, 2012).

50 See, e.g., the training manual developed by The Carter Center in Liberia, *Handbook for Civil Society Partners Community Education and Awareness Program on the Rule of Law* (2008): www.cartercenter.org/resources/pdfs/peace/conflict_resolution/liberia/Civil-Society-Partner-Handbook.pdf

knowing is of course also a form of knowing – it is just a form of knowing that does not register positively with the given concept. Just as repudiation is acceptance in negative form, to not know the law is to know law *otherwise.*

The littoral law of Liberia

When confronted with a law that does not talk with you, one response is laughter; another is to take the law in its given form and ground it in such a way that it *does* talk with you. Communities in Liberia are doing exactly this at the moment in the process of articulating what one government official referred to as their own Constitutions.[51] I was given a copy of one of these Constitutions, entitled the *Rules and Regulations Governing the Town of Killiwu.*[52] The choice of title reflects the national legislation that has regulated the lives of Liberia's "indigenous" peoples since 1905, and which since 1949 has been referred to as the *Rules and Regulations Governing the Hinterland.*[53] More generally, as a written text, its format and language reflects an Act of the Liberian legislature or of an official delegated authority. Thus on the face of it this Constitution expresses the law of Killiwu in an official form; and yet, just as the museum official had to point through the door to the street in order to give a full account of the "communication drum", this Constitution has to point through its text to another source in order to give a full account of the law. Or to put that another way, this Constitution too is defined by a blank space that must be known otherwise.

Section I(b) of the Constitution states: "All laws governing our sacred institutions (Poro, Sande, and their associates) shall be respected at all times by all persons living in the territorial limit of Killiwu Town". Section II(c) also refers to the "moral guidelines" set forth in the sacred institutions ("violators of 'section II b' shall pay a fine in addition to our sacred institutions as per their moral Guideline set forth"). And yet, apart from the prohibition on violence in section II(b), the Constitution does not specify the laws of the sacred institutions. Nor can it. Only those who are initiated through the sacred institutions might know and speak of its laws.[54] To specify these laws of Killiwu in this document would be to violate these laws of Killiwu. And so it is by pointing to the sacred institutions through a blank space that the Constitution of Killiwu succeeds in articulating law in an official form that nonetheless connects with its subjects normatively.

From the perspective of the people of Killiwu, this overcomes the contradiction in the national law. By leaving the text blank as to "the law", referring through it to the sacred institutions of *poro* and *sande*, the Constitution gives form to both "national" and "local" law. As an official expression of law – signed by officials of

51 Author interview with Li19.

52 *Rules and Regulations Governing the Town of Killiwu*, Zorzor District, Lofa County, Liberia, 8 August 2013.

53 *Revised Rules and Regulations Governing the Hinterland of Liberia*, Government of Liberia, 7 January 2001.

54 The "sacred institutions" of *poro* and *sande* ("and their associates") are often referred to as secret societies for this reason. See also note 30 above.

the Ministry of Internal Affairs and filed in the Office of the Paramount Chief – it is also grounded in and through the subjects of Killiwu. Thus the blank space of law, which opens the law to contradiction when it takes form, can be seen to provide a positive opening for the people of Killiwu to articulate their own law in conversation with the national law. This would be a littoral law *par excellence.* But as such, resolving the contradiction in this way – by having it talk back, by making the national law of Liberia fundamentally local – does not finally overcome the contradiction in law. The law, inverted under the Constitution of Killiwu, is at best inconsistent with and at worst repugnant to the national law under the Constitution of the Republic, with the law of the sacred institutions covering subject matter that the national government has arrogated to itself, and legalising practices that are unlawful under the national law. This includes the authority to take life. Indeed, in this form the law under the Constitution of Killiwu might be said to undermine "the rule of law". The charge might be that this verges on a state in which there is no proper ordering of law, where law takes form arbitrarily and in contradictory ways. Such an inordinate rule of law (the argument would go) is no such thing at all. And without doubt this does violate that sole and indubitable order of law. But in the harmony of voices that fearfully question whether it is wise "to deprive ourselves of that one law" – of certain order imposed from somewhere outside and above – and promote the rule of law as the very thing that would avoid such an inordinate state, the response continues to resound so discordantly on the ground: *how can you have the rule of law when we don't even know our own laws?*

Thus a contradiction that began with the constitutional act of 1820, when the Board of Managers of the American Colonization Society laid down a law defined by a blank space, continues to inform law in Liberia. However, as I have sought to show through this chapter, the contradiction does not undermine the national law of Liberia to the point that it is simply "not law". The national law might be subverted by chiefs and traditional leaders, it might be perverted by its own legal authorities, it might be ignored by its subjects, and ultimately flipped on its head – and yet at the same time, *and because of this*, the national law is taking form as law. Repudiation might define the plurality of ways in which the national law is accepted in Liberia today, its authority being undermined by its subjects and authorities alike, but this does not negate the fact of its acceptance nor does it completely negate its authority. On the contrary, its adverse treatment is what makes acceptance of the national law also the opposite of empty rhetoric, and what grounds its authority in Liberia. By making resistance a constitutive dimension of acceptance, the idea of the law under the Constitution of Liberia – an otherwise groundless vision of how things ought to be – is taking form on the ground in ways that leave it open to its responsive possibility as law. Undermined by a blank space, it has place to take root.

The result is an unavoidable pluralism in law – a pluralism that is not the perversion of legal order but its very life-blood.[55] Thus there remains an objectivity to

55 I discuss this further in Shane Chalmers, 'Law's Pluralism: Getting to the Heart of the Rule of Law', *Law, Culture and the Humanities* (2017): dx.doi.org/10.1177/

law, and legal ordering of the world, but to truly understand this law it also needs to be approached from the perspective of its subjects, to see how subjects, being made over by the law, are always also making over the law as their own.[56] Law might be seen to take form in contradictory ways as a result, with the law on the ground only law to the extent that it is also not the law, but then such is its life as law: a contradictory form that is acceptable precisely because it is defined by a blank space that requires its settlement to be written into it again and again. That is why for Liberians "the problem of our laws" is not whether the national law ought to be accepted or repudiated, but how it might be accepted *and* repudiated at the same time. In answer to Kafka's question – how is it possible for a people to repudiate the sole and indubitable law of the nobility? – Liberians appear to be answering: by accepting it *through and through*. Grounding it as their own, rather than rejecting it outright, the existence of the national law is no longer apparent in "whatever the nobles do" but in all manner of other ways.

1743872117707276 [print forthcoming]. See also Roderick A Macdonald, 'Custom Made – For a Non-Chirographic Critical Legal Pluralism', *Canadian Journal of Law and Society*, vol 26, no 2 (2011); Martha-Marie Kleinhans and Roderick A Macdonald, 'What is a *Critical* Legal Pluralism?', *Canadian Journal of Law and Society*, vol 12 (1997); Margaret Davies, *Law Unlimited: Materialism, Pluralism, and Legal Theory* (Abingdon: Routledge, 2017); Margaret Davies, 'Pluralism and Legal Philosophy', *Northern Ireland Legal Quarterly*, vol 57, no 4 (2006); Margaret Davies, 'The Ethos of Pluralism', *Sydney Law Review*, vol 27 (2005); Desmond Manderson, 'Beyond the Provincial: Space, Aesthetics, and Modernist Legal Theory', *Melbourne University Law Review*, vol 20 (1995).

56 See Macdonald, 'Custom Made'.

6 Facing the contradiction

Mediation of law

At the end of Chapter 3 I considered the Liberian Government's vision for the country post-war – a vision that suggests the continuation, if not intensification, of a logic that treats the subject as wholly an object of law (reifying their separation). In Chapter 4 I then examined the framework that promises to consolidate this vision through the establishment of a State based on the rule of law. This peace framework is informed by another logic that is supposed to resolve the contradiction in law by making the law identical with its subjects (plastering over the separation). In this state there would be no distinction between the subject as an object of law, and the subject as a subject of law. In this state, *the law is the law*. That analysis ended with a caution, however: the arrangement of "peace through justice" is a highly combustible one, requiring law's rule to be both forceful and just. This is a delicate balance at the best of times. It becomes especially fragile when the "justice" of law's rule is not in fact just, and merely violent, as during the First Republic of Liberia when the forceful justice represented and propelled by the image of Matilda Newport was experienced as an instrument of domination by the vast majority of Liberians.

It was with that in mind that I turned in the last chapter to examine how the national law is taking form on the ground post-war. This showed two things: one, the justice of the national law as conceived by the Government and its international supporters is not perceived as "just" by the majority of Liberians; but two, the national law is nonetheless taking form in ways that might make it just. Thus, against the logic of capital, which reifies the separation by rendering the subject wholly an object of law, law could be seen to remain an object of the subject of law. That is, the subject could be seen to remain a legal author/ity. However, this is not a situation in which "the law is the law". The subject might remain an author/ity of law, but this does not overcome the contradiction. Thus, also against the logic of security, the subjective expression of law and the experience of the law as expressed were seen to remain separate.

The analysis in Chapter 5 raises another problem, however. If the proposition "peace through justice" is to secure the state/State of Liberia, and not destroy it, the institution of the rule of law has to be open to the contradiction that makes the national law only law to the extent that it is also not law. That is, "peace through justice" requires the rule of an *illogical* law – a law that remains responsive to the contradictory demands of justice it confronts on the ground. The problem, in other words, is that such a framework for peace would be grounded in contradiction – indeed it would require facing the contradiction in law, and its rule, on a daily basis.[1] Whether, and how, such a response is possible is the question to which I turn in this chapter.

To answer that question I now take the third perspective, focusing on the "process of law". Recall that so far I have considered law in Liberia from two viewpoints. Thus Chapters 3 and 4 took the conceptual or articulate perspective, focusing on how law provides a medium for giving form to existence while providing a medium for different logics to inform its ends. Chapter 5 then took the nonconceptual or abject perspective, focusing on how law remains more and other than expressed, taking form in and through its subjects in a plurality of ways that contradict its given forms. Now neither of these two views is entirely satisfactory, as these chapters showed. Seen from the first standpoint, law risks becoming tyrannical, the act of articulation becoming an instrument of domination. Seen from the second standpoint, law risks becoming lawless, its expressions no more than what its subjects express it to be. Neither is entirely satisfactory, and yet neither can be entirely avoided. Law must remain *decisive*, giving form to existence, and law must remain *responsive*, articulating normativity in a way that leaves the law open to its subjects. The question now – the question of the "process of law" – is how to deal with this "double demand of modernity", as Peter Fitzpatrick puts it: "the demand for assured position integrated with a responsiveness to all that is beyond position, a demand to be met now without resort to erstwhile solutions of a transcendent kind".[2] If law is enlivened by these contradictory demands, indeed by the insatiable need for both, then where does this leave a legal system?

To answer that question I begin in this chapter by considering how law can become both over-mediated, articulating normativity "from outside", as well as under-mediated, articulating normativity "from within", and how the critical function of a legal system is to mediate the contradiction to ensure law does not come to rest on either extreme. I then turn to examine what is taking place in reforming Liberia's national legal system, and how it might be made responsive to the contradiction in law. On one hand this shows how a logic of "liberal internationalism" is exploiting both the separation and the nonseparation of subject and object simultaneously. Thus subjects are treated as subjects and not as mere objects to be worked upon; and yet at the same time their subjectivity is reduced to an empirical individuality that denies their subjective differences. As an empirical individual the subject becomes the object of a universal subjectivity that makes it

1 On the possibility of such a "rule of law", see Desmond Manderson, *Kangaroo Courts and the Rule of Law* (Abingdon: Routledge, 2012); Desmond Manderson, 'Modernism, Polarity, and the Rule of Law', *Yale Journal of Law and Humanities*, vol 24 (2012).

2 Peter Fitzpatrick, *Modernism and the Grounds of Law* (Cambridge: Cambridge University Press, 2001), 2.

not only legitimate but a categorical humanitarian imperative to assist in developing it to its full potential as such. This logic, I show, is informing the attempt to institute "the rule of law" in Liberia in response to the contradiction in law; but there are also other responses that point to a radically different "rule of law". It is upon this that I reflect in the book's Conclusion – on what the contradiction in law might mean for law's rule.

Over-mediated law

When an expression of law has little basis in its object, the law is potentially radically transformative, and potentially an instrument of domination. One way this occurs is when law does not articulate the normative disposition of its subject and instead articulates an other sense of normativity as the law and imposes that vision on them. This occurs "from outside" when the law is expressed primarily from a standpoint external to its subject. When the concern is to *transform* the subject as a normative matter, the intervention is from outside to the extent that it reflects an other's dissatisfaction with the norm more than internal revolt. Individuals and groups might come to identify with the law in this form and seek to bring their normative disposition in line with it from within. Even so, the more the law is used to bring about radical transformation, by imposing an other sense of how things ought to be, the more over-mediated law becomes, and the more likely the contradiction will manifest in a violent reaction.[3]

The intention might be to bring about social change by law, but it might also be concerned only with enforcement. Of course these alternatives are extremes: on one side, attempting to bring about a radical transformation by law from a standpoint that is set against the subject; on the other side, enforcing the law as given in total disregard of the subject. Yet despite their differences – one directed at transforming what is before the law, the other directed at enforcing what is posited by law – they are highly complementary. In the absence of a responsive dimension to the process of law, enforcement provides a means of containing the unavoidable reaction. Enforcement makes law "responsive" in a perverse way, with force providing a proxy for critical reflection. Through an enforced transformation, rather than a genuinely responsive one, an over-mediated legal regime might sustain itself, at least as long as those who control expressions of law also control the use of force.

Law enforcement is generally directed at informing the minds of subjects about "the law" through the use of force. The aim might be to bring subjects closer to the law as expressed, but it might merely be to make them *compliant* – to remind them of the law without necessarily intending to bring them closer to it as a

3 Sarat and Kearns discuss a similar approach to law in terms of "instrumentalism", which they contrast with a "constitutive" approach: Austin Sarat and Thomas R Kearns, 'Beyond the Great Divide: Forms of Legal Scholarship and Everyday Life', in Austin Sarat and Thomas R Kearns (eds), *Law in Everyday Life* (Ann Arbor: University of Michigan Press, 1993).

normative matter. Either way, enforcement is about overcoming the impotence of what is posited by law, by trying through force to make the law identical with the experience of its subjects, or at least *felt* by them. In modern state legal systems still one of the most popular means of achieving this is through the use of brute force.[4] With brute force the law is laid down on the bodies of subjects, with the rationale that this will inform their minds. In this way "the law" is brought closer to a subject as a matter of fact; and in a very real way, the law, brought violently into contact with the body, could be no closer. But as a normative matter, brute enforcement also has the opposite effect. By realising the contradiction in law with such visceral means, brute force acts to reify the separation of the law from its subject. The more brute force is used, the more the body recoils, the more the contradiction is reinforced as a physical reality, to the point where the law becomes a mere instrument of domination, bludgeoning the subject as if it were nothing more than an inanimate object. At this point the true nature of brute enforcement is clear: rather than working to bring the law closer to its subject, it *maintains* the contradiction in law through sheer force; and the result only aggravates the situation.[5]

A genuinely responsive law enforcement, by contrast, involves the use of force in a way that is critically concerned with a subject *as subject* – with the fact that every subject of law is always also a "law-maker" and not merely an object to be beaten into subjection.[6] A "responsive" use of force thus aims to bring about a change in behaviour from within the minds of subjects.[7] This is still a violent process. Whether brutish or responsive, the need for enforcement is always a function of law's impotence.[8] That law is always in a state of failure as a result of its separation from subjects is not the problem, however. The critical problem is not the fact of the contradiction in law, which makes the law a violent conceit, but

4 But compare this with the regulatory scholarship on other forms of regulation, such as the use of supportive tools to assist regulatees to comply: see, e.g., Ian Ayres and John Braithwaite, *Responsive Regulation: Transcending the Deregulation Debate* (Oxford: Oxford University Press, 1992); John Braithwaite, 'Fasken Lecture: The Essence of Responsive Regulation', *UBC Law Review*, vol 44, no 3 (2011); Neil Gunningham and Peter Grabosky, *Smart Regulation: Designing Environmental Policy* (Oxford: Clarendon Press, 1998); John Braithwaite and Peter Drahos, *Global Business Regulation* (Cambridge: Cambridge University Press, 2000); Hilary Charlesworth and Christine Chinkin, 'Regulatory Frameworks in International Law', in Christine Parker, et al (eds), *Regulating Law* (Oxford: Oxford University Press, 2004); Jeremy Matam Farrall and Hilary Charlesworth (eds), *Strengthening the Rule of Law through the UN Security Council* (Abingdon: Routledge, 2016).

5 This has motivated the search for alternative approaches to regulation, such as "responsive" and "smart" regulation; see, e.g., ibid.

6 See Martha-Marie Kleinhans and Roderick A Macdonald, 'What Is a *Critical* Legal Pluralism?', *Canadian Journal of Law and Society*, vol 12 (1997); Roderick A Macdonald, "Custom Made – For a Non-Chirographic Critical Legal Pluralism", *Canadian Journal of Law and Society*, vol 26, no 2 (2011).

7 Compare the work on "responsive regulation", e.g., Braithwaite, 'Fasken Lecture'.

8 On the "impotence" of law, see Chapter 2 of this book.

how the contradiction is dealt with. That is my concern in this chapter, in examining what is taking place in reforming Liberia's national legal system.

What the analysis shows is a Government supported by a coalition of international actors intent on reforming the national legal system in a way that would make it articulate normativity "from outside" the vast majority of its subjects. However, there is also a genuine responsiveness to the reform process that might ensure the national legal system articulates normativity "from within". The problem is that this is overshadowed by a "security sector reform" that is set to provide the Government with the means to enforce its law against the subjects who are talking back in the process of reforming the legal system. The result points to the institutionalisation of an over-mediated law that depends on brute force to uphold its rule.

Under-mediated law

Another set of problems arise when the medium through which law is expressed is dysfunctional. "Under-mediated", a legal system is incapable of mediating the articulation of normativity. To the extent that the system functions at all, what takes form as the law is no less arbitrary than when law's acts of articulation are over-mediated. The arbitrariness of the law is no longer that it gives expression to an other vision and forces subjects to conform to that vision. The arbitrariness of an under-mediated law is that law takes form subjectively, according to the contradictory ways in which its subjects give expression to it in everyday life, from moment to moment, without certainty, consistency, or equality. In other words, if the problem of over-mediation is the reification of the *separation* of law from its subjects, then the problem of under-mediation is the opposite: the more the articulation of normativity is under-mediated, the more the contradiction in law manifests in terms of the *inseparability* of law and its subjects. This is potentially no less violent than an over-mediated legal system. The more "the law" is indistinguishable from the normative disposition of the subject who gives expression to it, the more "the law" is disconnected from other subjects, for whom law in this form is only experienced as an arbitrary will. This is the "corruption" of law: when what is the law is indistinguishable from what a subject expresses it to be. This is "corruption" in the sense of dissolution: when the chasmic structure of law collapses to the point that "law" and "the law" appear the same. In this state, the will of the expressive subject is all-but equivalent to the law – and potentially terrifyingly so, the more powerful the subject.[9]

The more dysfunctional a legal system, the more prone law is to such corruption. Yet even the most dysfunctional legal system mediates the articulation of normativity to some extent and limits the degree to which law is merely a

9 Recall from Chapter 1 of this book that the "subject" might be an individual subject or a collective subject. Thus, as I discuss below, "the will of the subject" might be the will of a police officer on patrol who demands a bribe in the name of the law, or it might be the will of a mob who lynch a man in the name of the law.

subjective act of articulation. Law might be corrupted in the process, but there is still a system to speak of. When a situation is said to be "lawless" more often than not this reflects a failure to see the system that mediates the madness. Although that is not necessarily the case. It may be that there is no functioning system at all – no structuring medium – in which case law takes form *unmediated*. On one hand, this would be the absolute corruption of law; on the other hand, it would be the purest expression of normativity. Unmediated, law loses all positive constraint and takes form in an uncontrolled outburst: a subject giving immediate expression to how things ought to be at that very moment – indeed how they *will be*. At this point law and normativity collapse in on each other. As the articulation of normativity this is law in its most negative form; and as an entirely negative force it is incapable of articulating normativity in any positive way. As a result, law is wholly normative, and normativity wholly law: a form of law that is simultaneously the antithesis of law, and a form of normativity that cannot realise itself in any positive way. *This* is lawlessness: a pure expression of normativity without any positive dimension, erupting straight from its subjective source with all the force of law.

For those who know law primarily through a highly mediated legal system, and in terms of the orthodoxy of modern legal positivism, which sets "the law" in opposition to something called "lawlessness", an unmediated form of law – a law without jurisprudence, without institutions, without lawyers – can only appear lawless, as utterly other than what is the law. It may no longer be contentious to say that law takes many forms; however, it is still contentious to say that one of those forms is lawlessness itself. Acting lawfully and rioting are surely opposites: one respects the rule of law, the other manifests a complete disregard for it. And yet, as opposites, so-called "lawfulness" and "lawlessness" are identical in one decisive respect: both involve the articulation of normativity. The difference, which is a difference of quality, is *how* the act of articulation is mediated. That is my other concern here, which I turn to in the final part of the chapter in examining the dysfunction in Liberia's national legal system and its connection not only to increasing police and judicial corruption, but also rising incidences of mob violence. Both official corruption and mob violence, I argue, are instances of an under-mediated law, in which the law takes form in terms of the will of the expressive subject who articulates the law. I then return to the threatened "April 12" protests discussed in the previous chapter and consider how the threat of revolutionary violence might be understood in terms of an unmediated law.

Beginning again

Access to justice

In 2010, officers of Liberia's Ministry of Justice and the judiciary sat down with chiefs, traditional leaders and members of civil society for the first time since the end of the war to consider the relationship between "statutory", "customary", and "traditional" law in Liberia.[10] The occasion was the National Conference on Enhancing Access to Justice,[11] and on the agenda was the very contradiction in law: how the national legal system could be reformed in light of the fact that the national law is not law for the vast majority of Liberians, and other law is not law in fundamental ways under the Constitution of Liberia. In her opening statement the President of Liberia, Ellen Johnson Sirleaf, made clear that the Conference was about nothing less than beginning again, by facing this contradiction:

> If you look across Africa our peoples and governments have made significant progress in developing truly African approaches to justice. In many countries, diverse groups have come together and developed ways to enhance access to justice for all people – the rich, the poor, ethnic minorities and majorities alike. This conference should be the beginning of such a process in Liberia.[12]

The Minister of Justice echoed the President in her foreword to the report on the Conference proceedings: this "is not the end of the process – in many ways, it is a beginning", to make law "responsive to the basic desires and values of all Liberian people".[13]

Getting to this beginning was not straightforward. By 2010 the Government of Liberia might have "taken to heart" the importance of reforming the national legal system in light of the plurality of difference that animates law in the country,[14] but in the years leading up to that point, and even still, the idea of reforming the national legal system in light of law's pluralism has met strong resistance from government officials as well as Liberia's ruling class more generally. For foreign actors involved in the process,[15] it is obvious why members of government have resisted and continue to resist the idea. For those in power in Monrovia the national law as it stands *is* law. For the judiciary and members of the national legal profession, but also for Liberia's ruling class, with its predominantly

10 Author interview with UN officials, 24 May 2013 (MU1 and MU2). The term "statutory law" is used in Liberia to refer to the law articulated by Liberia's legislative and judicial organs of government. The term "customary law" refers to the law articulated by members of the Liberia's executive organ of government, primarily in the Ministry of Interior, most frequently chiefs. "Traditional law", by contrast, refers to the law articulated by "unofficial" organs, such as the sacred institutions of the *poro* and *sande* societies (see Chapter 5).

11 Held 15–17 April, 2010, Gbarnga, Bong County, Liberia.

12 Ellen Johnson Sirleaf, 'Special Remarks at the National Conference on Enhancing Access to Justice' (15 April 2010), 4–5.

13 Christiana Tah, 'Foreword from the Minister of Justice', *Report on the National Conference on Enhancing Access to Justice* (Monrovia: 2010), viii.

14 Amanda C Rawls, 'Policy Proposals for Justice Reform in Liberia: Opportunities under the Current Legal Framework to Expand Access to Justice', *Traditional Justice: Practitioner's Perspectives* (IDLO Working Paper Series, 2011), 4.

15 UNMIL, The Carter Center in Liberia, and The United States Institute of Peace were instrumental in initiating and facilitating the process leading up to and beyond the 2010 Conference on Access to Justice, over several years and against significant resistance from government.

Americo-Liberian heritage and/or socialisation in the US, "traditional law" is not law properly so-called[16]; rather, it persists anachronistically as an outmoded social form that will eventually wither away with modernisation.[17] From this perspective, if Liberia is to "modernise" then the only logical development is towards the abolition of traditional law.[18]

This mindset might be at an extreme end of how Liberia's ruling class thinks about legal pluralism in the country, but there is at least a common reluctance to commit scarce resources to strengthening "traditional practices" in the course of establishing a state based on the rule of law. As a UN official said to me, reflecting on the difficulty faced by UNMIL in convincing the Government to "buy-in" to the process that led to the Access to Justice Conference: "They see no reason why we should be spending time and energy on other law".[19] This is not surprising, given that many if not most members of Liberia's ruling class have no connection with "other law". The same UN official, echoing what I heard elsewhere, put it like this: "How do you sell this idea to people who are not subject to it, and will never be subject to it – and in any event, over generations, over a hundred years, it hasn't ever applied to them?"[20]

For many politically and economically powerful Liberians, returning to the country from abroad post-war and concerned with turning Liberia into a modern "middle-income country",[21] there is nothing self-evident about the need to address law's pluralism.[22] Or at least, if the problem was initially recognised, then

16 Thus it is called "informal justice", "traditional justice", "customary justice", "alternative dispute resolution", amongst other terms, but not "law". This reflects the terminology used by international actors as well as Western governments. For instance, in 2007, in explaining why Australia voted against the *United Nations Declaration of Indigenous Peoples Rights*, Australia's Ambassador to the UN, Robert Hill, argued that "[c]ustomary law is not 'law' in the sense that modern democracies use the term; it is based on culture and tradition", effectively limiting law properly so-called to "state law" and repeating the positivist cliché that state law has no basis in culture or tradition. See UN Doc A/61/PV.107 (13 September 2007), 11; see also Laura Grenfell, *Promoting the Rule of Law in Post-conflict States* (Cambridge: Cambridge University Press, 2013), 54. For a critique of the orthodox separation of "law" and "culture", see Macdonald, 'Custom Made'.

17 Grenfell makes a similar observation with respect to the attitude in many international organisations: see Laura Grenfell, 'The UN and "Rule-of-Law Constitutions"', in Farrall and Charlesworth (eds), *Strengthening the Rule of Law*, 128.

18 This is how one senior member of the national legal profession sees it. When asked by UNMIL officers about the idea of initiating a process to "harmonise" statutory law and customary law, I was told he replied: "Why do you want to do this? Let's just abolish this customary law. Let's just have the statutory system". Author interview with MU1 and MU2.

19 Ibid.

20 Ibid. The same point was repeated by another informant working within the Ministry of Justice: author interview with government officer, 28 May 2013 (MG3).

21 See Republic of Liberia, *Agenda for Transformation: Steps Toward Liberia Rising 2030. Liberia's Medium Term Economic and Development Strategy (2012–2017)* (Monrovia: Republic of Liberia, 2012).

22 See also Peter Chapman and Chelsea Payne, '"You Place the Old Mat with the New Mat": Legal Empowerment, Equitable Dispute Resolution, and Social Cohesion in

it was not prioritised as such in the first six years of post-war reform. Whatever the reason for this, significant persuasion was required to get the Government to the point of beginning again. UNMIL might take credit for getting the Government to this point,[23] but as an organisation and as a mission UNMIL was even less prepared to see the need to address law's pluralism as part of its mandate to provide "rule-of-law reform" assistance. To start with, the UN Security Council resolution establishing UNMIL did not give it an explicit mandate to do so, nor has the Council done so in subsequent resolutions amending the Mission's mandate. The work done by UNMIL's Legal and Judicial Services Support Division on "informal justice systems", which largely underwrote the Access to Justice process, only came about as a result of a generous interpretation of the mandate by UN officials who took a personal interest in the issue of legal pluralism.[24]

The turning point in the process came in 2009 with the publication of the United States Institute of Peace study led by Deborah Isser, Stephen Lubkemann, and Saah N'Tow, of "Liberian experiences with and perceptions of local justice options".[25] Building on the work of Liberian common law jurist, Philip Banks, this was the first in-depth empirical study of "how both formal and customary justice systems are perceived and utilized by Liberians".[26] As discussed in the preceding chapter, the results provided undeniable evidence of the relevancy of local legal systems for the vast majority of Liberians, and the impotency of the national legal system. At the same time, with the backing of UNMIL's Legal and Judicial System Support Division, as well as The Carter Center Liberia, the US Institute of Peace facilitated the formation of a Legal Working Group made up of Liberian scholars from government, the national legal profession, and civil society.[27] The Legal Working Group's terms of reference were "to engage both members of the legal community and traditional leaders in discussions about justice reform in Liberia, in particular regarding the dual legal system".[28] Their findings, reflecting the US Institute of Peace study, confirmed the need to address the serious "capacity and legitimacy shortfalls" of the national legal system.[29] Indeed the "key policy question" asked by the Group in light of the national legal system's "legitimacy shortfall" was how to make the national law more reflective: "As Liberia considers the future of its justice, how can it move toward a system that inclusively reflects the values of the Liberian people?"[30]

Post-Conflict Liberia', *Open Society Justice Initiative* (autumn 2013), 15. Chapman worked for The Carter Center Liberia at the time, while Payne was the Country Representative and Access to Justice Project Lead for The Carter Center Liberia.

23 Author interview with MU1 and MU2.

24 Ibid.

25 Deborah H Isser, Stephen C Lubkemann, and Saah N'Tow, *Looking for Justice: Liberian Experiences with and Perceptions of Local Justice Options* (Washington, DC: USIP Peaceworks, 2009).

26 Ibid, 3.

27 Author interview with MU1 and MU2; see also Rawls, 'Justice Reform in Liberia', 2.

28 *Findings of the Legal Working Group* (Monrovia: adopted 10 December 2009), 1.

29 Ibid, 5.

30 Ibid, 7 (my italics).

The recommendations of the Legal Working Group, combined with the US Institute of Peace study and feedback from a series of national consultations held in the lead-up to the 2010 Conference, amounted to a call that could not be ignored by government; and yet the mindset that gave rise to the Government's initial resistance had not changed. All of this culminated in the 2010 Conference on Access to Justice, and the result was a fundamental tension running through the proceedings. A US lawyer who was working within the Liberian Ministry of Justice at the time, and who was close to the process, notes that the Government's preference was always "for building trust in the formal legal system and using law and policy to change beliefs and behaviors".[31] At the same time the Government could not ignore the evidence that Liberians not only use, but prefer, their "local" legal systems.

The Government's preference for a policy of social transformation thus came up against the need to make the national legal system more reflective, or at least more responsive to Liberia's diverse social body. To the Government's credit, the fact that the Conference took place with high-level attendance, on top of a series of nationwide consultations, demonstrated a degree of responsiveness by the Government. And yet the responsiveness was highly selective, framed by an ideological opposition between what is thought "modern" and what is denigrated as "traditional". For the organisers of the Conference – the Ministry of Justice, the Ministry of Internal Affairs, and the Supreme Court[32] – the bottom line running through the Conference was that the very integrity of a "modern" legal system does not admit certain aspects of "tradition". Or more to the point, if the national legal system is to be reformed as one of the core institutions of a "modern" Liberia, it cannot *also* be "traditional". Other systems of law might be part of the national legal system, but they must be modernised in the process. This is what is meant by "harmonisation", the catchword used by the Government under the influence of its international partners to describe their solution to law's pluralism. Like the pre-1980 policy of National Unification,[33] national harmonisation is directed at resolving the problem of pluralism by ensuring local expressions of law are at one with the national law, dissolving *them* within *it* without compromising the integrity of the national legal system.

This limited responsiveness is reflected in the way the organisers of the Conference framed the proceedings in their agenda.[34] The three main discussion themes were "enhancing customary justice", "enhancing the formal justice

31 Rawls, 'Justice Reform in Liberia', 6.

32 The official organisers were the Ministry of Justice, the Ministry of Internal Affairs, and the Supreme Court, "with support from the Ministry of Gender and Development, the National Traditional Council, the United States Institute of Peace, the Carter Center, the United Nations Mission in Liberia (UNMIL), the United Nations Development Programme (UNDP)": *Report on the National Conference on Enhancing Access to Justice* (2010).

33 Discussed at the end of Chapter 3.

34 *Report on the National Conference on Enhancing Access to Justice* (2010), Annex 1, 68–74.

system", and "reforming both systems to increase access to justice for all Liberians".[35] The session on "enhancing customary justice" was set to open with a discussion of "the empirical data on onerous customary practices" and "potential mechanisms that could be developed to address such practices in the customary system".[36] The subgroup was then to consider two questions in breakout sessions:

> Breakout Question 1: *How should trial by ordeal be addressed?*[37]
>
> - What are the alternatives to trial by ordeal?
> - Apart from making trial by ordeal illegal, what steps can the Government of Liberia take to discourage the practice?
>
> Breakout Question 2: Cooperation between the formal and customary systems. *How can we change the way the two justice systems interact to better address issues of customary beliefs and practices that the formal system finds problematic?*
>
> - Should there be specific types of cases that are under initial jurisdiction of the customary system?
> - How should cases be appealed from the customary system?
> - How can the formal system provide better alternatives to problematic customary practices?[38]

Meanwhile another subgroup was to consider "enhancing the formal justice system", beginning with consideration of "the empirical data on unjust practices in both systems [...] before beginning a discussion of potential mechanisms that could [be] developed to address [the] problems".[39]

> Breakout Question 1: Making formal courts more effective in rural areas.
>
> - How can the Government best combat corruption, and prevent bias in the formal system?
> - When corruption or bias is encountered in the formal system, how should the parties, chiefs, or other leaders respond?
>
> Breakout Question 2: Relationship between formal courts and customary Chiefs.
>
> - What types of cases should be heard first by traditional leaders?
> - What types of cases should be heard first in formal courts?[40]

35 Ibid.
36 Ibid, 70.
37 "Trial by ordeal" is the English term used to describe judicial procedures for determining guilt and innocence. "Sassywood", which is often used synonymously for trial by ordeal in Liberia, is one such procedure, whereby poison extracted from the bark of a tree is administered in the form of a drink to the accused person.
38 *Report on the National Conference on Enhancing Access to Justice*, 71 (italics in original).
39 Ibid, 72.
40 Ibid.

The juxtaposition of these two sessions is revealing. While discussion of the "formal justice system" focused on its institutional dysfunction – ineffectiveness, corruption, bias – discussion of "customary justice" focused on the "traditional practices" themselves, and specifically on their unacceptability. To put this another way, the normativity of the formal system was never put in question, while "onerous customary practices" framed the line of enquiry on "enhancing customary justice".

It is also not surprising that "trial by ordeal" was singled-out as exemplary of "onerous customary practices".[41] Trial by ordeal represents in spectacular form precisely what modernity has worked so hard to overcome, and what a modern-liberal ideology finds so repugnant: a theory of causation that uses a powerful ritual to enact a knowledge of what is right that does not separate out the individual person from the community.[42] As a method of addressing conflict within a community, trial by ordeal is not about what is right for any particular individual but what is right for individuals-in-community. In this, both scientific knowledge and individual rights are stepped over by a rationality that does not stop in the final analysis at the individual human or individuated cause and effect. To a liberal mind, especially one initiated into the Anglo-American common law, what appears to take place in a trial by ordeal is thus a violation of "natural justice": a potentially innocent individual suffering harm without being accorded due process (based on a scientific determination of guilt).

Such "traditional practices" are intolerable to the international interveners engaged in reforming Liberia's legal system, such as The Carter Center, the US Institute of Peace, and the UN,[43] whether because they personally find such practices repugnant from a liberal standpoint, and/or because institutionally they are required to uphold the normative order of international human rights law. The result is also intolerable to members of the Government of Liberia, whether because of their personal convictions (many having been raised and/or educated in liberal societies such as the US), or because funding from Western states and international organisations is contingent upon ensuring the national law is "consistent with international human rights norms and standards".[44]

41 On "trial by ordeal" see note 37 above.

42 On how modern law takes its identity in opposition to such mythical forms, see Peter Fitzpatrick, *The Mythology of Modern Law* (Abingdon: Routledge, 1992).

43 As the UN Secretary-General wrote to the UN Security Council in a 2016 report on UNMIL: "Deeply entrenched harmful traditional practices such as female genital mutilation, forcible initiation into secret societies, trial by ordeal and ritualistic killing, which disproportionally affect the most vulnerable, including women and children, have had a negative impact on human rights": UN Doc S/2016/968 (15 November 2016), para 18. That might be so, but framing these practices in this way represents an arrogance marked by a refusal to attempt to see what these practices mean for the Liberians who practise them. To take the easiest example, what is "forcible initiation into secret societies" from one perspective is "going to school" from another; indeed, it would be just as easy to frame a Western educational system as "forcible initiation into a secret society" (see the discussion of the *poro* and *sande* "secret societies" in Chapter 5).

44 See the UN Secretary-General's definition of the rule of law, which requires a state's laws to be "consistent with international human rights norms and standards": UN Doc S/2004/616 (23 August 2004), para 6.

And yet, despite this commitment to a liberal normative order, and a policy of changing Liberians' beliefs and behaviour to bring them in line with it, the Government opened these questions up to debate during both the pre-Conference consultations and the Conference itself. And the result was *truly modern*: a littoral cacophony.[45] Having framed the debate in a way that reflected the organisers' standpoint, presumably with the hope of directing discussion towards the "right" answer, the response was a resounding chorus of voices supporting "onerous customary practices", and above all trial by ordeal (also referred to here as sassywood):

> A Maryland chief from the National Traditional Council noted that there is a need to understand what is meant by trial by ordeal.
>
> A National Traditional Council Chairman from River Gee added [...] we need to distinguish genuine sassywood from fake sassywood.
>
> The Paramount Chief from Bong County agreed that there is a need to test sassywood practitioners to check if they are genuine. However, he added that the Government cannot do away with the tradition. He asked whether the Government was willing to change its Constitution.
>
> The National Traditional Council Chairwoman from Bong County said that sassywood is effective, but human rights are confusing traditional justice cases.
>
> A female Clan Chief from Nimba County said that the administering of sassywood is good. She gave an example of one Kollie-tambo who used to perform his Marico (traditional drum) to identify witchcraft during President Doe's time.
>
> A representative from the Ministry of Gender and Development noted that people do not want to give up sassywood, and that there are no alternatives to sassywood in certain cases.
>
> A Women's Representative from Grand Cape Mount pointed out that there are non-harmful ways of administering sassywood. She also noted that magic is real.[46]

This, then, was the beginning for a government that could no longer deny the need to be responsive but found itself caught between an agenda for transformation and subjects demanding greater critical reflection in the process of reforming the national legal system. It is this tension, running through the dialogue that

45 See Manderson, *Kangaroo Courts.*

46 These "voices" are recorded in the official report on the Conference proceedings: *Report on the National Conference on Enhancing Access to Justice*, 31–34. On law and magic in a different context, see Miranda Forsyth and Richard Eves, 'The Problems and Victims of Sorcery and Witchcraft Practices and Beliefs in Melanesia: An Introduction', in Miranda Forsyth and Richard Eves (eds), *Talking it Through: Responses to Sorcery and Witchcraft Beliefs and Practices in Melanesia* (Canberra: ANU Press, 2015); Miranda Forsyth, 'A Pluralist Response to the Regulation of Sorcery and Witchcraft in Melanesia', in Forsyth and Eves (eds), *Talking it Through.*

began in the wake of the US Institute of Peace study and into the Conference sessions, that ensures "access to justice" remains a critical concept in Liberia, denying the possibility of law becoming a positive expression of either a "modern-liberal" or a "traditional-customary" mindset. For the Government and its international supporters, who continue to see the national law as the only law properly so-called, access to justice means overcoming the "justice vacuum" that results from not having a functioning national legal system.[47] If other systems of law have to be brought within the national legal system to make it effective, then those other systems must become "modern" in the process.[48] At the same time, for very many Liberians, access to justice has the opposite meaning: if the national legal system is to be truly modern, then it must be capable of articulating normativity "responsably", in a way that is able to respond to the normative disposition of its subjects.[49]

Security sector reform

If this is the possibility of beginning again, to make Liberia's national legal system more responsive, it is taking place in the shadow of another process that currently dominates national and international efforts to establish Liberia as a state based on the rule of law. As UNMIL began to draw down its military and civilian components, with a complete withdrawal scheduled for the end of April 2018,[50] building the capacity of Liberia's "security sector" became the main priority for the first time since the peace operation began in 2003.[51] Fearful of a security vacuum that would allow non-government actors to challenge the Government's monopoly on the use of force, especially in the interior, the Government's priority was to build the capacity of its police force. As discussed in Chapter 4, one of the main security sector projects at this time was the development of five Regional Justice and Security Hubs, a project that appears to have very little to do with the kind of "access to justice" being discussed at the 2010 Conference and everything to do with strengthening the police force in the interior. But as such, the Hubs are entirely consistent with the Government's preferred direction on "access to justice". Indeed, the Hubs were originally conceived by the Government as regional command centres for the Liberian National Police to have "forward operating bases" in the interior.

47 See *Report on the National Conference on Enhancing Access to Justice*, 71.
48 See also ibid, 71–72.
49 "'The law' thence would be an unconditional law of utter responsiveness to the other, a responsability, to revive an old usage". Peter Fitzpatrick, 'The Revolutionary Past: Decolonizing Law and Human Rights', *Metodo: International Studies in Phenomenology and Philosophy*, vol 2, no 1 (2014), 128.
50 UN Doc S/Res/2333 (23 December 2016), para 10.
51 As discussed in Chapter 4, while "security sector reform" was part of UNMIL's mandate since 2003, building the capacity of Liberia's security sector, with a focus on the Liberian National Police in particular, only become the top priority with UNMIL's withdrawal. See also UNMIL's updated mandate for the anticipated final year of the mission: ibid, para 11, and see para 17.

It is surely no coincidence that, just as the Government and its international supporters began to focus their attention and resources on security sector reform and building up a police presence in the interior, the initiative on "access to justice" began to go backwards. After the 2010 Conference an inter-ministerial Committee on Access to Justice was formed to consider policy options on legal system reform in light of the recommendations coming out of the Conference. Since then nothing has happened. Not only has the Committee not built on the momentum leading into the Conference, but in 2013 a newly appointed Solicitor-General, taking over the Chair of the Committee, was considering returning to the start with more research and consultations.

Thus at the same time as the Government was being held to account at the 2010 Conference on Access to Justice in a way that was offering a glimpse of the possibility of the national legal system being reformed in light of its "legitimacy deficit", the Government was moving ahead with a deal to build a series of Justice and Security Hubs in the interior.[52] Brought together within the same complex, "justice" and "force" would complement each other just as the Government and the UN hoped they would: a new police force deployed in the interior, with courthouses and lawyers co-located on-site for processing offenders of the national law. Without the need for the hard critical reflection demanded by the delegates at the 2010 Access to Justice Conference, the national law *would be* law.

Legal empowerment

Thus the 2010 Conference on Access to Justice might have represented a new beginning in a national dialogue on legal system reform in Liberia, but it is not taking place in isolation. Outside of these meeting rooms both government and communities across Liberia are working to strengthen their hand in the reform process. For the Government this largely means strengthening the "security sector" to maintain "peace and stability" as it pursues its policy of transforming beliefs and behaviour. For many communities, however, it means strengthening their capacity to engage with the Government and international actors to ensure they remain responsive in the process of reforming the legal system.

To this end, local and international non-government organisations are working to empower Liberians as both subjects and authorities of law. The two most prominent NGOs working in this field of "legal empowerment" are The Carter Center and the Liberian Catholic Justice and Peace Commission. These two organisations work in partnership to provide legal advisory and dispute resolution services in communities, and to strengthen traditional leaders' dispute resolution capabilities. While The Carter Center provides financial, technical, and capacity-building support to the Justice and Peace Commission, primarily in the form of

52 For a global perspective on the rule-of-law industry that also helps explain the lack of concern for justice on the ground, see Veronica L Taylor, "Big Rule of Law©®^{SMTM} (pat. pending): Branding and Certifying the Business of the Rule of Law", in Farrall and Charlesworth (eds), *Strengthening the Rule of Law*.

"monitoring and mentoring",[53] the Justice and Peace Commission engages directly with Liberians through its nationwide network of offices. The major component of their legal empowerment work takes place through their Community Justice Advisor programme, a national legal service that employs and trains local Liberians to provide free legal education, advice, and dispute resolution services to towns and remote communities throughout the country.[54]

The Carter Center and the Justice and Peace Commission are not alone in this work. The Norwegian Refugee Council pioneered a community-based dispute resolution and legal education programme in relation to land, and the Liberian Sustainable Development Initiative has been at the forefront of policy development on land rights and dispute resolution. Other local and international NGOs are carrying out similar work in the area of human rights. What brings these otherwise distinctive organisations together is their approach to law's pluralism. At the heart of their work is a motivation to "bridge the gap" between different systems of law, by increasing Liberians' knowledge of and material access to the national legal system while at the same time supporting community legal systems. As two practitioners who worked on the Access to Justice Project for The Carter Center in Liberia explain: "Legal empowerment can promote locally driven processes of change capable of supporting peaceful and equitable outcomes in the near term, while simultaneously enabling citizens to influence institutional structures". "Rather than taking a top-down, Monrovia-centered approach, supporting legal empowerment can provide a means to incorporate community aspirations into justice reform".[55]

Such legal empowerment thus seeks to bring about social change "from within", transforming the legal landscape in a way that respects and even strengthens local systems of law. At the same time, however, it has a missionary agenda: to bring about normative transformation according to a modern-liberal understanding of right. Just as the organisers of the 2010 Access to Justice Conference were selective in their response to what "legal system reform" might look like in a modern nation-state – tolerating the idea of bringing other systems of law within the national legal system as long as they are harmonised with it in the process – the organisations working to support legal empowerment in Liberia are selective in what can be "empowered". And the limit of their tolerance is more or less the same, based on a particular view of what they deem normatively acceptable. In short: if legal empowerment is directed at bridging the gap between

53 See The Carter Center, *Handbook for Civil Society Partners – Community Education and Awareness Program on the Rule of Law* (Monrovia: TCC, 2008). See also Walter Leitner International Human Rights Clinic, *A Handbook for the Justice and Peace Commission: Best Practices of Community Legal Advice Programs, Program Assessment and Recommendations* (Fordham Law School, 2008), commissioned by The Carter Center and the Justice and Peace Commission.

54 See also Chapman and Payne, '"You Place the Old Mat with the New Mat"', 26.

55 Ibid. On legal empowerment, see Stephen Golub, 'The Legal Empowerment Alternative', in Thomas Carothers (ed), *Promoting the Rule of Law Abroad: In Search of Knowledge* (Washington, DC: Carnegie Endowment for International Peace, 2006).

local and national systems of law, then the "bridge" is conceived as a one-way route to a liberal Western modernity. For instance, from my conversations with the members of these organisations who were working on legal empowerment, it was clear that their vision is circumscribed by a commitment to human rights as the standard of what is acceptable,[56] and by a concept of the state that admits only one legal system within which all expressions of law must be harmonised.

This vision of legal empowerment hardly diverges from that of the Government and Western international interveners, and in this sense remains over-mediated to the extent that it is under-written by an agenda to transform the minds of Liberians according to an other normative disposition. There are differences, however, in how these legal empowerment actors are trying to achieve their mission. For one, rather than deploying security forces they are providing Liberians with information through education campaigns and material access to the institutions of government.[57] Another important difference is the involvement of Liberians. The Carter Center, the Justice and Peace Commission, the Norwegian Refugee Council, the Sustainable Development Initiative, as well as others working on legal empowerment, could not do this work without Liberians responding to their offers of support. Many Liberians that engage with these organisations want to influence the changes taking place in their country. In this way the legal empowerment initiatives are also dependent on the organisations being responsive to the communities they are motivated to transform.

These differences matter. While the members of the organisations with whom I spoke were unapologetic about their organisations' missionary agenda, what that actually means, at this point in history, is not obvious. The parallel with the nineteenth-century colonial mission to civilise Africa, and the use of equivalent "legal empowerment" and "rule-of-law reform" interventions to realise that vision, is striking. But the conclusion that what is taking place in post-war Liberia is simply a neocolonial intervention is complicated by the fact that the current process in Liberia is being led in fundamental ways by Liberians. A powerful example is the women's movement in Liberia. Throughout the country there is a broad constituency of women aligned with the national and international intervention to end "onerous customary practices", such as female genital cutting, and more broadly patriarchal domination, which finds expression in the extremely high rates of violence against girls and women by men. For these women – who greatly influenced the election and re-election of Ellen Johnson Sirleaf to the Presidency in 2005 and 2011 – the national legal system holds out the potential to provide a critical medium for challenging oppressive community norms and articulating another vision of how they can continue to be together with men.[58]

As such, "legal empowerment" is about working with Liberians to bring about a normative shift that is already taking place but remains contentious – to bring about a

56 See also the discussion of the perceived inevitability of human rights in Chapter 5.
57 See, e.g., the handbooks in note 53 above.
58 See African Women and Peace Support Group, *Liberian Women Peacemakers* (Trenton: African Women and Peace Support Group, 2004).

transformation "from outside" that is already under-way "from within" but that has not been resolved into any broadly accepted normative position. Because "things have changed", because "you can't go back" – but even more importantly, because most Liberians do not *want* to "go back" – the problem becomes as much or more of an internal struggle over how a people ought to continue to be together in society.[59]

Facing the contradiction

The fact that Liberia's national legal system articulates normativity in a way that remains fundamentally disconnected from most Liberians is compounded by the fact that the national legal system is also severely dysfunctional. This dysfunction leaves law open to becoming a terrifyingly violent expression of "mob justice"; but it also opens up law to unofficial mediation, which points to the possibility of a genuinely responsive legal system.

Mob justice

The structural problems in the national legal system discussed at the 2010 Conference on Access to Justice are symptomatic of a legal system that is seriously under-mediated: unaffordable, inaccessible, and untimely; non-transparent and un-accountable; and generally ineffective in "delivering justice".[60] The Liberian National Police is no exception. Ranked by Liberians in national surveys as the most corrupt institution of government, the police force is not only dysfunctional but also exploitative.[61] At the same time incidents of mob violence have risen since the end of the war, spiking in 2013,[62] the same year that Human Rights Watch published its findings on police corruption in Liberia.[63] It would be naïve to view these increasing incidents of mob violence as irrational outbursts disconnected from the dysfunction and corruption in the national legal system. The rationality of "mob justice", and its connection to the dysfunction in the national legal system, was pointed out to me during one of my trips in a "bush taxi" in the interior of Liberia in 2013,[64] when a news report on the radio prompted three of my fellow male passengers to swap stories about their experiences with the national legal system. Their stories invariably ended with a line about how one could not expect to get justice from the police or the courts. When I asked how they could get justice, given the dysfunction in the national legal system, they laughed. "We have to get it ourselves". They might have been laughing but they

59 See discussion in Chapter 5.

60 See also Isser, Lubkemann, and N'Tow, *Looking for Justice*, 3.

61 See Human Rights Watch, *'No Money, No Justice': Police Corruption and Abuse in Liberia* (New York: HRW, August 2013).

62 Author interview with UN official, 11 October 2013 (MU6). See also UN Doc S/ 2013/479 (12 August 2013); UN Doc S/2014/123 (18 February 2014).

63 Human Rights Watch, *'No Money, No Justice'.*

64 "Bush taxis" are shared taxis that provide one of the only transport options throughout the country, operating on relatively fixed routes.

were not joking. Throughout my stay in Liberia I read and heard reports on a regular basis of mostly young men responding in this way – getting justice for themselves – by burning trucks, buses, and cars that had hit a motorcycle or pedestrian, or beating up people caught stealing in the market. In one major incident in 2013 the members of the motorcycle transport union in Gbarnga, apparently fed up with gangs operating in the town, responded by attacking the residential quarters where the "criminals" lived. As a newspaper reported the incident:

> At least one person was reported dead and several others seriously wounded after motorcyclists went on the rampage in Gbarnga and its environs last Saturday destroying ghettoes. According to our Bong County correspondent the riot began after the motorcyclists visited a police station in the city in demand of a suspect detained for allegedly stealing a motorcycle which they claimed belong to a colleague of theirs. As police rejected their demand to turn over the suspect to them hundreds of them took to the streets of Gbarnga carrying cutlasses, axes and other metals destroying ghettoes on grounds that they were hide-ups for criminals.[65]

Fewer than two weeks earlier the police had held "peace talks" with the same motorcycle transport union at the Gbarnga Regional Justice and Security Hub. For several years motorcycle taxi drivers, many of whom are former combatants who fought in the wars as children and young men, had clashed with government security forces in Gbarnga, as well as elsewhere in the country. According to the President of the Bong Chapter of the Liberia Motorcyclist Transport Union, harassment by police was a major reason they had taken up arms, and the peace talks were intended to find a way to work together to maintain "peace and stability". While the talks suggested a responsive approach to the problem, the dialogue nonetheless took place within the fortified walls of the Gbarnga Justice and Security Hub. That could send only one message, and it was the same message that the Minister of Defence issued in the lead-up to the threatened "April 12" protest.[66] In a statement that sought to justify a threat he had made earlier to use lethal force against the protesters, the Minister of Defence declared:

> You can understand; when a Liberian says, "I want to demonstrate" he has that right to demonstrate under the law, nobody stop you. We've had demonstrations here; you follow the provisions as stipulated under the law, you go and have your demonstration. But then when you hear a Liberian saying "we will not stop until the Government comes down", what you want me to do? Put my hand in my back pocket and go and sit down?[67]

65 'In Gbarnga Riot One Dead Several Injured', *New Dawn*, Monrovia, 23 September 2013.

66 See discussion in Chapter 5.

67 Wade Williams, '"No Apologies" – Liberia's Defense Chief Stands By Pre-April 12 Statement', *Front Page Africa*, Monrovia, 22 April 2013.

Like the motorcycle transport unionists who threatened to give expression to the law on their own terms, and Liberians who felt they had to get justice for themselves through mob violence, the April 12 protest threatened something far more dangerous than a random act of massive violence. It threatened to give expression to a sense of right in an entirely negative form. As a newspaper commented, not even the "positive intentions of the organisers" would be able to channel this demonstration through a "lawful" protest.[68] The Defence Minister saw this threat, as did the police, when they made clear their own threat to use lethal means to maintain peace and stability. "We are here to maintain peace", a police spokesperson sought to reassure the public after a display of force in the days leading up to April 12. "The men wearing police uniform are here for peace. We are sending a message to those who think they can undermine the peace of this country".[69]

Here too was "peace talk" in response to the threat of Liberians giving immediate expression to their normative disposition in a way that would threaten "peace and stability". Without doubt the threat was of a short-sighted law, a revolutionary law, set against a short-sighted peace; but the extreme violence of this threatened act of articulation was a response to the extreme violence of this peace. And yet, despite the violence of this state of peace, in the end the April 12 protest was called off. For a majority of Liberians, who know from experience the terrifying destructiveness of war and revolution, it was still preferable to face the contradictions inherent in this state/State of peace and that are felt with such violence by the majority on a daily basis than to be subject again to revolution. This was a passionate, knowledgeable, and indisputable preference to begin again on 13 April by facing the contradiction of peaceful violence secured through the rule of law rather than return to the rule of mob justice.

Peace-builders

It is in this preference to face the contradiction on a daily basis, rather than through another revolutionary event, that Liberians are realising the emancipatory possibilities of law. Largely out of sight of the national legal system reform process and the Government's concern with harmonising expressions of the law, communities throughout Liberia are engaging in a more radical process of mediating the articulation of normativity in a way that makes difference the basis of the law. These mediators are the everyday "peace-builders" found throughout Liberia, in each town and village,[70] working to rebuild relationships between people whose shared histories are of intimate friendship and bloody conflict. Women's leaders, youth leaders, religious leaders, elders, concerned members of the community – whether "up-skilled" in Alternative Dispute Resolution by Western interveners, or drawing on their own knowledge and experience as members of legal traditions that long predate the West's modern discovery of ADR – it is these women and

68 'Observing the Law in Protest', *New Democrat*, Monrovia, 1 April 2013.

69 'Police Flex Muscles', *New Democrat*, Monrovia, 8 April 2013.

70 At least in every place I visited.

men who are facing the contradiction on the ground in Liberia. These diverse Liberians share an awareness that their communities, and by extension the nation, can only continue to be together as communities and a nation if the cleavages that run through them are made the basis of the law.[71]

The differences between the approach taken by these "peace-builders" and the approach taken by the national legal system are deeply considered and discussed throughout Liberia. One reason is that the differences mirror the differences between the African legal traditions in Liberia, which are often described as "restorative", and the Anglo-American common law tradition that was introduced by the African-American settlers and that continues to inform the national legal system. As discussed in the preceding chapter, the main difference is between a restorative approach that is based on compromise and community wellbeing and a concern for the past and future, and an approach that seeks a determination of individualised blame and remedy through an oppositional trial process concerned only with a temporally limited set of facts. To quote a veteran peace-builder in the northwest of Liberia who discussed these differences with me:

> If we are in court, the law is talking about what I did, and to quote the law that I was wrong, and I'm guilty. And I have to go to jail for 30 years, or pay a fine of one million dollars. And then the judge is finished with it. He is not looking at the future, what will happen – even with reference to your generation and the next man's generation. [...] The legal system seeks to promote the organic law of the land. It's the law that they are protecting, the Constitution. If you kill, you must be killed. There is no compromise.
>
> [By contrast, our approach] is looking at relationship-building between the parties, their children. These people came from the community, they are going to be living together, they are mourning. [Our approach is to have] both parties sit down together, look at the positive side of one another in the community, before coming over to where they had a misunderstanding. [We then focus on] how do they work together to make their future brighter, for the benefit of their offspring.[72]

I met many others who echoed this understanding of the different approaches to law, and they were not just Liberians with a vocation in community "peace-building". Government administrators as well as official legal and para-legal officers frequently made the same point in conversations with me. This may not be a comprehensive sample, but it reflects the broader pattern of evidence about how Liberians tend to think about the relationship between law, justice, and peace. It also highlights the fact that "ADR" is increasingly being promoted and advanced as part of the national legal system, despite strong resistance from the national

71 Compare J Wood, C Shearing, and J Froestad, 'Restorative Justice and Nodal Governance', *International Journal of Comparative and Applied Criminal Justice*, vol 35, no 1 (2011).

72 Author interview with elder and civil society actor, 16 September 2013 (Li25).

legal profession. This is remarkable because it suggests a critical awareness within government that has the potential to inform the rule of law in Liberia.

Thus, at a point in history when Liberia is facing its contradictions in a way that it has not before, perhaps the most important work is being done in communities throughout the country in everyday acts of "mediation". At the same time as the Government is beginning again to reform the national legal system – seeking to harmonise expressions of law under the Constitution of the Republic while strengthening its enforcement through the security sector – in an effort to overcome the contradictions that are seen to be the cause of conflict, these community-based peace-builders are doing the opposite. The elder quoted above described the law that emerges in the process of the community peace-builders' mediation when he spoke of how "both parties sit down together, look at the positive side of one another in the community, before coming over to where they had a misunderstanding". Facing one another, the parties articulate how they can continue to be together. The "parties", however, are not just the individual disputants but also the community members who have been divided by the cleavage that is manifesting through the disputing individuals. That is why the mediation takes place in a public space, such as a palava hut, with the community inseparably a part of the process. This system of law is not about resolving conflict by providing an answer either this way or that way, in favour of this outcome or that outcome (by law: "it is this"; or by law: "it is that"). Such an approach, which characterises the national legal system, denies the contradiction between this and that and makes the denial the basis of the law (thus the judge rules: it *is* this and *not that*). As Liberians repeated to me again and again, the law that emerges from the national legal system is set against peace. It resolves the confusion analytically, dividing "right" from "wrong", the "right party" from the "wrong party". But as the elder made clear, if there is to be reconciliation then there must be a *coming over*. What is wrong must be included within the very definition of what is right, so that what is right can become the law in light of the fact that at its heart is a wrong that cannot be dissolved and must live on through the law.

Facing the contradiction

After a decade of peace, and more than three decades after the overthrow of the First Republic, Liberians are reforming their national legal system in the process of establishing a state based on the rule of law. In doing so they are facing a contradiction in law that holds the potential to return the nation to war, but also to realise the possibility of being together post-war. On one hand Liberians are seeking to bring about radical social transformation through the national legal system; on the other hand, Liberians are demanding fundamental reform to this system, to make it better reflect them; while out of hand – outside of the national legal system – Liberians are mediating the articulation of normativity in their own ways. In every case, law, force, and justice are at play, and in every case, Liberia is in a truly revolutionary position of beginning again.

Figure 6.1 Painting of a palava hut by F B Yekehson (2012)

Through this chapter I have considered how a legal system might articulate normativity in ways that make law more or less reflective and more or less transformative. The critical question, however, is not whether the intention is to bring about normative change according to law or to make the law better reflect the normative dispositions of its subjects. For one, “the law” as expressed can never be at one with its object. Moreover, while the contradiction opens law up to being an instrument of domination, it also makes law potentially emancipatory, by providing a means for breaking through oppressive norms and articulating different ways of being together. Thus the critical question is not whether the intention is to make the law more or less reflective or transformative, because neither outcome can be entirely avoided, and neither is necessarily good or bad in itself. What is *critical* is how responsive the process of articulating normativity is. This is the critical concern of a legal system: not *what* takes form as "the law", but *how* the articulation of normativity is mediated. Under-mediated, the system is incapable of structuring the process of law; over-mediated, the system is unconcerned with remaining responsive to the subjects of law; and either way, what takes form as the law becomes an arbitrary expression, and potentially terrifyingly so.

I began the chapter by examining how law can be mediated in ways that make the law more or less transformative and more or less reflective, to the point where law becomes an instrument of domination or a lawless outburst – but also potentially a critical medium of peace-building. With this in mind I then examined how the Government of Liberia is beginning to reform the national legal system post-war. The view was of a national legal system that is being reformed in a way that risks making it both a medium of a liberal internationalist agenda for transformation and an instrument of domination, with a strong state security sector enforcing through brute force the liberal internationalist regime. According to the logic of this regime every recognised subject is seen to be equivalent, reducing them to an empirical individuality that denies their subjective differences. As an "empirical individual" the subject becomes the object of a universal subjectivity that makes it not only legitimate but a categorical humanitarian imperative to assist in developing it to its full potential as such. On this logic law's pluralism is seen as a problem that will be transcended as subjects gain access to the system of the one true and just law.

As I also showed, the state security sector, with its "justice-chain" of police, courts, and corrections facilities, is being developed to facilitate access to this justice throughout Liberia. At the same time, international and national non-government organisations are assisting Liberians to gain access to this justice through "legal empowerment". Like the Government's vision of an enforced transformation, there is little doubt that their agenda is also transformative, informed by the same logic of liberal internationalism; and yet they remain responsive to the communities they are seeking to empower. Indeed, in many instances community members are leading the transformation, as in the case of the Liberian women who are using international human rights law to overcome gender violence.[73] The result nonetheless is reform to the national legal system that risks making the national law an over-mediated instrument of transformation. That the push for change is coming both from outside and from within does not make this law any less over-mediated.

Finally, I examined how the national legal system remains dysfunctional, marked by corruption of the police and courts as well as rising incidences of mob violence. Both, I argued, are expressions of under-mediated law, in which the law is taking form in terms of the will of the expressive subject who articulates "the law". Alongside this, however, outside the national legal system, communities are also mediating the articulation of normativity in ways that make the process of law more genuinely responsive. What is critical about these community peace-builders,

73 See also Sally Engle Merry, *Human Rights and Gender Violence: Translating International Law into Local Justice* (Chicago: University of Chicago Press, 2006).

I argued, is not the law that takes form in the process, but *how* they make conflict the basis of legal resolution. The "peace" they work to uphold every day is a peace riven by conflict. Their aim is not to overcome these conflicts that separate individuals, families, neighbours, communities; they recognise that living together in Liberia means living inseparably apart. This means ensuring the law is not simply "this" but that the law is "this" always in respect of the fact that it is also "not this". To recall the elder, this means crossing both ways: "both parties sit down together, look at the positive side of one another in the community, before coming over to where they had a misunderstanding". Crossing both ways: what is wrong is included within what is right. Without doubt the result is unstable, contradictory – but that is why Liberians are beginning again each day, to face the contradiction.

Conclusion

Law's rule

A portrait of law

In the course of researching this book I stayed a few weeks in the small town of Zorzor in the north-west of Liberia. Each day I would spend several hours sitting in the street-side tea shops that line the town's dusty, and more often muddy, main road. The structure of these open-air joints is usually little more than a zinc roof nailed over three wooden walls, with stools and sometimes a table or two, in which a variety of coffee and tea is served including the local favourite, Chinese Gunpowder Tea (the ingredients of which I never worked out, but it seemed to keep the motorcycle-taxi drivers going all day and long into the night). Across Liberia these tea shops provide the meeting place for mostly men to gather throughout the day, to discuss current affairs, debate intellectual puzzles ("what is the difference between respect and fear?", "what do Liberians have in common?", "how can you have the rule of law when we don't even know our own laws?") – the men coming and going, joining a common table to listen or standing at the head lecturing to the group; or else questioning a stranger.

Alongside one of these tea shops in Zorzor is an art gallery. It too is little more than a zinc roof with three wooden walls. The owner, who is also the artist, is a man of very few words, and I never heard his story, but one of his small water-colour paintings caught my eye (Figure C.1). It shows five women who appear to be walking together, their bodies identified in bold black outline and yet remaining amorphous, blending in to each other as well as into the background; while the background, which is also the foreground, is a montage of colourful block-like strokes, at once firm expressions, precise in their measure, and yet a messy patchwork, with the blocks overlapping and leaving gaps exposed. *Here* is what I had come to Liberia to examine; here is an image that expresses the dialectical life of law.

Like that painting, this book is a portrait of the dialectic that animates law, seen from the vantage of a tea shop. And like that painting, this book presents an image of law as a common experience, animated by a dialectic of normativity, and a portrait of that dialectic as it plays out in Liberia. Consider again the painting by Yekehson of the Liberian women. Its significance is not merely its illustrative quality. The painting *is* illustrative, but its significance is also the painting's form as an artwork. Even more, its significance is what the social scientist might learn from

Figure C.1 Painting of Liberian women by F B Yekehson (2010)

the method of analysing the artwork. To understand this is to understand the three main arguments that run through this book.

Thus as an *illustration*, Yekehson's painting can be seen as a portrayal of the dialectic that I have argued animates law. The dialectic can be seen in the relation of the montage of block-colours and the amorphous social grouping. Like the blocks of colour, expressions of the law provide a social-structural background/foreground, although there is no easy analytical separation. The relation is dialectical, with law giving form to the social body as well as to the individual bodies, and everything else besides, while the shifting dispositions of the bodies gives form to law. To see this is to see how law gives form, *vividly*, and how law takes form, *socially*, in a dialectic between the act of articulation and what is being articulated. In this, a dialectic can be seen to connect the forms of expression and the amorphous subject of the portrait, without the two finally merging or remaining entirely separate. This is the irresolvable contradiction in law presented in the abstract in Chapter 2. But of course, much is missed if the portrait is seen ahistorically, as an empty signifier. Yekehson's painting expresses horror and heartbreak. Blood is everywhere. Blood soaks the women's hair. Blood smears their faces. Blood covers their bodies. The women walking together appear as ghosts, spectres of the recent wars that tore Liberia apart. This does not make the painting merely an illustration of the past any more than it simply presents an illustration in empty and homogenous time and space. It is precisely as *spirits* that the women in this painting remain, as much part of Liberia now as the empirical individuals who continue to recall their names.

I have argued that law is only really meaningful, or whole, when seen in relation to its subjects, and as such, pluralism has to be understood as law's essential condition. This is not only true of present expressions of law, as if law only takes place on a horizontal-spatial plane. As can be seen in Yekehson's painting, present expressions are not enlivened by subjects isolated in time. What *has been* – historically – informs the present, mediating how it is now, just as historical representations are mediated through-and-through by the present and can only be grasped as contemporary figurations of what has been.[1] Just as there is nothing "historical" that is not a matter of the here and now, there is nothing "here and now" that is not a matter of history.[2] As in Yekehson's painting there is a temporal depth to law, a temporal legal pluralism, that makes what has been part of its expressions now.[3] It is this temporal dimension that makes the question of how law manifests an historical question as much as an empirical one. Just as spirits

1 See Walter Benjamin, *The Arcades Project* (Cambridge: Belknap Press, 1999), 463.

2 As Benjamin writes, while it is a dialectical image that is illuminated in this discursive construction of history, this is nonetheless "genuinely historical", against the "vulgar historical naturalism" that lays claim to history by amassing facts and "establishing a causal nexus" between them in "empty and homogenous time": Walter Benjamin, 'On the Concept of History', *Gesammelte Schriften*, vol 1, no 2 (1974): Adendum A. See also Benjamin, *The Arcades Project*, 461–462. Compare this with the approach to history influenced by Quentin Skinner that "dominates Anglophone history today", according to which "historical texts must not be approached anachronistically in light of current debates, problems and linguistic usages or in the search for the development of canonical themes, fundamental concepts or timeless doctrines". For discussion, see Anne Orford, 'The Past as Law or History? The Relevance of Imperialism for Modern International Law', *Institute for International Law and Justice Working Paper 2012/2* (2012); Anne Orford, 'On International Legal Method', *London Review of International Law*, vol 1, no 1 (2013).

3 See also Desmond Manderson, *Temporalities of Law in the Visual Arts* (Cambridge: Cambridge University Press, 2018).

mediate life in Liberia,[4] the spirit world mediates the life of law; indeed, law cannot be separated from its human subjects any more than it can be separated from its spirits. When the Liberian elder spoke of including what is wrong within every expression of right, he understood this: that there is a temporal depth to law that makes the spirit world part of law no less than the empirical confusion that makes law always also not law on the ground.[5] Whether they are the spirits of the civil dead, whose bodies have been decimated by the logic of capital; the spirits of the civil wars, whose bodies have been laid to rest; or the spirits of the living dead, whose bodies, yet to be buried, defy – and even *mock* – the frameworks that confine them: these spirits mediate expressions of law.

Recall the scene in Liberia's Central Prison, where the book began. Recall the drawing on the prison wall: an exact representation of the Liberian coat of arms, with its image of a ship sailing towards the west African shore carrying the free people of colour who would establish what would become the Republic of Liberia. Hanging over this coat of arms was a slightly larger than usual banner – and here, I suggested, the prisoner's hand must have lingered a moment, a flicker of a smile must have crossed his face, for a moment, if not a burst of laughter, shaking the foundations of the Central Prison as he reprinted the line: *The love of liberty brought us here*. This was an act of articulation that confronted an institution of law with its history, that placed this history in juxtaposition with the material reality of this institution. The prisoner's drawing required this history to be seen from the perspective of the prisoner within this institution, but it also required this institution to be seen from the perspective of this history. The effect was to place the institution in history – to make it a matter not only of the here and now but also a matter of what has been. The effect was also to draw out the history from the institution – to make the history of Liberia a matter of what is taking place here and now.

What this historical-materialist act pointed to was a fundamental contradiction, writ large on the prison wall, concentrating the ironies of law's life in Liberia in one scene. We can see this now: there is the nineteenth-century vision of liberty that resulted in civil death for the majority of Liberians; there is the ship chartered by the American Colonization Society that brought the Constitution for the Government of the African Settlement at , which made the law of Liberia a littoral one par excellence, its lawfulness requiring a restless process of talking and talking back; and there they are, represented on the inside of a cell-block of Liberia's Central Prison – a fortification designed to secure a state/State of peace by containing within it any body that contradicts its logics. This drawing was an act of articulation of a living-dead man playing with the logics that frame him in the most concrete way. This was an act of talking back that confronted the institution of law with the spirits of Liberia's capitalist-colonial history.

4 See also M C Jedrej, 'Cosmology and Symbolism on the Central Guinea Coast', *Anthropos*, vol 81, no 4 (1986); William C Siegmann, 'Spirit Manifestation and the Poro Society', *Ethnologische Zeitschrift Zürich*, vol 1 (1980).

5 See Chapter 6.

Thus, as Walter Benjamin was so good at showing, it is in the refuse of scattered off-cuts that the crystal of the totality might be discovered; not the totality *itself*, but in the assemblage of the smallest and least remarkable data a composite that refracts a dialectical image of it.[6] The dialectical image of law that I have sought to illuminate through this discursive configuration may not be "law" as it is known by its concept, and yet it is by representing law configuratively, through the imaginative work of the scholar, that one might obtain an image of it that is more real than its concept can admit on its own. That is what I have attempted to create here, portraying through a constellation of scenes the life of law in Liberia. The result is a view that makes the subject who remains abject before the law *critical* to law, in both positive and negative senses of the word. "Positively", the subject can be seen to *constitute* how law takes form; but for this very reason, "negatively", the subject can also be seen to *critique* the given form of law. Thus law must remain responsive to its subjects, if it is not to become synonymous with death. While law may not avoid the grim association with death, the two are not identical.[7] Against the absolution of death, law holds out the possibility of a *living* death. This is not necessarily a hopeless condition. As the prisoners in Liberia's Central Prison testify, the living dead are never mere bodies but always also subjects capable of critical acts of articulation, no matter how well an institution succeeds in containing their expression.[8] Against the logics of capital, security, or a liberal-internationalist regime that would reduce the subject to a universally exchangeable object, the subject remains, until finally death comes. But at that point, too, *in* death, law has no power.[9]

This is not only about Liberia. It is also a general argument about law as a common experience. It is in its *form* as an artwork that the painting by Yekehson suggests how this book can be about both – how it can be both a singular portrayal of law in Liberia, enlivened by humans and spirits alike, as well as a generic argument about the life of law. Thus Yekehson's painting expresses a content that is singular, being of a particular time and place and experiences of that time and place that are without equivalence; and yet its form leaves its content open to be seen in the light of different times and places and experiences. This also points to the book's methodology, in its attempt to drive a theoretical

6 This was central to Adorno's sociology too, as exemplified in Theodor W Adorno, *Minima Moralia: Reflections from Damaged Life* (Dennis Redmond, members.efn.org, 2005). On how *Minima Moralia* can be read as a work of sociology, see Matthias Benzer, *The Sociology of Theodor Adorno* (Cambridge: Cambridge University Press, 2011), 44–46.

7 See Austin Sarat, 'Introduction: On Pain and Death as Facts of Legal Life', in Austin Sarat (ed), *Pain, Death, and the Law* (Ann Arbor: University of Michigan Press, 2001). This also returns to Mbembe, discussed in the Introducion, on how expressions of sovereignty can create "death worlds", "in which vast populations are subjected to conditions of life conferring upon them the status of *living dead*". Achille Mbembe, 'Necropolitics', *Public Culture*, vol 15, no 1 (2003), 40 (italics in original).

8 See further, Shane Chalmers, 'The Chameleon Subject – Representation, Law, and the Problem of Living Dead', *Law, Culture and the Humanities* (forthcoming).

9 See Sarat, 'On Pain and Death'.

approach into sociological research in a way that engages both the "empirical" and the "imaginary". In the same way that an image might be analysed to see how its form makes a work of expression both singular and generic, expressing a particular material history without the two becoming identical, so too might law be analysed, as an expressive form that articulates normativity without its expressions becoming identical with its object.

Law's rule, in Liberia (and elsewhere)

If we are to understand law in this way, as a medium for subjects to give expression of themselves without the law becoming identical with its subjective expression, then this has implications for how we understand the rule of law. I have pointed to these implications throughout the book, but only in passing. I will now, by way of conclusion, consider them more directly.

There is a dominant tendency to cast "the rule of law" as a proposition for finally resolving the contradiction in law, to ensure it is law and not humans that rules. This can be seen for instance in the work of Albert Dicey, the English jurist famous for popularising the term "the rule of law" in the nineteenth century.[10]

Like theorists before and after him, Dicey set the rule of law in opposition to arbitrariness:

> It means, in the first place, the absolute supremacy or predominance of regular law as opposed to the influence of arbitrary power, and excludes the existence of arbitrariness, of prerogative, or even of wide discretionary authority on the part of the government.[11]

As can be seen here, Dicey was especially concerned with the arbitrariness of discretionary treatment by law. While he did not conflate "arbitrariness" and "discretion", he brought the two together in opposition to the rule of law. Thus he wrote: "the rule of law is contrasted with every system of government based on the exercise by persons in authority of wide, arbitrary, or discretionary powers of constraint", before observing:

> a study of European politics now and again reminds English readers that wherever there is discretion there is room for arbitrariness, and that in a republic no less than under a monarchy discretionary authority on the part of the government must mean insecurity for legal freedom on the part of its subjects.[12]

10 See Albert V Dicey, *Introduction to the Study of the Law of the Constitution* (London: Macmillan, 1948), Chapter IV.

11 Ibid, 202.

12 Ibid, 188.

In formulating his concept of the rule of law Dicey was looking across the English Channel at continental Europe, where he saw a wide exercise of discretion by government officials.[13] He contrasted this with what he saw as a fundamental principle of the British Constitution: that the law should be applied equally to everyone, regardless of their position. Indeed this, for Dicey, is one of the three core attributes of the rule of law: "equality before the law, or the equal subjection of all classes to the ordinary law of the land administered by the ordinary law courts".[14] Elsewhere Dicey sharpened his definition of "equality before the law", making its point "the universal subjection of all classes to one law administered by the ordinary courts".[15]

And yet Dicey also recognised the essentiality of discretion in law, to ensure it remains responsive to difference. As an English common law jurist Dicey was especially aware of the importance of discretion in judicial decision-making. But this gives rise to a problem: the principle of equality before the law comes up against the experience of the subject who remains abject before it – an experience that calls for differential treatment by law. Facing this, Dicey equivocated. Mindful of the importance of the standard measure to the liberal principle of equality, he set the rule of law against the exercise of discretion; and yet he was unable to naïvely advocate a legal system without the exercise of discretion. Thus to begin with, Dicey reasoned, the rule of law "excludes the existence of arbitrariness", and therefore must exclude the exercise of discretion for the reason that "wherever there is discretion there is room for arbitrariness"; but with an eye to law's life on the ground, Dicey stopped short of an absolute exclusion of discretion, excluding only "wide discretionary authority on the part of the government"; and so in the end, the rule of law, set in opposition to arbitrariness, but left open to the exercise of discretion, is left open to arbitrariness.

Dicey's ambivalence – setting the rule of law against arbitrariness, and yet, unable to close it entirely in the face of its subjects, leaving it open to arbitrariness – does not reflect his shortcomings as a legal theorist. Rather, his ambivalent theorisation of the rule of law reflects the contradiction that is at its heart as a proposition, a contradiction that has frustrated scholars before and after Dicey. As Brian Tamanaha has observed: "The idea of 'the rule of law, not man', powerful as it is, has been forever dogged by the fact that laws are not self-interpreting or applying. The operation of law cannot be sequestered from human participation".[16] This condition is not exclusive to the rule of law, though. As discussed in the Introduction and elaborated in Chapter 2, it is the very condition of the modern institution, the foundations of which ultimately rest upon – or rather in, and through – its subjects.[17] Jacques Derrida considers this problem in his essay on "Declarations of

13 Ibid, 188–189.

14 Ibid, 202–203.

15 Ibid, 193.

16 Brian Z Tamanaha, *On the Rule of Law: History, Politics, Theory* (Cambridge: Cambridge University Press, 2004), 123–124.

17 For discussion of how the rule of law in the "classical jurisprudence" of Hobbes and Rousseau was supposed to resolve the contradiction between the state and society, see

Independence", in which he examines the act of articulation that is said to found an institution.[18] The problem for Derrida is the inability to decide whether the act of articulation is constative – a mere statement of what *is* as matter of fact; or performative – bringing about the fact through the act of articulating what "is". In the US Declaration of Independence, which Derrida is examining, "the good people" declare their freedom and independence. On one hand this suggests a mere statement of fact, which the Declaration enshrines in law. On the other hand, it also appears that the subject who signs the Declaration "by right" – the good people – creates its subjectivity in fact, as a free and independent people, through this act. That is, the signature as matter of law appears to create the signer as matter of fact in a "fabulous retroactivity" that transforms what "ought to be" into what *is*.[19] This leaves two contradictory possibilities: a movement from fact to norm, and a movement from norm to fact. There is an echo of Dicey's agony in Derrida's indecision over which of these movements is at work. Thus to begin with, the instituting act of articulation is clearly performative: "such an act does not come back to a constative or descriptive discourse. It performs, it accomplishes, it does what it says it does"[20]; and yet this performance remains *intentional* and not ontic: it requires an ongoing engagement by "the signers" for it to achieve what it says it achieves; but this is problematic because it leaves an instituting act that "does what it says it does", that never quite does what it says it does. Without a constative beginning, and without a constative end, the resulting institution is left suspended in an ongoing performance. Indeed both "beginning" and "end" appear to be positioned *in* this performance, leaving its foundations ever in need of founding – undermined by the very subjects that give the institution its name.

The same paradox has haunted theorists of the rule of law, who have long asked: *how can law rule over the subject that is its source?*[21] How can law rule over its maker, whether that maker is a monarch or the people? Or in Derrida's terms: how can what is instituted through an act of articulation be the author(ity) of the act of articulation? The logical answer is that this is simply impossible. A law-maker *cannot* be subordinate to the law it makes, any more than the signature can create the signer in a "fabulous retroactivity". That would be self-contradictory – pure absurdity. It would be a situation in which law-maker and made-law are *both* supreme.[22] As it turns out this is precisely what Dicey appears to suggest in his

Robert Fine, *Democracy and the Rule of Law: Marx's Critique of the Legal Form* (Caldwell: The Blackburn Press, 2002), Chapter 1.

18 Jacques Derrida, 'Declarations of Independence', in Elizabeth Rottenberg (ed), *Negotiations: Interventions and Interviews, 1971–2001* (Stanford: Stanford University Press, 2002).

19 Ibid, 50.

20 Ibid, 47.

21 For a modern, or rather modernist, consideration of this question, see Desmond Manderson, *Kangaroo Courts and the Rule of Law* (Abingdon: Routledge, 2012).

22 See also Brian Z Tamanaha, 'The Rule of Law for Everyone?', *Current Legal Problems*, vol 55, no 1 (2002): 105–109.

chapter on "The Rule of Law: Its Nature and General Applications", which begins with the observation:

> Two features have at all times since the Norman Conquest characterised the political institutions of England.
>
> *The first of these features is the omnipotence or undisputed supremacy throughout the whole country of the central government.* This authority of the state or the nation was during the earlier periods of our history represented by the power of the Crown. The King was the source of law and the maintainer of order. The maxim of the courts, *tout fuit in luy et vient de lui al commencement* [all was his, and all proceeded originally from him], was originally the expression of an actual and undoubted fact. This royal supremacy has now passed into that sovereignty of Parliament which has formed the main subject of the foregoing chapters.
>
> *The second of these features, which is closely connected with the first, is the rule or supremacy of law.* This peculiarity of our polity is well expressed in the old saw of the courts, "*La ley est le plus haute inheritance, que le roy ad; car par la ley il meme et toutes ses sujets sont rules, et si la ley ne fuit, nul roi, et nul inheritance sera*" ["the law is the greatest heritage that the King has for by the law he and all his subjects are governed, and if the law did not exist, there would be no King and no heritage"].[23]

On the face of it these two features are in striking contradiction. How can law-maker and made-law both be "supreme", a quality that means by definition "highest in authority"? On one hand the law-maker is said to have undisputed supremacy; on the other hand it is said to be *by law* that the law-maker is supreme. Indeed it is said that by law the law-maker *exists* as an entity; and yet it is this very law-maker that is said to be the source of law – the source of the law that brings the law-maker into existence. Surely this is impossible; logically something must be missing from the analysis. Something else – something from outside this tautological proposition – must intervene, to ground the proposition and make the rule of law possible. "To have meaning *and* an effect, there must be a last instance".[24]

In the case of the US Declaration of Independence, Derrida shows, "God is the name – the best one – for this last instance and this ultimate signature".[25] By (in the words of the Declaration) "appealing to the Supreme Judge of the world" as the ultimate authority of the act of articulation,[26] the performance acquires a constative quality – and so in the end the Declaration comes to rest, not on an abyssal indeterminacy, but on an unchanging truth. In the case of the rule of law God has also provided the last instance and ultimate authority from time to time.

23 Dicey, *Introduction*, 183–184 (italics added). The translation of the "old saw of the courts" is from Robert French, 'Public and Private Law: the Intersection', La Trobe Lecture, 30 October 2009.
24 Derrida, 'Declarations of Independence', 52 (italics in original).
25 Ibid.
26 Declaration of Independence of the USA (1776), preambular para 5.

This can be seen for instance in Thomas Aquinas's thirteenth-century *Treatise on Law*, where he considers the question "whether all are subject to the law?" (Question 96, Article 50). In answering the question Aquinas first sets out the problem, or objection: "*Obj. 3.* Further, the jurist says that *the sovereign is exempt from the laws.* But he that is exempt from the law is not bound thereby. Therefore not all are subject to the law". Aquinas then sets out his argument in response:

> *Reply Obj. 3.* The sovereign is said to be *exempt from the law*, as to its coercive power; since, properly speaking, no man is coerced by himself, and law has no coercive power save from the authority of the sovereign. Thus then is the sovereign said to be exempt from the law, because none is competent to pass sentence on him, if he acts against the law. Wherefore on Ps. L. 6: *To Thee only have I sinned*, a gloss says that *there is no man who can judge the deeds of a king.* – But as to the directive force of law, the sovereign is subject to the law by his own will, according to the statement *(Extra, De Constit.* cap. *Cum omnes)* that *whatever law a man makes for another, he should keep himself. And a wise authority says: "Obey the law that thou makest thyself".* Moreover the Lord reproaches those who *say and do not;* and who *bind heavy burdens and lay them on men's shoulders, but with a finger of their own they will not move them* (Matth. xxiii. 3, 4). Hence, in the judgement of God, the sovereign is not exempt from the law, as to its directive force; but he should fulfil it of his own free-will and not of constraint. – Again the sovereign is above the law, in so far as, when it is expedient, he can change the law, and dispense in it according to time and place.

Aquinas thus begins by upholding the sovereign's position above the law, on the rational basis that, "properly speaking, no man is coerced by himself, and law has no coercive power save from the authority of the sovereign"; but then having done so he *also* upholds the rule of law, by holding the sovereign "subject to the law"; and thus in the end the result appears to be a situation where law and law-maker both rule, with one subject to the other's authority. Aquinas gets out of the paradox, however, and he does so by making the sovereign subject to the law, not by the coercive power of the law made by the sovereign but by "the judgement of God". By invoking God as the last instance and ultimate authority, "all are subject to the law", including the human law-maker – a resolution that does not contradict the supremacy of the sovereign but also does not exempt the sovereign from law's rule.

That resolution might be acceptable in times when the judgement of God has real force of law, but as a "modern" proposition the rule of law cannot be seen to depend on a god-given law to secure its foundations. And yet, if modernity cannot provide a transcendental authority to break the tautology and secure law's rule against its pluralism, the rule of law appears to be left in the impossible position – and so again the question: how is it possible? The answer, which remains the bedrock of a modern common sense of law, is to posit a legal objectivity that overcomes its subjectivity.[27] As Matthew Kramer writes in preface to his book *Objectivity and the Rule of law:* "Legal objectivity, in its manifold aspects, is what marks the divide between the rule of law and the rule of men".[28] Above all it is the judiciary, as the last instance of law, that must be (or must be seen to be) objective, its rulings carried out by independent, impartial officers, whose professionalism ensures it is law and not humans that ultimately rules. And indeed, this is what appears to resolve the contradiction in the passage by Dicey discussed above, where he sets out the simultaneous supremacy of law-maker and made-law. Recall: to begin with Dicey observes that "[t]he King was the source of law", a fact he establishes by repeating "[t]he maxim of the courts, *tout fuit in luy et vient de lui al commencement* [all was his, and all proceeded originally from him]". So here is the familiar paradox: the source of law is the King, and the source of the King's authority is law… But now on closer inspection, something can be seen to intervene to break the tautology. In the end it is the courts that declare the sovereignty of the King. Just as for Aquinas the judgement of God provides the last instance that makes the law-maker subject to the law, for Dicey it is the judgement of the courts that provides the last instance and ultimate authority.

So too today: faced with a situation in which "the rule of law" and "the rule of humans" cannot be finally separated, for the reason that law cannot be separated from its subjects, the judiciary is said to provide the ultimate authority that secures law's rule over humans (whose subjection to law is in the last instance enforced by the courts) without compromising their position as the source of law (which again is upheld in the last instance by the courts). And yet, having resolved the contradiction in this way, by making the courts the ultimate authority of law, a new problem of course appears: how do the courts escape the paradox of the modern institution? If the judiciary's foundations are also subjective, then does this not undermine *its* position as the last instance and ultimate authority? If "it" – the institution of the courts – is enlivened by an other, or rather by others, does this not make *them* the authority? And are "they" none other than the subjects of law who are now signing the instituting act under the disguise of a wig?

27 For Peter Fitzpatrick the contradiction is overcome in myth. Thus in *The Mythology of Modern Law*, Fitzpatrick begins by examining an opposition that "marks the major divide in modern jurisprudence – that is, the opposition between law as autonomous doctrine and law as dependent on society" (3), before showing how the contradiction between these opposed views of law, as objective ("distinct, unified and internally coherent") and as subjective (socially contingent), is resolved in and through the mythology of modern law. Or, as Collier has written in review of Fitzpatrick's book, "the 'rule of law' has replaced the 'rule of God' as the foundation myth of Western democracies": Jane F Collier, 'Book review: *The Mythology of Modern Law* by Peter Fitzpatrick', *Contemporary Sociology*, vol 22, no 5 (1993): 713. See also Manderson, *Kangaroo Courts*, 36–37.

28 Matthew Kramer, *Objectivity and the Rule of Law* (Cambridge: Cambridge University Press, 2007), xii.

We know the answer: of course they are.[29] We also know the usual answer to the answer, which is to sublate the subjective performance within an objective framework that is said to render the problem in fact unproblematic. This modern positivist response, which rests on an unproblematic objectivity that transcends law's problematic subjectivity, would have surely struck Aquinas as a secular riff on his own theological answer. Adorno's words come to mind: "the constitutive forms of socialisation, of which that mystification is one, maintain their unconditional supremacy over human beings, as if they were divine providence".[30] By "that mystification" Adorno is referring to "the law of capitalist accumulation" that has become "nature-like due to the character of its inescapability under the dominating relationships of production",[31] but he might as well have been referring to the objectivity that is said to ground law's rule, an objectivity that has the same constative quality as any other constitutive form of socialisation.

Whether through a theology of natural law, or a mythology of modern law, law's rule might be rendered constative, its institution acquiring a "natural lawfulness" by being "hypostasized as an immutable given fact of nature".[32] Not only does this provide a solid basis for the performance to go on, but it also provides a medium for the logic to reproduce itself through the institution. Thus Aquinas's theory of the rule of law was as much an instantiation of the King's sovereign authority as it was an instantiation of a legal theology. Likewise, the modern positivist belief in objectivity is what enables an organisation like the World Bank to state:

> it has long been established that the rule of law – which at its core requires that government officials and citizens be bound by and act consistently with the law – is the very basis of the good governance needed to realize full social and economic potential.

This not only reduces law to an instrument of the Bank's development ideology, but also perpetuates that ideology through the institutionalisation of this "rule of law" around the world.[33]

The problem is that such responses fail to take law's contradictory condition seriously. The World Bank admits as much when it writes in its 2017 World Development Report on *Governance and the Law*:

29 See Desmond Manderson, 'Modernism, Polarity, and the Rule of Law', *Yale Journal of Law and Humanities*, vol 24 (2012); Manderson, *Kangaroo Courts*; Paul Kahn, *The Reign of Law: Marbury v Madison and the Construction of America* (New Haven: Yale University Press, 1997); Keith J Bybee, *All Judges Are Political – Except When They Are Not: Acceptable Hypocrisies and the Rule of Law* (Stanford: Stanford University Press, 2010); Douglas E Edlin, *Common Law Judging: Subjectivity, Impartiality, and the Making of Law* (Ann Arbor: University of Michigan Press, 2016).

30 Theodor W Adorno, *Negative Dialectics* (Dennis Redmond, members.efn.org, 2001), 347–351.

31 Ibid.

32 Ibid, 347–351.

33 World Bank Group, *World Development Report 2017: Governance and the Law* (Washington, DC: World Bank Group, 2017), 83.

> This Report sidesteps these philosophical debates [on "what is law"] and uses the term *law* or *formal law* in its most conventional sense to mean positive state laws – that is, laws that are officially on the books of a given state – at the national or subnational level, whether they were passed by a legislature, enacted by fiat, or otherwise formalized. Law here means the de jure rules.[34]

But if the objectivity of this "most conventional sense" of law begins and ends in a subjective performance, then surely it is not good enough to sidestep the debate and rest assured that the subjective is in fact objective, or sufficiently objective – *especially* for an organisation with as much power and influence as the World Bank.

Dismissing the contradiction in the rule of law on the basis of a modernist faith in determinacy is not the only response, however.[35] At another extreme, under the influence of a postmodernist belief in indeterminacy, the contradiction is also seen as a fatal flaw. The Critical Legal Studies movement, and more recently the field of law and literature, has tended to this conceit,[36] and it is no less absolutist, with the basis of law's rule appearing to dissolve in a subjective morass. However, there is also a third response to the contradiction, which seeks to hold both subjective and objective views of law together. This is the most promising for getting to the life of the rule of law, and yet even within this approach there is a certain institutional fixation, a tendency to render the subjective objective by institutionally fixing the grounds of law.

Consider for instance the opening chapter of *Getting to the Rule of Law*, the 50th volume of the Yearbook of the American Society for Political and Legal Philosophy. In this chapter Jeremy Waldron addresses the contradiction in the rule of law in terms of a tension between "the formal requirements [of a legal system] that relate to the determinacy of legal norms", and a legal system's procedural requirements that open the law to argumentation. "These are not just arguments about what the law *ought to be*", Waldron emphasises; "they are arguments of reason that present competing arguments about what the law *is.* [...] Law, in other words, becomes a matter of argument".[37] Thus against a modern positivist account of the rule of law, according to which "the most important thing that people need from the law that governs them is certainty and predictability in the conduct of their lives and businesses", Waldron reminds us that law is *essentially* contested, with "the law" emerging inter-subjectively, and that this is fundamental

34 Ibid, 84 (italics in original).

35 On the usual responses to the contradiction in the rule of law, see Manderson, *Kangaroo Courts*, 1–8. As Manderson argues, if the problem is not ignored, or seen as a fatal flaw – and therefore reason to abandon the ideal of the rule of law in favour of another, such as literature, politics, or ethics – then it is seen as a problem to be resolved.

36 Ibid, 3.

37 Jeremy Waldron, 'The Rule of Law and the Importance of Procedure', in James E Flemming (ed), *Getting to the Rule of Law: Nomos L* (New York: New York University Press, 2011), 18–19 (italics in original).

to the rule of law.[38] Waldron is no postmodernist, however, any more than he is a legal positivist. Law might emerge inter-subjectively, but above all "law is a mode of governing people".[39] As such, while Waldron holds in his chapter two views of law – an objective view of law as external to its subjects (a mode of governing over them, as law-receivers), and a subjective view of law as internal to its subjects (emerging through them, as law-makers) – he ultimately resolves the contradiction between the two by institutionalising law's subjectivity (with law "made" by subjects institutionally rather than in everyday life). This is the limitation: the "culture of argumentation" that Waldron recognises is limited to the one "that a legal system frames, sponsors, and institutionalises".[40] As such, law might be enlivened by its subjects, but this is regulated by institutionalised procedures; or as Waldron puts it, "law comes to life *in institutions*".[41]

We have seen this view of law before: a man from the country comes before a law "that treats them with respect, as though they had a view or perspective of their own to present on the application of the norm to their conduct and situation".[42] Without doubt this law before which the countryman comes has a dignitarian ethos:

> applying a norm to a human individual is not like deciding what to do about a rabid animal [...] it embodies a crucial dignitarian idea – respecting the dignity of those to whom the norms are applied as *beings capable of explaining themselves.*

But it is still the dignity of the human "entity" that is free to present their arguments before the law.[43]

While Kafka's parable "Before the Law" leaves readers uneasy with the view of law it presents, Waldron's version is even more unsettling. Whereas in Kafka's parable the contradiction between the countryman and the law is its central theme (which is what makes it unsettling), in Waldron's chapter the contradiction appears to have been resolved. This is even more unsettling because, while Waldron recognises that the rule of law is "not a magic that somehow absolves us from human rule",[44] this recognition does not result in a troubling situation, when it should. It does not result in a troubling situation because the human is cast as "an active intelligence" that shapes what the law "is" through reasonable argumentation mediated by institutionalised procedures. In other words, the human who comes before the law is supposed to be capable of finding itself recognised in its rationality. And yet, as Adorno observed in response to Hegel's *Philosophy of Right*:

38 Ibid, 21.
39 Ibid, 15.
40 Ibid, 22.
41 Ibid, 14 (italics in original).
42 Ibid, 15–16.
43 Ibid, 16 (italics in original).
44 Ibid, 25.

> That the individual feels so easily wronged, when the antagonism of interest drives it into the juridical sphere, is not, as Hegel would like to argue, its own fault, such that it would be too deluded to recognize its own interest in the objective legal norm and its guarantee; rather it is that of the constituents of the legal sphere itself.[45]

That the human remains before the law, arguing their side of the story to the day of their death, having never finally passed into it, is not the human's fault but the result of a lack of equation between their legal subjectivity and the rationality of this law. *This* is the troubling situation made so apparent in Kafka's parable; while the troubling situation in Waldron's chapter is that this is no longer apparent. By institutionalising law's subjective dimension, Waldron equates it with the internal rationality of a legal system, leaving the many suspended at the gate while observing that it remains open to them.[46]

By placing pluralism at the heart of the institution, Waldron's concept does not result in a positivist objectivity, with the content of "the law" remaining subjectively determined, but it nonetheless views law as a mode of governing over the many, rendering its *form* effectively objective. Thus there remains a modernist desire to impose objective controls on the subjectivity of law, a desire that only appears to be enflamed by the recognition that its institution ultimately comes to rest in its subjects. This can be seen in Tamanaha too, who, having observed that "the operation of law cannot be sequestered from human participation",[47] goes on to argue that law nonetheless *must* be sequestered from everyday political struggles to protect the rule of law from becoming a means through which actors struggle for power.[48] A fearful vision of chaos is evoked as the foil for Tamanaha's vision of the good:

> The root danger can be stated summarily: In situations of sharp disagreement over the social good, when law is perceived as a powerful instrument, individuals and groups within society will endeavor to seize or co-opt the law in every way possible; to fill in, interpret, manipulate, and utilize the law to serve their own ends. This will spawn a Hobbesean conflict of all against all carried on within and through the legal order. Rather than function to maintain social order and resolve disputes, as Hobbes suggested was the role of law, combatants will fight to control and use the implements of the law as weapons in social, political, religious, and economic disputes. Law will thus generate disputes as much as resolve them. [...] Spiralling conflicts will ensue with no evident halting point or termination short of exhaustion of resources or total

45 Adorno, *Negative Dialectics*, 303–305.
46 Compare the critique of H L A Hart and Ronald Dworkin in Fitzpatrick, *The Mythology of Modern Law*, 4–6 and Chapter 6.
47 Tamanaha, *On the Rule of Law*, 123–124.
48 Brian Z Tamanaha, *Law as a Means to an End: Threat to the Rule of Law* (Cambridge: Cambridge University Press, 2006). See also the critique in Manderson, *Kangaroo Courts*, 83–84.

> conquest by one side. Such struggles over and through law are openly visible today, and worsening.[49]

And yet, if "the operation of law cannot be sequestered from human participation", then how can law be isolated from the "social, political, religious, and economic disputes" and "sharp disagreements" that animate the everyday life of a social body? Securing law from its own chaotic condition, to ensure the realm of law's rule remains one of institutionalised order and stability, does not resolve the original contradiction in law. The opposite, it imposes on the rule of law the rule of particular humans who would uphold law's rule in the name of the many. This would require deciding over which "human participation" might be safely included, and which must be excluded. This is no less arbitrary, and potentially more dangerous, than the threat Tamanaha identifies because it seeks to master what remains, as life, beyond the confines of any conceptual order. But, as I have sought to show through this book, it is this very conflicted life of law that keeps it from becoming authoritarian or lifeless. To reduce law to an institutional arrangement for governing over the many is, once again, to forget law's pluralism.

And yet the rule of law cannot be *equivalent* to the rule of the many either. Law can no more become identical with its subjects than it can be totally separated from them. This is the paradoxical condition of law and its rule. On one hand Tamanaha is correct to fear the implication of "the rule of law" being no different to "the rule of humans", as this would totally negate its integrity as a concept. On the other hand, as Tamanaha also observes, the rule of law cannot be separated from the rule of humans. But if that is correct – if law cannot be sequestered from those who "fill in, interpret, manipulate, and utilize" it – then where does this leave the rule of law?

One answer is suggested by the striking image of Leviathan that Peter Fitzpatrick draws attention to in his reading of Thomas Hobbes, where Fitzpatrick addresses how (citing Hobbes):

> the very laws made by Leviathan, the civil laws, are found in a sense to bind Leviathan, for, just as "men" have been able to create a sovereign Leviathan, "so also have they made Artificiall Chains, called *Civill Lawes*, which they themselves, by mutual covenants, have fastened at one end to the lips of that Man, or Assembly, to whom they have given the Soveraigne Power, and at the other end to their own ears".[50]

The image of a chain connecting subjects and sovereign evokes a relationship that recognises the supreme authority of institutional expressions of law, while binding the institutional organ of articulation – the lips of the sovereign – to its subjects, whose every movement pulls upon, persuades, aggravates, and no doubt slurs its

49 Tamanaha, *Law as a Means to an End*, 1–2.

50 Peter Fitzpatrick, 'Legal Theology: Law, Modernity and the Sacred', *Seattle University Law Review*, vol 32 (2009): 332.

expression of law. If this is the objective institutional structure of the rule of law, whereby both ruler and ruled are regulated by a common bond of law, then it is an institution that is not set over and above the heads of its subjects in a detached way but is attached directly to their every push and pull. These subjects of law might be bound to listen, but they are not bound to be *passive* listeners. Indeed, to isolate the rule of law from the commotion of everyday life, to isolate it from the disorder and instability that animates every social body, would be to cut the chain that binds the lips of the sovereign to its subjects and raise the institution to a place beyond the reach of the many, to be guarded by a select few. Even *if* this could be achieved, it would leave an authoritarian in the place of Hobbes's more democratic Leviathan, which Hobbes did not present as being in simple opposition to a situation of "conflict of all against all" but rather as the institutionalisation of this conflict. That was the point of Leviathan: to ensure that the "conflict of all against all" would be "carried on within and through the legal order", rather than outside of it, which would be a "state of nature".[51]

The negative-dialectical approach that I have sought to model through this study of law in Liberia allows one to appreciate this: law's simultaneous singularity, incorporating all subjects within jurisdiction, and plurality, taking form in non-identical ways, enlivened by the subjects over whom law rules. But it also points to a more radical rule of law, one which is not wholly contained by an institutional structure. The point is not just that law is animated by pluralism, but that law also rules *in* and *through* this pluralism. This opens the frame around "the rule of law" in two ways in particular. On one side, the "law" that is seen to rule would not be equated with official acts of articulation, and would include law that is made sensible through the richly expressive media of human culture. And on the other side, the "rule" of this law would not be equated with an institutional mode of governance, with the everyday lives of legal subjects instead providing the critical locus of law's rule. In short, it provides an approach to "the rule of law" that opens its concept to the nonconceptual, making the living realities of law's rule critical to the conceptual schemas deployed to institute it. As Manderson observes with reference to Clifford Geertz's work, it is to appreciate "local knowledge" of "the cultural, communal and individual construction of legality" when examining the rule of law.[52]

Opening the frame in this way thus allows the rule of law to be seen culturally, not as *itself* a culture, as in a "rule of law culture" that might be brought about by changing the attitude and behaviour in societies that are said to lack such a culture, but as already having a cultural life in places and times that on the West's institutional measures are made to appear to lack "rule of law". At a time when international organisations, governments as well as non-government organisations

51 See also Peter Fitzpatrick, 'Leveraging Leviathan', in Charles Barbour and George Pavlich (eds), *After Sovereignty: On the Question of Political Beginnings* (Abingdon: Routledge, 2009).

52 Desmond Manderson, 'Beyond the Provincial: Space, Aesthetics, and Modernist Legal Theory', *Melbourne University Law Review*, vol 20 (1995), 1069.

and civil society actors are working to build the rule of law around the world, understanding this could not be more important.[53] For those who repeat the mantra, "context matters", this is what it means to take context seriously; for those who care about understanding "rule of law cultures",[54] *this* is the cultural life of the rule of law, in Liberia, and elsewhere.

53 See, e.g., World Bank, *WDR 2017*, 14–15.
54 Compare Leanne McKay, *Toward a Rule of Law Culture: Exploring Effective Responses to Justice and Security Challenges* (Washington, DC: United States Institute of Peace, 2015).

Appendix

Interview list

Interviews in Monrovia, Liberia

Code	*Position*	*Date*
	Government of Liberia	
MG1	Ministry of Internal Affairs	22 May 2013
MG2	Ministry of Internal Affairs	15 May 2013
MG3	Ministry of Internal Affairs	28 May 2013
MG4	Ministry of Justice	15 May 2013
MG5	Land Commission	14 August 2013
MG6	Land Commission	7 August 2013
MG7	Land Commission	14 August 2013
MG8	Land Commission	14 August 2013
MG9	Ministry of Internal Affairs	15 August 2013
	United Nations in Liberia	
MU1	United Nations Mission in Liberia	24 May 2013
MU2	United Nations Mission in Liberia	24 May 2013
MU3	United Nations Mission in Liberia	15 August 2013
MU4	United Nations Development Program	19 June 2013
MU5	United Nations Development Program	30 July 2013
MU6	United Nations Mission in Liberia	11 October 2013
	Foreign government agencies in Liberia	
MB1	US State Department/Pacific Architects & Engineers	5 June 2013
MB2	US Agency for International Development	5 August 2013

Code	*Position*	*Date*
MB3	German International Cooperation (GIZ)	12 August 2013
MB4	Australian Agency for International Development	8 October 2013
	Non-government organisations	
MN1	The Carter Center	9 April 2013
MN2	The Carter Center	13 April 2013
MN3	The Carter Center	6 August 2013
MN4	Former legal adviser to The Carter Center	25 April 2013
MN5	Sustainable Development Institute	15 August 2013
MN6	Norwegian Refugee Council	16 August 2013
	Civil society	
MC1	Journalist	1 April 2013
MC2	Researcher	14 May 2013

Interviews in Liberia outside of Monrovia

Code	*Position*	*Date*
Li1	Ministry of Justice	26 August 2013
Li2	Rural Human Rights Activists	26 August 2013
Li3	Superintendent	10 August 2013
Li4	Land Commissioner	13 August 2013
Li5	City Mayor's Office	11 August 2013
Li6	Refugee Repatriation & Resettlement Commission	10 August 2013
Li7	Magistrate	12 August 2013
Li8	Magistrate	12 August 2013
Li9	Public Defender	9 August 2013
Li10	United Nations Mission in Liberia	10 August 2013
Li11	United Nations Mission in Liberia	9 August 2013
Li12	FIND	11 August 2013
Li13	Lofa Network of Local NGOs	7 August 2013

Code	*Position*	*Date*
Li14	Journalist	7 August 2013
Li15	Youth leader, member of county Peace Committee	10 August 2013
Li16	Journalist	30 August 2013
Li17	Journalist	2 September 2013
Li18	Land Commission	29 August 2013
Li19	Paramount Chiefdom Clerk	2 September 2013
Li20	Paramount Chiefdom Assistant Clerk	2 September 2013
Li21	Town leader	2 September 2013
Li22	Magistrate	2 September 2013
Li23	Police Commander	3 September 2013
Li24	City Mayor	16 September 2013
Li25	Lutheran Trauma Healing & Reconciliation	16 September 2013
Li26	City Mayor's Office	18 September 2013
Li27	Magistrate	19 September 2013
Li28	Ears for the Masses	19 September 2013
Li29	Paramount Chief	19 September 2013
Li30	United Nations Mission in Liberia	23 September 2013
Li31	Community Peace Hut	23 September 2013
Li32	Magistrate	24 September 2013
Li33	Magistrate	24 September 2013
Li34	Catholic Justice and Peace Commission	24 September 2013
Li35	Catholic Justice and Peace Commission	26 September 2013
Li36	City Mayor	26 September 2013
Li37	United Nations Mission in Liberia	26 September 2013
Li38	United Nations Mission in Liberia	27 September 2013
Li39	Land Commission	27 September 2013

Interviews in New York City, USA

Code	*Position*	*Date*
NY1	United Nations Department of Peacekeeping Operations	20 June 2013
NY2	United Nations Department of Peacekeeping Operations	25 June 2013
NY3	United Nations Department of Peacekeeping Operations	25 June 2013
NY4	United Nations Department of Peacekeeping Operations	20 June 2013
NY5	United Nations Department of Peacekeeping Operations	17 June 2013
NY6	United Nations Department of Peacekeeping Operations	25 June 2013
NY7	United Nations Department of Peacekeeping Operations	22 June 2013
NY8	United Nations Department of Peacekeeping Operations	21 June 2013
NY9	United Nations Department of Political Affairs	26 June 2013
NY10	United Nations Development Program	26 June 2013
NY11	United Nations Development Program	27 June 2013
NY12	Human Rights Watch	18 June 2013

Bibliography

Abasiattai, Monday B, 'European Intervention in Liberia with Special Reference to the "Cadell Incident" of 1908–1909', *Liberian Studies Journal*, vol 14, no 1 (1989).

Adorno, Theodor W, *Hegel: Three Studies* (Cambridge: MIT Press, 1963).

Adorno, Theodor W, 'Society', *Salmagundi*, vol 10/11 (fall 1969–winter 1970).

Adorno, Theodor W, 'The Actuality of Philosophy', *Telos*, vol 31 (1977).

Adorno, Theodor W, *Negative Dialectics* (Dennis Redmond, members.efn.org, 2001).

Adorno, Theodor W, *Minima Moralia: Reflections from Damaged Life* (Dennis Redmond, members.efn.org, 2005).

African Women and Peace Support Group, *Liberian Women Peacemakers* (Trenton: African Women and Peace Support Group, 2004).

Agamben, Giorgio, *Homo Sacer: Sovereign Power and Bare Life* (Stanford: Stanford University Press, 1998).

Akingbade, Harrison, 'The Pacification of the Liberian Hinterland', *Journal of Negro History*, vol 79, no 3 (1994).

Akingbade, Harrison, 'The Liberian Problem of Forced Labor 1926–1940', *Africa: Rivista Trimestrale di Studi e Documentazione dell'Istituto Italiano per l'Africa e l'Oriente*, vol 52, no 2 (1997).

Allen, William E, 'Liberia and the Atlantic World in the Nineteenth Century: Convergence and Effects', *History in Africa*, vol 37 (2010).

Anker, Kirsten, *Declarations of Interdependence: A Legal Pluralist Approach to Indigenous Rights* (Aldershot: Ashgate, 2014).

Aquinas, Thomas, *Treatise on Law (Summa Theologica, Questions 90–97)* (Chicago: Henry Regnery Company, 1949).

Arthurs, Harry, *'Without the Law': Administrative Justice and Legal Pluralism in Nineteenth-Century England* (Toronto: University of Toronto Press, 1985).

Austin, John, *Lectures on Jurisprudence, or the Philosophy of Positive Law, vol 2* (London: John Murray, 1873).

Ayres, Ian and John Braithwaite, *Responsive Regulation: Transcending the Deregulation Debate* (Oxford: Oxford University Press, 1992).

Azikiwe, Nnamdi, 'In Defense of Liberia', *Journal of Negro History*, vol 17, no 1 (1932).

Azikiwe, Nnamdi, *Liberia in World Politics* (Westport: Negro Universities Press, 1970).

Bacon, Francis, *The New Organon, or True Directions Concerning the Interpretation of Nature* (Adelaide: ebooks@Adelaide, 2014).

Badiou, Alain, 'Affirmative Dialectics: From Logic to Anthropology', *International Journal of Badiou Studies*, vol 2, no 1 (2013).

Barr, Olivia, *A Jurisprudence of Movement: Common Law, Walking, Unsettling Place* (Abingdon: Routledge, 2016).

Benjamin, Walter, 'On the Concept of History', *Gesammelte Schriften*, vol 1, no 2 (1974).

Benjamin, Walter, *The Arcades Project* (Cambridge: Belknap Press, 1999).

Benjamin, Walter, 'Critique of Violence', in Marcus Bullock and Michael W Jennings (eds), *Walter Benjamin: Selected Writings, Volume 1, 1913–1926* (Cambridge: Belknap Press, 2002).

Benzer, Matthias, *The Sociology of Theodor Adorno* (Cambridge: Cambridge University Press, 2011).

Bergling, Per, Jenny Ederlöf, and Veronica Taylor (eds), *Rule of Law Promotion: Global Perspectives, Local Applications* (Uppsala: Iustus Förlag, 2009).

Beyan, Amos J, *The American Colonization Society and the Creation of the Liberian State: A Historical Perspective, 1822–1900* (Lanham: University Press of America, 1991).

Beyan, Amos J, *African American Settlements in West Africa: John Brown Russwurm and the American Civilizing Efforts* (New York: Palgrave Macmillan, 2005).

Blume, Till, 'Review Essay: Security, Justice and the Rule of Law in Peace Operations', *International Peacekeeping*, vol 15, no 5 (2008).

Boley, G E Saigbe, *Liberia: The Rise and Fall of the First Republic* (London: Macmillan, 1983).

Bowden, Brett, Hilary Charlesworth, and Jeremy Matam Farrall (eds), *The Role of International Law in Rebuilding Societies after Conflict: Great Expectations* (Cambridge: Cambridge University Press, 2009).

Braithwaite, John, 'Fasken Lecture: The Essence of Responsive Regulation', *UBC Law Review*, vol 44, no 3 (2011).

Braithwaite, John and Peter Drahos, *Global Business Regulation* (Cambridge: Cambridge University Press, 2000).

Buchanan, Ruth and Sundhya Pahuja, 'Legal Imperialism: Empire's Invisible Hand?', in Paul A Passavant and Jodi Dean (eds), *Empire's New Clothes: Reading Hardt and Negri* (New York: Routledge, 2004).

Buck-Morss, Susan, *The Origin of Negative Dialectics: Theodor W Adorno, Walter Benjamin, and the Frankfurt Institute* (New York: The Free Press, 1977).

Buell, Raymond Leslie, *Liberia: A Century of Survival, 1847–1947* (Philadelphia: University of Pennsylvania Press, 1947).

Burin, Eric, *Slavery and the Peculiar Solution: A History of the American Colonization Society* (Gainesville: University Press of Florida, 2005).

Bybee, Keith J, *All Judges are Political – Except When They Are Not: Acceptable Hypocrisies and the Rule of Law* (Stanford: Stanford University Press, 2010).

Carothers, Thomas (ed), *Promoting the Rule of Law Abroad: In Search of Knowledge* (Washington, DC: Carnegie Endowment for International Peace, 2006).

Chalmers, Shane, 'Law's Imaginary Life on the Ground: Scenes of the Rule of Law in Liberia', *Law and Literature*, vol 27, no 2 (2015).

Chalmers, Shane, 'Law's Pluralism: Getting to the Heart of the Rule of Law', *Law, Culture and the Humanities* (2017a).

Chalmers, Shane, 'Civil Death in the Dominion of Freedom: Liberia and the Logic of Capital', *Law and Critique*, vol 28, no 2 (2017b).

Chalmers, Shane, 'The Visual Force of Justice in the Making of Liberia', in Desmond Manderson (ed), *Law and the Visual: Representations, Technologies, and Critique* (Toronto: University of Toronto Press, 2017c).

Chalmers, Shane, 'The Beginning of Human Rights: The Ritual of the Preamble to Law', *Humanity*, vol 9, no 1 (2018).

Chalmers, Shane, 'The Chameleon Subject – Representation, Law, and the Problem of Living Dead', *Law, Culture, and the Humanities* (forthcoming). Available at: https://ssrn.com/abstract=3097575

Chalmers, Shane and Jeremy Matam Farrall, 'Securing the Rule of Law through United Nations Peace Operations', *Max Planck Yearbook of United Nations Law*, vol 18 (2014).

Chapman, Peter and Chelsea Payne, '"You Place the Old Mat with the New Mat": Legal Empowerment, Equitable Dispute Resolution, and Social Cohesion in Post-Conflict Liberia', *Open Society Justice Initiative* (autumn 2013).

Charlesworth, Hilary and Christine Chinkin, 'Regulatory Frameworks in International Law', in C Parker, C Scott, N Lacey, and J Braithwaite (eds), *Regulating Law* (Oxford: Oxford University Press, 2004).

Cheesman, Nick, 'Law and Order as Asymmetrical Opposite to the Rule of Law', *Hague Journal on the Rule of Law*, vol 6, no 1 (2014).

Cheesman, Nick, *Opposing the Rule of Law: How Myanmar's Courts Make Law and Order* (Cambridge: Cambridge University Press, 2015).

Ciment, James, *Another America: The Story of Liberia and the Former Slaves Who Ruled It* (New York: Hill and Wang, 2013).

Clegg III, Claude A, *The Price of Liberty: African Americans and the Making of Liberia* (Chapel Hill: University of North Carolina Press, 2004).

Collier, Jane F, 'Book Review: The Mythology of Modern Law by Peter Fitzpatrick', *Contemporary Sociology*, vol 22, no 5 (1993).

David, John Seh, *The American Colonization Society and the Founding of the First African Republic* (Bloomington: iUniverse, 2014).

Davies, Margaret, 'The Ethos of Pluralism', *Sydney Law Review*, vol 27 (2005).

Davies, Margaret, 'Pluralism and Legal Philosophy', *Northern Ireland Legal Quarterly*, vol 57, no 4 (2006).

Davies, Margaret, *Law Unlimited: Materialism, Pluralism, and Legal Theory* (Abingdon: Routledge, 2017).

De Colquhoun, Patrick Mac Chombaich, *A Summary of the Roman Civil Law: Volume 3* (London: V and R Stevens and Sons, 1849).

Deranty, Jean-Philippe, 'Adorno's Other Son: Derrida and the Future of Critical Theory', *Social Semiotics*, vol 16, no 3 (2006).

Derrida, Jacques, 'Force of Law: The "Mystical Foundation of Authority"', *Cardozo Law Review*, vol 11 (1989–1990).

Derrida, Jacques, *Of Grammatology* (Baltimore: Johns Hopkins University Press, 1997).

Derrida, Jacques, 'Declarations of Independence', in Elizabeth Rottenberg (ed), *Negotiations: Interventions and Interviews, 1971–2001* (Stanford: Stanford University Press, 2002).

Derrida, Jacques, *Fichus* (Paris: Galilee, 2002).

Derrida, Jacques, 'Differance', in Julie Rivkin and Michael Ryan (eds), *Literary Theory: An Anthology* (Malden: Blackwell, 2004).

Dews, Peter, 'Adorno, Post-Structuralism and the Critique of Identity', *New Left Review*, vol 157 (May–June 1986).

Dicey, Albert V, *Introduction to the Study of the Law of the Constitution* (London: Macmillan, 1948).

Dop, Henk and Phillip T Robinson (eds), *Travel Sketches from Liberia: Johann Buttikofer's 19th Century Rainforest Explorations in West Africa* (Leiden: Brill, 2013).

Dorsett, Shaunnagh, 'Mapping Territories', in Shaun McVeigh (ed), *Jurisprudence of Jurisdiction* (Abingdon: Routledge, 2007).

Dorsett, Shaunnagh and Shaun McVeigh, *Jurisdiction* (Abingdon: Routledge, 2012).

Du Bois, W E B, 'Liberia, the League and the United States', *Foreign Affairs*, vol 11, no 4 (1933).

Dunn, D Elwood, *Liberia and the United States During the Cold War: Limits of Reciprocity* (New York: Palgrave Macmillan, 2009).

Dunn, D Elwood and Svend E Holsoe, *Historical Dictionary of Liberia* (Metuchen: Scarecrow Press, 1985).

Edlin, Douglas E, *Common Law Judging: Subjectivity, Impartiality, and the Making of Law* (Ann Arbor: University of Michigan Press, 2016).

Fahnbulleh, Varney J, 'A Concise Synopsis of the Tubman National Unification Policy', in Department of Internal Affairs, Republic of Liberia: William V S Tubman Papers (Bloomington: Liberian Collections, Indiana University Libraries, 1967).

Fairhead, James, Tim Geysbeek, Svend E Holsoe, and Melissa Leach (eds), *African-American Exploration in West Africa: Four Nineteenth-Century Diaries* (Bloomington: Indiana University Press, 2003).

Farrall, Jeremy Matam, 'Recurring Dilemmas in a Recurring Conflict: Evaluating the UN Mission in Liberia (2003–2006)', *Journal of International Peacekeeping*, vol 16 (2012).

Farrall, Jeremy Matam, 'Rule of Accountability or Rule of Law? Regulating the UN Security Council's Accountability Deficits', *Journal of Conflict and Security Law*, vol 19 (2014).

Farrall, Jeremy Matam and Hilary Charlesworth (eds), *Strengthening the Rule of Law through the UN Security Council* (Abingdon: Routledge, 2016).

Fine, Robert, *Democracy and the Rule of Law: Marx's Critique of the Legal Form* (Caldwell: The Blackburn Press, 2002).

Fine, Robert, 'Debating Human Rights, Law, and Subjectivity: Arendt, Adorno, and Critical Theory', in Lars Rensmann and Samir Gandesha (eds), *Arendt and Adorno: Political and Philosophical Investigations* (Stanford: Stanford University Press, 2012).

Fine, Robert, 'Natural Law and Critical Theory: Bringing Rights Back In', *Journal of Classical Sociology*, vol 13, no 2 (2013).

Firestone Plantations Company, *Liberia and Firestone: The Development of a Rubber Industry, a Story of Friendship and Progress* (Akron: Firestone, 1956)

Fischer-Lescano, Andreas, 'A "Just and Non-violent Force"? Critique of Law in World Society', *Law and Critique*, vol 26, no 3 (2015).

Fitzpatrick, Peter, *The Mythology of Modern Law* (London: Routledge, 1992).

Fitzpatrick, Peter, *Modernism and the Grounds of Law* (Cambridge: Cambridge University Press, 2001).

Fitzpatrick, Peter, 'Why the Law is also Non-Violent', in Austin Sarat (ed), *Law, Violence and the Possibility of Justice* (Princeton: Princeton University Press, 2001).

Fitzpatrick, Peter, 'Legal Theology: Law, Modernity and the Sacred', *Seattle University Law Review*, vol 32 (2009a).

Fitzpatrick, Peter, 'Leveraging Leviathan', in Charles Barbour and George Pavlich (eds), *After Sovereignty: On the Question of Political Beginnings* (Abingdon: Routledge, 2009b).

Fitzpatrick, Peter, 'Foucault's Other Law', in Ben Golder (ed), *Re-Reading Foucault: Law, Power, Rights* (Abingdon: Routledge, 2013).

Fitzpatrick, Peter, 'The Revolutionary Past: Decolonizing Law and Human Rights', *Metodo: International Studies in Phenomenology and Philosophy*, vol 2, no 1 (2014).

Fitzpatrick, Peter, 'Necessary Deceptions: Kafka and the Mystery of Law', in Maria Aristodemou, Fiona Macmillan, and Patricia Tuitt (eds), *Crime Fiction and the Law* (Abingdon: Routledge-Birkbeck Law Press, 2017).

Ford, Martin, *Ethnic Relations and the Transformation of Leadership among the Dan of Nimba, Liberia (ca. 1900–1940)* (PhD Thesis: State University of New York at Binghamton, 1990).

Forsyth, Miranda, 'A Pluralist Response to the Regulation of Sorcery and Witchcraft in Melanesia', in Miranda Forsyth and Richard Eves (eds), *Talking it Through: Responses to Sorcery and Witchcraft Beliefs and Practices in Melanesia* (Canberra: ANU Press, 2015).

Forsyth, Miranda and Richard Eves, 'The Problems and Victims of Sorcery and Witchcraft Practices and Beliefs in Melanesia: An Introduction', in Miranda Forsyth and Richard Eves (eds), *Talking it Through: Responses to Sorcery and Witchcraft Beliefs and Practices in Melanesia* (Canberra: ANU Press, 2015).

Fraenkel, Merran, *Tribe and Class in Monrovia* (London: Oxford University Press, 1964).

Galtung, Johan, 'Twenty-Five Years of Peace Research: Ten Challenges and Some Responses', *Journal of Peace Research*, vol 22, no 2 (1985).

Gerdes, Felix, *Civil War and State Formation: The Political Economy of War and Peace in Liberia* (Frankfurt: Campus Verlag, 2013).

Gershoni, Yekutiel, 'Liberia's Unification Policy and Decolonization in Africa: A Parallel Process', *Asian and African Studies*, vol 16 (1982).

Gershoni, Yekutiel, *Black Colonialism: The Americo-Liberian Scramble for the Hinterland* (Boulder: Westview Press, 1985).

Gershoni, Yekutiel, 'The Formation of Liberia's Boundaries, Part 1: Agreements', *Liberian Studies Journal*, vol 17, no 1 (1992a).

Gershoni, Yekutiel, 'The Formation of Liberia's Boundaries, Part 2: The Demarcation Process', *Liberian Studies Journal*, vol 17, no 2 (1992b).

Gibbs Jr, James L, 'Poro Values and Courtroom Procedures in a Kpelle Chiefdom', *Southwestern Journal of Anthropology*, vol 18, no 4 (1962).

Gibbs Jr, James L, 'The Kpelle Moot: A Therapeutic Model for the Informal Settlement of Disputes', *Africa: Journal of the International African Institute*, vol 33, no 1 (1963).

Glenn, H Patrick, 'Sustainable Diversity in Law', *Hague Journal on the Rule of Law*, vol 3, no 1 (2011).

Golder, Ben and Peter Fitzpatrick, *Foucault's Law* (Abingdon: Routledge, 2009).

Golub, Stephen, 'The Legal Empowerment Alternative', in Thomas Carothers (ed), *Promoting the Rule of Law Abroad: In Search of Knowledge* (Washington, DC: Carnegie Endowment for International Peace, 2006).

Greene, Graham, *Journey without Maps* (London: Vintage, 2002).

Grenfell, Laura, *Promoting the Rule of Law in Post-Conflict States* (Cambridge: Cambridge University Press, 2013).

Grenfell, Laura, 'The UN and "Rule-of-Law Constitutions"', in Jeremy Matam Farrall and Hilary Charlesworth (eds), *Strengthening the Rule of Law through the UN Security Council* (Abingdon: Routledge, 2016).

Grossberg, Lawrence, 'On Postmodernism and Articulation: An Interview with Stuart Hall', *Journal of Communication Inquiry*, vol 10, no 2 (1986).

Guannu, Joseph Saye, *A Short History of the First Liberian Republic* (Monrovia: Star Books, 2010a).

Guannu, Joseph Saye, *Liberian History since 1980* (Monrovia: Star Books, 2010b).

Gunningham, Neil and Peter Grabosky, *Smart Regulation: Designing Environmental Policy* (Oxford: Clarendon Press, 1998).

Hallifax, Samuel, *An Analysis of the Roman Civil Law, Compared with the Laws of England* (Cambridge: printed by J Archdeacon Printer to the University, 1774).

Harley, George W, *Notes on the Poro in Liberia* (New York: Kraus Reprint Corporation, 1968).

Hatchard, John and Amanda Perry-Kessaris (eds), *Law and Development: Facing Complexity in the 21st Century* (London: Routledge, 2003).

Herman, Johanna and Olga Martin-Ortega, 'Narrowing Gaps in Justice: Rule of Law Programming in Liberia', in Chandra Lekha Sriram, Olga Martin-Ortega, and Johanna Herman (eds), *Peacebuilding and Rule of Law in Africa: Just Peace?* (Abingdon: Routledge, 2011).

Higate, Paul and Marsha Henry, *Insecure Spaces: Peacekeeping, Power and Performance in Haiti, Kosovo and Liberia* (London: Zed Books, 2009).

Hill, Alfred Boima, *Rule of Law through International State-Building: A Study of Liberia's Judicial Institute and its Magistrates Program* (MA Thesis: International Institute for the Sociology of Law, University of the Basque Country, 2012).

Hobbes, Thomas, *Leviathan* (Oxford: Oxford University Press, 2008).

Holsoe, Svend E, 'The Manipulation of Traditional Political Structures among Coastal Peoples in Western Liberia', *Ethnohistory*, vol 21, no 2 (1974).

Holsoe, Svend E, 'Notes on the Vai Sande Society in Liberia', *Ethnologische Zeitschrift Zürich*, vol 1 (1980).

Holsoe, Svend E, 'Matilda Newport: The Power of a Liberian-Invented Tradition', *Liberian Studies Journal*, vol 32, no 2 (2007).

Horkheimer, Max, 'Traditional and Critical Theory', in Max Horkheimer (ed) *Critical Theory: Selected Essays* (New York: Continuum, 1972).

Howard, Michael, 'The Concept of Peace', *Encounter*, vol 61, no 4 (1983).

Huberich, Charles Henry, *The Political and Legislative History of Liberia* (New York: Central Book Company, 1947).

Humphreys, Stephen, *Theatre of the Rule of Law: Transnational Legal Intervention in Theory and Practice* (Cambridge: Cambridge University Press, 2012).

International Commission of Enquiry (ICE), 'The 1930 Enquiry Commission to Liberia', *Journal of the Royal African Society*, vol 30, no 120 (1931)

Innes, William, *Liberia* (New York: Books for Libraries Press, 1831).

Isser, Deborah H, Stephen C Lubkemann, and Saah N'Tow, *Looking for Justice: Liberian Experiences with and Perceptions of Local Justice Options* (Washington, DC: USIP Peaceworks, 2009).

Jameson, Frederic, *Late Marxism: Adorno, or the Persistence of the Dialectic* (London: Verso, 1990).

Janse, Ronald, 'A Turn to Legal Pluralism in Rule of Law Promotion?', *Erasmus Law Review*, vol 6, no 3/4 (2013).

Jay, William, *An Inquiry into the Character and Tendency of the American Colonization and American Anti-Slavery Societies* (New York: R G Williams, 1837).

Jedrej, M C, 'Cosmology and Symbolism on the Central Guinea Coast', *Anthropos*, vol 81, no 4 (1986).

Jensen, Erik G and Thomas C Heller (eds), *Beyond Common Knowledge: Empirical Approaches to the Rule of Law* (Stanford: Stanford University Press, 2003).

Johnson, Charles S, *Bitter Canaan: The Story of the Negro Republic* (Piscataway: Transaction Books, 1987).

Johnston, Harry, *Liberia* (London: Hutchinson & Co, 1906).

Kafka, Franz, 'The Problem of Our Laws', in *The Collected Short Stories of Franz Kafka* (London: Penguin, 1988).

Kahn, Paul, *The Reign of Law: Marbury v Madison and the Construction of America* (New Haven: Yale University Press, 1997).

Kazanjian, David, 'The Speculative Freedom of Colonial Liberia', *American Quarterly*, vol 63, no 4 (2011).

Kazanjian, David, 'Hegel, Liberia: A Review of Susan Buck-Morss, Hegel, Haiti, and Universal History', *Diacritics*, vol 40, no 1 (2012).

Keane, Rory, 'Reviewing the Justice and Security Hub Modality as Piloted in Liberia', *Stability: International Journal of Security and Development*, vol 1, no 1 (2012).

Kieh Jr, George Klay, 'Post-Conflict Peacebuilding in Liberia: An Assessment of the Liberal Model', *Liberian Studies Journal*, vol 35, no 1 (2010).

Kleinhans, Martha-Marie and Roderick A Macdonald, 'What is a Critical Legal Pluralism?', *Canadian Journal of Law and Society*, vol 12 (1997).

Knörr, Jacqueline and Wilson Trajano Filho (eds), *The Powerful Presence of the Past: Integration and Conflict Along the Upper Guinea Coast* (Leiden: Brill, 2010).

Kramer, Matthew, *Objectivity and the Rule of Law* (Cambridge: Cambridge University Press, 2007).

Krever, Tor, 'The Legal Turn in Late Development Theory: The Rule of Law and the World Bank's Development Model', *Harvard International Law Journal*, vol 52, no 1 (2011).

Krygier, Martin, 'The Rule of Law: Pasts, Presents, and Two Possible Futures', *Annual Review of Law and Social Science*, vol 12 (2016).

Larking, Emma, *Refugees and the Myth of Human Rights: Life Outside the Pale of the Law* (Farnham: Ashgate, 2014).

Latrobe, John H B, *Liberia: Its Origin, Rise, Progress and Results* (Washington, DC: American Colonization Society, 1883).

Liebenow, J Gus, *Liberia: The Evolution of Privilege* (Ithaca: Cornell University Press, 1969).

Locke, John, *The Second Treatise of Government and a Letter Concerning Toleration* (New York: Dover, 2002).

Lubkemann, Stephen C, Deborah Isser, and Peter Chapman, 'Neither State nor Custom – Just Naked Power: The Consequences of Ideals-Oriented Rule of Law Policy-Making in Liberia', *Legal Pluralism and Unofficial Law*, vol 63 (2011).

Luckham, Robin and Tom Kirk, 'Security in Hybrid Political Contexts: An End-User Approach', *Justice and Security Research Program* (Paper 2, 2012).

Luckham, Robin and Tom Kirk, 'The Two Faces of Security in Hybrid Political Orders: A Framework for Analysis and Research', *Stability: International Journal of Security and Development*, vol 2, no 2 (2013).

Lyon, Judson M, 'Edward Blydon: Liberian Independence and African Nationalism', *Phylon*, vol 41, no 1 (1980).

Macdonald, Roderick A, 'Custom Made – For a Non-Chirographic Critical Legal Pluralism', *Canadian Journal of Law and Society*, vol 26, no 2 (2011).

Maley, William, 'Peace, Needs and Utopia', *Political Studies*, vol 33, no 4 (1985).

Manderson, Desmond, 'Beyond the Provincial: Space, Aesthetics, and Modernist Legal Theory', *Melbourne University Law Review*, vol 20 (1995).

Manderson, Desmond, *Kangaroo Courts and the Rule of Law* (Abingdon: Routledge, 2012a).

Manderson, Desmond, 'Modernism, Polarity, and the Rule of Law', *Yale Journal of Law and Humanities*, vol 24 (2012b).

Manderson, Desmond, 'Ad 2014: A Review Essay of Eve Darian-Smith, Laws and Societies in Global Contexts – Contemporary Approaches', *Law and Humanities*, vol 8, no 1 (2014).

Manderson, Desmond, 'Bodies in the Water: On Reading Images More Sensibly', *Law and Literature*, vol 27, no 2 (2015).
Manderson, Desmond, *Temporalities of Law in the Visual Arts* (Cambridge: Cambridge University Press, 2018).
Manderson, Desmond and Honni van Rijswick, 'Introduction to Littoral Readings: Representations of Land and Sea in Law, Literature, and Geography', *Law and Literature*, vol 27, no 2 (2015).
Marin, Louis, *Portrait of the King* (Minneapolis: University of Minnesota Press, 1988).
Marx, Karl, *Capital: A Critique of Political Economy: Volume 1* (London: The Electric Book Company, 1998).
Massoud, Mark Fathi, *Law's Fragile State: Colonial, Authoritarian, and Humanitarian Legacies in Sudan* (New York: Cambridge University Press, 2013a).
Massoud, Mark Fathi, 'Legal Poverty and the Rule of Law in Strife-Torn States', *Whittier Law Review*, vol 34, no 2 (2013b).
Mattei, Ugo and Laura Nader, *Plunder: When the Rule of Law is Illegal* (New York: Wiley-Blackwell, 2008).
May, Christopher, *The Rule of Law: The Common Sense of Global Politics* (Cheltenham: Edward Elgar, 2014).
Mbembe, Achille, 'Provisional Notes on the Postcolony', *Africa: Journal of the International African Institute*, vol 62, no 1 (1992).
Mbembe, Achille, *On the Postcolony* (Berkeley: University of California Press, 2001).
Mbembe, Achille, 'Necropolitics', *Public Culture*, vol 15, no 1 (2003).
McVeigh, Shaun (ed), *Jurisprudence of Jurisdiction* (Abingdon: Routledge, 2007).
Mehler, Andreas, 'Why Security Forces Do Not Deliver Security: Evidence from Liberia and the Central African Republic', *Armed Forces and Society*, vol 38, no 1 (2012).
Melissaris, Emmanuel, *Ubiquitous Law: Legal Theory and the Space for Legal Pluralism* (Farnham: Ashgate, 2009).
Merry, Sally Engle, *Human Rights and Gender Violence: Translating International Law into Local Justice* (Chicago: University of Chicago Press, 2006).
Mgbako, Chi and Kristina Scurry Baehr, 'Engaging Legal Dualism: Paralegal Organizations and Customary Law in Sierra Leone and Liberia', in Jeanmarie Fenrich, Paolo Galizzi, and Tracy E Higgins (eds), *The Future of African Customary Law* (Cambridge: Cambridge University Press, 2011).
Minkkinen, Panu, 'The Radiance of Justice: On the Minor Jurisprudence of Franz Kafka', *Social and Legal Studies*, vol 3, no 3 (1994).
Minkkinen, Panu, *Thinking without Desire: A First Philosophy of Law* (Oxford: Hart Publishing, 1999).
Mnookin, Robert and Lewis Kornhauser, 'Bargaining in the Shadow of the Law: The Case of Divorce', *Yale Law Journal*, vol 88, no 5 (1979).
Moran, Mary H, *Civilised Women: Gender and Prestige in Southeastern Liberia* (Ithaca: Cornell University Press, 1990).
Moran, Mary H, *Liberia: The Violence of Democracy* (Philadelphia: University of Pennsylvania Press, 2006).
Moses, Wilson Jeremiah (ed), *Liberian Dreams: Back-to-Africa Narratives from the 1850s* (University Park: Pennsylvania State University Press, 1998).
Mutua, Makau, 'Africa and the Rule of Law', *Sur: International Journal on Human Rights*, vol 13, no 23 (2016).
Nancy, Jean-Luc, *Hegel: The Restlessness of the Negative* (Minneapolis: University of Minnesota Press, 2002).

Neumann, Hannah and Joel Gwyn Winckler, 'When Critique is Framed as Resistance: How the International Intervention in Liberia Fails to Integrate Alternative Concepts and Constructive Criticism', *International Peacekeeping*, vol 20, no 5 (2013).

Nilsson, Desirée and Mimmi Söderberg Kovacs, 'Different Paths of Reconstruction: Military Reform in Post-War Sierra Leone and Liberia', *International Peacekeeping*, vol 20, no 1 (2013).

Norrie, Alan, *Law and the Beautiful Soul* (London: The Glasshouse Press, 2005).

Onoma, Ato Kwamena, 'Transition Regimes and Security Sector Reforms in Sierra Leone and Liberia', *The ANNALS of the American Academy of Political and Social Science*, vol 656, no 1 (2014).

Orford, Anne, 'The Past as Law or History? The Relevance of Imperialism for Modern International Law', *Institute for International Law and Justice Working Paper 2012/2* (2012).

Orford, Anne, 'On International Legal Method', *London Review of International Law*, vol 1, no 1 (2013).

Pahuja, Sundhya, 'Power and the Rule of Law in the Global Context', *Melbourne University Law Review*, vol 28, no 1 (2004).

Pahuja, Sundhya, *Decolonising International Law: Development, Economic Growth and the Politics of Universality* (New York: Cambridge University Press, 2011).

Palombella, Gianluigi and Neil Walker (eds), *Relocating the Rule of Law* (Oxford: Hart Publishing, 2008).

Pascal, Blaise, *Pascal's Pensées* (New York: E P Dutton & Co, 1958).

Peerenboom, Randy, 'The Future of Rule of Law: Challenges and Prospects for the Field', *Hague Journal on the Rule of Law*, vol 1, no 1 (2009).

Rainey, Timothy A, 'Buffalo Soldiers in Africa: The US Army and the Liberian Frontier Force, 1912–1927', *Liberian Studies Journal*, vol 21, no 2 (1996).

Rajagopal, Balakrishnan, 'Invoking the Rule of Law in Post-Conflict Rebuilding: A Critical Examination', *William and Mary Law Review*, vol 49, no 4 (2008).

Rancière, Jacques, 'Who is the Subject of the Rights of Man?', *South Atlantic Quarterly*, vol 103, no 2/3 (2004).

Rawls, Amanda C, 'Policy Proposals for Justice Reform in Liberia: Opportunities under the Current Legal Framework to Expand Access to Justice', *Traditional Justice: Practitioner's Perspectives* (IDLO Working Paper Series, 2011).

Reeves, Craig, '"Exploding the Limits of Law": Judgment and Freedom in Arendt and Adorno', *Res Publica*, vol 15, no 2 (2009).

Reeves, Craig, 'Criminal Law and the Autonomy Assumption: Adorno, Bhaskar, and Critical Legal Theory', *Journal of Critical Realism*, vol 13, no 4 (2014).

Reeves, Craig, 'Adorno, Freedom and Criminal Law: The "Determinist Challenge" Revitalised', *Law and Critique*, vol 27, no 3 (2016).

Reno, William, 'Predatory Rebellions and Governance: The National Patriotic Front of Liberia, 1989–1992', in Ana Arjona, Nelson Kasfir, and Zachariah Mampilly (eds), *Rebel Governance in Civil War* (New York: Cambridge University Press, 2015).

Rowlands, Michael, 'Civilization, Violence and Heritage Healing in Liberia', *Journal of Material Culture*, vol 13, no 2 (2008).

Rush, Peter, 'An Altered Jurisdiction: Corporeal Traces of Law', *Griffith Law Review*, vol 6 (1997).

Sannerholm, Richard Zajac and Frida Wall, 'Rule-of-Law Assistance in UN Peace Operations: Securitisation, Sectorisation and Goal Displacement', in Jeremy Matam Farrall and Hilary Charlesworth (eds), *Strengthening the Rule of Law through the UN Security Council* (Abingdon: Routledge, 2016).

Sannerholm, Richard Zajac, Frida Möller, Kristina Simion, and Hanna Hallonsten, *UN Peace Operations and Rule of Law Assistance in Africa 1989–2010: Data, Patterns and Questions for the Future* (Stockholm: Folke Bernadotte Academy, 2012).

Sarat, Austin, 'Introduction: On Pain and Death as Facts of Legal Life', in Austin Sarat (ed), *Pain, Death, and the Law* (Ann Arbor: University of Michigan Press, 2001).

Sarat, Austin and Thomas R Kearns, 'Beyond the Great Divide: Forms of Legal Scholarship and Everyday Life', in Austin Sarat and Thomas R Kearns (eds), *Law in Everyday Life* (Ann Arbor: University of Michigan Press, 1993).

Sawyer, Amos, *The Emergence of Autocracy in Liberia: Tragedy and Challenge* (San Francisco: Institute for Contemporary Studies Press, 1992).

Sawyer, Amos, 'Challenges of Governance Reform in Liberia', in Cassandra R Veney and Dick Simpson (eds), *African Democracy and Development: Challenges for Post-Conflict African Nations* (Plymouth: Lexington Books, 2013).

Schröder, Ursula C and Johannes Kode, 'Rule of Law and Security Sector Reform in International State-Building: Dilemmas of Converging Agendas', *Hague Journal on the Rule of Law*, vol 4, no 1 (2012).

Sevareid, Peter, 'The Case of the Unreturned Goat: Dispute Resolution by a Mano Court in Liberia', *Temple International and Comparative Law Journal*, vol 7 (1993).

Shick, Tom W, *Behold the Promised Land: A History of Afro-American Settler Society in Nineteenth-Century Liberia* (Baltimore: Johns Hopkins University Press, 1980).

Siegmann, William C, 'Spirit Manifestation and the Poro Society', *Ethnologische Zeitschrift Zürich*, vol 1 (1980).

Slaughter, Joseph, 'Enabling Fictions and Novel Subjects: The Bildungsroman and International Human Rights Law', *PMLA*, vol 121, no 5 (2006).

Sohn-Rethel, Alfred, *Intellectual and Manual Labour: A Critique of Epistemology* (Atlantic Highlands: Humanities Press, 1978).

Starr, Frederick, *Liberia: Description, History, Problems* (Chicago: publisher not identified, 1913).

Stevens, Caleb J, 'The Legal History of Public Land in Liberia', *Journal of African Law*, vol 58, no 2 (2014).

Stewart, Reed F, 'Liberia's Boundaries: A Preliminary Study', Conference on Social Science in Liberia (Stanford, 1–2 August 1969).

Stromseth, Jane, David Wippman, and Rosa Brooks (eds), *Can Might Make Rights? Building the Rule of Law after Military Interventions* (Cambridge: Cambridge University Press, 2006).

Sundiata, I K, 'Prelude to Scandal: Liberia and Fernando Po, 1880–1930', *Journal of African History*, vol 15, no 1 (1974).

Tamanaha, Brian Z, 'The Rule of Law for Everyone?', *Current Legal Problems*, vol 55, no 1 (2002).

Tamanaha, Brian Z, *On the Rule of Law: History, Politics, Theory* (Cambridge: Cambridge University Press, 2004).

Tamanaha, Brian Z, *Law as a Means to an End: Threat to the Rule of Law* (Cambridge: Cambridge University Press, 2006).

Tamanaha, Brian Z, 'The Rule of Law and Legal Pluralism in Development', *Hague Journal on the Rule of Law*, vol 3, no 1 (2011).

Taylor, Veronica L, 'Frequently Asked Questions About Rule of Law Assistance (and Why Better Answers Matter)', *Hague Journal on the Rule of Law*, vol 1, no 1 (2009).

Taylor, Veronica L, 'Big Rule of Law©®SMTM (pat. pending): Branding and Certifying the Business of the Rule of Law', in Jeremy Matam Farrall and Hilary Charlesworth (eds),

Strengthening the Rule of Law through the UN Security Council (Abingdon: Routledge, 2016).

Trebilcock, Michael J and Ronald J Daniels, *Rule of Law Reform and Development: Charting the Fragile Path of Progress* (Cheltenham: Edward Elgar, 2008).

Trubek, David M and Alvaro Santos, *The New Law and Economic Development: A Critical Appraisal* (New York: Cambridge University Press, 2006).

Unruh, Jon D, 'Land Rights in Postwar Liberia: The Volatile Part of the Peace Process', *Land Use Policy*, vol 26 (2009).

Waldron, Jeremy, 'Is the Rule of Law an Essentially Contested Concept (in Florida)?', *Law and Philosophy*, vol 21, no 2 (2002).

Waldron, Jeremy, 'The Rule of Law and the Importance of Procedure', in James E Flemming (ed), *Getting to the Rule of Law: Nomos L* (New York: New York University Press, 2011).

Watson, Irene, *Aboriginal Peoples, Colonialism and International Law: Raw Law* (Abingdon: Routledge, 2015).

Waugh, Colin M, *Charles Taylor and Liberia: Ambition and Atrocity in Africa's Lone Star State* (London: Zed Books, 2011).

Weah, Aaron, 'Hopes and Uncertainties: Liberia's Journey to End Impunity', *International Journal of Transitional Justice*, vol 6, no 2 (2012).

Wiley, Bell I (ed), *Slaves No More: Letters from Liberia 1833–1869* (Lexington: University Press of Kentucky, 1980).

Wilkeson, Samuel, *A Concise History of the Commencement, Progress and Present Condition of the American Colonies in Liberia* (Washington, DC: printed at the Madisonian Office, 1839).

Wood, J, C Shearing, and J Froestad, 'Restorative Justice and Nodal Governance', *International Journal of Comparative and Applied Criminal Justice*, vol 35, no 1 (2011).

Zetterström, Kjell, 'Poro of the Yamein Mano, Liberia', *Ethnologische Zeitschrift Zürich*, vol 1 (1980).

Žižek, Slavoj, *The Sublime Object of Ideology* (London: Verso, 2008).

Zürn, Michael, André Nollkaemper, and Randy Peerenboom (eds), *Rule of Law Dynamics: In an Era of International and Transnational Governance* (Cambridge: Cambridge University Press, 2012).

Index

For Product Safety Concerns and Information please contact our EU representative GPSR@taylorandfrancis.com
Taylor & Francis Verlag GmbH, Kaufingerstraße 24, 80331 München, Germany

www.ingramcontent.com/pod-product-compliance
Ingram Content Group UK Ltd.
Pitfield, Milton Keynes, MK11 3LW, UK
UKHW011014180926
475701UK00004B/734
9780367893125